Black Sheep

TITLES IN THIS SERIES
(listed chronologically by date of publication)

LIBRARY OF NAVAL BIOGRAPHY

John F. Wukovits

Black Sheep
The Life of Pappy Boyington

NAVAL INSTITUTE PRESS
Annapolis, Maryland

This book has been brought to publication with the generous
assistance of Marguerite and Gerry Lenfest.

Naval Institute Press
291 Wood Road
Annapolis, MD 21402

Library of Congress Cataloging-in-Publication Data
Wukovits, John F.
  Black Sheep : the life of Pappy Boyington / John F. Wukovits.
    p. cm. — (Library of naval biography)
  Includes bibliographical references and index.
  ISBN 978-1-59114-977-4 (hardcover : acid-free paper) 1. Boyington, Gregory. 2.
World War, 1939–1945—Aerial operations, American. 3. World War, 1939–1945—
Campaigns—Oceania. 4. World War, 1939–1945—Prisoners and prisons, Japanese. 5.
Fighter pilots—United States—Biography. 6. Marines—United States—Biography. 7.
United States. Marine Corps—Biography. 8. United States. Marine Fighter Squadron,
214th. 9. Heroes—United States—Biography. 10. Prisoners of war—Japan—
Biography. I. Title.
  D790.473214th .W85 2011
  940.54'5973092—dc22
  [B]
                                                            2010044509

Printed in the United States of America.

19 18 17 16 15 14 13 12 11   9 8 7 6 5 4 3 2

To my granddaughter, Emma Lastra,
whose smile and cheerfulness
brighten a grandfather's day

Contents

Preface

Like many Americans, I first became aware of Gregory Boyington from the 1970s television series *Baa Baa Black Sheep*. Unfortunately, the program focused on the tabloid aspects of the famous Black Sheep Squadron, and the events it portrayed—practically all of them fictitious—bore little reality to the actual accomplishments of Boyington and his squadron in the South Pacific. For a few months they roamed the skies over the Solomon Islands in their flashy Chance-Vought Corsair F4U fighter aircraft, contributing their skills and their machines to the defeat of an enemy air power that had known little but triumph and conquest. Their efforts helped turn a near-calamitous situation into the start of a massive offensive pointing toward Tokyo.

My interest increased when I learned that one of the Black Sheep pilots, Fred Avey, lived only a few miles from my Michigan home. In the late 1980s I had the pleasure of visiting with Avey, whose informative material corrected the version depicted by the television series.

Boyington's life provides much fodder for the biographer—fodder he willingly supplied, albeit in exaggerated form, in his autobiography. Where Boyington walked, turmoil followed. He stomped and crashed his way through life like a bull, leaving hurt feelings and disillusioned loved ones in his path. Associates either loved or hated the man—nothing in between—and superior officers who had to corral him must have felt as if they had grabbed an electrical wire. In many ways, Boyington failed miserably as a human being.

To concentrate on the many flaws that characterized Boyington, however, would be to ignore his valuable contributions to the war in the South Pacific. Like the phoenix rising from the ashes, Boyington lifted himself from the mire fashioned by earlier disappointments and exhibited genuine leadership abilities in commanding the Black Sheep Squadron. The man may have neglected or ignored his other responsibilities, his family chief among them, but he knew how to lead men in battle. That quality alone makes Boyington deserving of study.

One historian with whom I corresponded while doing the research for this book told me bluntly that he held Boyington in low esteem because the flier was an alcoholic who mistreated loved ones. He is correct; however, dismissing the value of a man's life because he was flawed shows clouded judgment. When I informed the historian that I too am an alcoholic—and have not touched a drink since 1983—he replied that it would probably take an alcoholic to completely understand Boyington.

Possibly that has given me an edge; possibly not. I can only state with certainty that beneath the bluster and the anger, hidden by hurts real and imagined, lay a commander whom the men of his squadron revere to this day. To fully appreciate Boyington, one must peel away the layers and appraise each for what it is. In Boyington's case, that means examining both the massive negativity that informed much of his life and the contributions he made at a crucial time in America's history.

Other individuals lent considerable help as I researched and wrote this book. Former members of the American Volunteer Group, more commonly known as the Flying Tigers—particularly Frank Losonsky, Carl Brown, and Charles Baisden—offered their insights, as did survivors of the Black Sheep Squadron, especially James Hill and the late Fred Avey. In a lengthy interview Ray "Hap" Halloran, a B-29 airman incarcerated in a Japanese prisoner-of-war camp with Boyington, talked about life as a captive and about his long friendship with the aviator. Former Olympic track star and World War II aviator Louis Zamperini, still vibrant and active despite his nine decades, welcomed me to his home in 2008 for an interview in which he shared his thoughts; and Joseph Goicoechea, a veteran of the fighting at Wake Island, offered valuable information on prison camp life. Bruce Gamble, the author of his own biography of Boyington, kindly sent a copy of Boyington's 1977 tape-recorded reminiscences, *Pappy Boyington, World War II Ace,* and offered other suggestions and information. Henry Sakaida, the talented chronicler of aerial combat in the South Pacific, generously lent his assistance whenever asked. James Bradford's exquisite editorial skills and vast historical knowledge also aided me in producing this book.

Chronology

December 4, 1912	Boyington is born near Coeur d'Alene, Idaho
September 18, 1919	Clyde Pangborn takes Boyington for his first airplane ride
July 1934	Boyington marries Helene Clark
December 20, 1934	Boyington graduates from the University of Washington
May 24, 1935	Son Gregory Jr. is born
January 27, 1936	Boyington is sworn into the Marine Corps and assigned to flight training at Pensacola, Florida, where he earns his wings
January 28, 1938	Daughter Janet is born
July 1938	Boyington is assigned to the Philadelphia Navy Yard
January 1940	Boyington is assigned to VMF-2 of the 2d Marine Aircraft Group in San Diego, California
February 1940	Boyington qualifies aboard the carrier *Yorktown*
April 24, 1940	Daughter Gloria is born
October 1940	Boyington is promoted to first lieutenant and assigned to Pensacola as a flight instructor
August 4, 1941	Boyington joins the American Volunteer Group
September 24, 1941	Boyington leaves the United States for Burma
November 12, 1941	Boyington arrives in Rangoon, Burma
March 24, 1942	Boyington participates in the raid at Chiang Mai

April 21, 1942	Boyington resigns from the American Volunteer Group
January 7, 1943	Boyington leaves the United States for the South Pacific
March 11, 1943	Boyington is named executive officer of VMF-122 in the South Pacific
September 7, 1943	VMF-214, with Boyington as commanding officer, is officially formed
September 12, 1943	Boyington begins the first combat tour with VMF-214
September 16, 1943	Boyington shoots down five Japanese aircraft
October 4, 1943	Boyington shoots down three enemy fighters in sixty seconds
October 19, 1943	Boyington completes his first combat tour
November 27, 1943	Boyington begins his second combat tour with VMF-214
December 17, 1943	Boyington leads the first fighter sweep against Rabaul
January 3, 1944	Boyington ties Joe Foss and Eddie Rickenbacker as the top ace by downing his twenty-sixth Japanese aircraft and is shot down, picked up by a Japanese submarine, and taken to Rabaul
January 19, 1944	Headquarters Marine Aircraft, South Pacific, Fleet Marine Force Intelligence Section, prints and distributes *The Combat Strategy and Tactics of Major Gregory Boyington, USMCR*
March 7, 1944	Boyington arrives at Ofuna prison camp in Japan
March 1944	President Franklin Roosevelt awards the Medal of Honor to Boyington
April 16, 1945	Boyington arrives at Omori prison camp in Japan
August 29, 1945	Boyington is liberated from Omori prison camp
September 12, 1945	Boyington arrives in the United States to a warm welcome from his Black Sheep Squadron and begins an exhausting national bond tour

October 4, 1945	Boyington submits a supplemental action report that makes him the lead ace
October 5, 1945	Boyington receives the Medal of Honor from President Harry Truman in a White House ceremony
January 1946	Boyington weds Frances Baker
August 1, 1947	The Marine Corps places Boyington on the retired list
July 1958	Boyington's autobiography, *Baa Baa Black Sheep,* is published
October 1959	Boyington weds Dolores Shade
August 1975	Boyington weds Josephine Moseman
Fall 1976	The National Broadcasting Company airs the television series *Baa Baa Black Sheep*
January 11, 1988	Boyington dies in a Fresno, California, hospice
January 15, 1988	Boyington is buried at Arlington National Cemetery
February 2006	The Student Senate at the University of Washington debates honoring Boyington
August 2007	Officials rename the airport in Coeur d'Alene, Idaho, Coeur d'Alene Airport–Pappy Boyington Field

Black Sheep

Chapter One
"A Chained Animal Just Striding to Get Loose"

Mourners barely noticed the biting cold wind that whistled through Arlington National Cemetery on the morning of January 15, 1988. They had gathered to pay their final respects to an old warrior, a World War II Medal of Honor recipient who had, in small ways and large, touched their lives. A riderless horse signifying the deceased slowly led the procession—out in front, fittingly, just where the warrior would have been in aerial combat—and a horse-drawn caisson containing a flag-draped coffin followed close behind. A pair of reversed boots, symbolizing a fallen soldier, rested on the caisson near the coffin.

When the funeral procession arrived at the hero's final resting spot, veterans with creased faces and young Marine officers on current duty waited for the ceremony for Gregory "Pappy" Boyington to begin. A flyover—rare in Washington, D.C., even in those days—honored Boyington, officially the leading Marine ace in the Pacific war.

Ray "Hap" Halloran, a longtime friend who had languished in a Japanese prisoner-of-war camp along with Boyington, rose to deliver the eulogy. Halloran spoke of the people who would miss Boyington, especially the members of his famed Black Sheep Squadron, VMF-214, Marine aviators who compiled a stellar record while fighting the Japanese in the Solomon Islands in late 1943 and early 1944. These men and other aviators, he said, "consider Pappy one of their very best." He was "the original 'top gun'—a hero—a legend in his own time—an inspiration."[1]

1

James Hill, one of the Black Sheep pilots, said that Boyington "was the best damn commanding officer of a Marine fighter squadron during wartime." Others added that Boyington's inspired leadership enabled them to achieve more than their individual skills would have allowed, and that few squadrons had the outstanding esprit de corps of the Black Sheep.[2]

Not everyone would agree with those assessments. Some members of an equally famous unit, Claire Chennault's vaunted Flying Tigers, who prowled the China-Burma skies in 1941 and 1942 and bested the Japanese at their own game, fashion an image of Boyington at variance with the one formed by the Black Sheep. "Boyington himself was no friend of the AVG [Flying Tigers]," wrote one Flying Tiger veteran on the association's web site in 2003. "He was a drunk, the kind that gets mean when he has a snoot full. . . . I had a lot of respect and admiration for our AVG pilots but Boyington was not one of them."[3]

The dichotomy might confound the casual observer. How can the same individual be vilified by people with whom he worked in 1942 and venerated by those he commanded a mere seventeen months later? The split continues to the present. A Flying Tiger will cast Boyington in somber hues while a Black Sheep paints a vivid picture with broad, colorful strokes. That is the paradox that was Gregory Boyington, a complex man built of nearly impenetrable layers of emotions and motivations. He was at the same time the product of an abusive family who ignored his own children, the author of a successful book and contributor to a hit television series who had trouble paying his bills, and a man who detested taking orders from others and yet became a valued squadron commander. Problems—many of his own making—plagued Boyington his entire life, but in the end he could take comfort in having found one arena in which he could be free, one place where enthusiasm and talent met opportunity and exhilaration. At the controls of an aircraft, sitting confidently in the cockpit as he raced to the skies, Boyington's problems peeled away and his shackles eased. He was a man meant to seek high adventure in a plane, for above all else, as *Life* magazine said of him in 1945, "Boyington was born to be a swashbuckler."[4]

"Christmas day was repulsive to me"

The shackles that bound Boyington to a life of neglect and abuse were forged before his birth; discontentment seemed part of the family's gene pool. From the moment Boyington's grandfather, Joseph, planted family roots in Coeur d'Alene, Idaho, in 1902, the clan's saga spiraled downward out of control.

Joseph's son Charles—Boyington's father—left Idaho for Evanston, Illinois, to enroll in Northwestern University's school of dentistry. After earning his degree, Charles, who by now had exhibited a violent temper, returned to the Coeur d'Alene area. He opened a practice, married and divorced one woman in speedy fashion, then married Grace Gregory in January 1912. Pregnant within three months, Grace gave birth to their son, Gregory, on December 4, 1912, in a small wooden hospital next to a lake near Coeur d'Alene. A fire ravaged the hospital shortly after Gregory's birth, destroying his birth certificate along with other hospital records.

Little Gregory was the product of a dysfunctional couple who argued violently and did little to nurture their child. Grace's wild temperament more than matched Charles' vicious tendencies. She had flaunted social dictates as a girl by sneaking cigarettes and alcohol, and entered what society deemed the "shady" world of entertainment by playing music in theaters offering silent films. Knitting sweaters and baking cookies took a back seat to indolence and indulgence. Those rebellious tendencies more than once pitted her against Charles, who wanted a more subdued and traditional wife than the version Grace handed him. The couple argued often—over money, over behavior, over almost everything. Before Gregory's third birthday the ill-suited mates had reached the point of no return. Eventually Charles accused his wife of being unfaithful during his lengthy unexplained absences and produced evidence to support his claim. In June 1914 he abandoned his wife and child, claiming that he was not Gregory's father and would no longer be responsible for them. Grace filed for divorce, which a judge granted on March 4, 1915.

The cagey Grace, however, was far from desolated. She speedily took up with Ellsworth Hallenbeck, a man with whom Charles had earlier accused her of cheating, and they moved to tiny St. Maries, Idaho, a bleak lumberjack town twenty miles southeast of Coeur d'Alene where Hallenbeck went to work as a bookkeeper for a sawmill.

Despite the wooden shacks, mud, bars, and whorehouses that defined the rough-and-tumble St. Maries, Boyington's memories of the place were almost idyllic, as if he purposely focused on warm memories to mask the disturbing ones. He described the town as resting "in a beautiful location" at the fork of two rivers, with rolling meadows rising gently from the riverbanks. He remembered "walking through a meadow to go to this little school house. It looked like all the other company houses the sawmill had. It was about a mile from where we lived. I recall the meadowlarks that were in abundance, and I loved their calls. I still do to this day, and to hear the whine of the sawmill as they made the timber out of these logs. The mill ran three shifts, twenty-four hours a day."[5]

The tranquil memories helped blot out Ellsworth's distressing behavior. Like Charles Boyington a heavy drinker, he verbally abused those around him. Again the home resounded with the sounds of arguments as Ellsworth targeted one or the other of his family for insults. Ellsworth, however, camouflaged a sinister side that made Charles seem saintly in comparison. Though no evidence exists suggesting that Gregory was a victim, some family members and historians claim that Ellsworth sexually abused at least some of his children.

By the time Gregory had entered his first schoolroom, he had thus already been exposed to a frightening array of domestic violence, alcohol, frequent changes of residence, and perhaps pedophilia. Christmas, a time most children recall fondly, held only painful memories for Boyington, who watched as tempestuous relatives drank and argued the day away. He later wrote, "As far back as I could remember Christmas Day was repulsive to me. Ever since my childhood, it had always been the same. Relatives were forever coming to our house and kissing my brother and me with those real wet kisses children dread so much, and making a number of well-wishing compliments that none of them ever seemed to believe." The Christmas cheer would deteriorate after everyone "had a snout full of firewater, fighting and speaking their true thoughts. All Christmases were alike, my brother Bill and I ending up by going to a movie." Boyington added that even when he was older, he preferred celebrating the holiday with strangers in a bar to remaining in the sour atmosphere at home.[6]

Norman Rockwell never met a family like the Boyingtons. The safe, sheltered life that all parents owe their children never existed for Gregory Boyington.

"He can't be beat"

"Safe" and "sheltered" are not adjectives typically applied to Boyington—child or adult, in or out of the military. Much like the cloud of dirt that followed Pigpen in Charles Schulz's classic cartoons, injuries stalked Boyington from an early age. The carnage began at age two and involved, fittingly enough, traveling through the air. "I remember how I liked to get airborne even when I was two," Boyington recalled. In this case he was playing with his mother's comb and brush when he waddled over to an open window. The next thing he knew, he was hurtling downward through the air and landing headfirst in a flowerbed. The fall momentarily knocked him unconscious. "My mother happened to locate me there in the flowerbed, and brushed me off and washed me up and I was good as new."[7]

Unfazed by his experience with the second-floor window, Boyington next tried the water. On a visit to the beach, he later said, "and having no fear of water, I waded out promptly to where it was over my head." Boyington recalled looking upward toward the surface, whose movement reminded him of water swirling down a drain, but his reverie lasted only a moment before his mother's hand yanked him up to air and retribution. Though his mother was only feet away and Boyington was never in danger of drowning, "My mother fished me out and scolded me. I was coughing a little bit."[8]

Boyington was tested yet again when he was three years old. He and a friend, a little girl from the neighborhood, were playing near an upstairs window when he once more became airborne, "which seemed to be a habit that would stay with me throughout life. I landed on my head on the sidewalk below. Fortunately they were wooden sidewalks in those days, or I wouldn't be here today." He barely avoided serious injury in the incident. The impact knocked one of his eyes out of its socket, however, a sight that sent his mother into hysterics. Fortunately, a nurse who lived nearby came to the rescue. She opened Boyington's eye socket with her fingers and gently replaced the eyeball. "The cord wasn't broken connecting it to the inside," Boyington said, but "I had a bloodshot eye for six or seven months."[9]

Not surprisingly, Boyington admitted to an early fondness for heights. "Long before I could ever possibly be a pilot," he recalled in 1977, "I seemed to have a penchant for climbing in high places, like the tallest trees that were available." Trees dangling over a cliff's edge seemed made for Boyington, who somehow always avoided falling into the abyss below. The town's grain elevator was another favorite high spot. It had "two towers that connected together way over one hundred feet off the ground. I liked to go from the top of one grain elevator to the other on these beams, and of course you got a little breeze up there and it was quite precarious. You had to hold your hands out and balance like a tightrope walker. How I ever survived all these things I got mixed up into—my poor mother never will know. . . . [A]pparently I have been blessed with nine lives."[10]

An incident with a horse that occurred when Gregory was in the fourth grade may have used up another of those nine lives. Boyington loved riding horses, and one day he noticed a horse being sold by a Native American from a nearby reservation. The nine-year-old Boyington was instantly obsessed with the thought of owning the stallion, and he applied all his persuasive powers to convince his stepfather to buy it. Before agreeing, though, Ellsworth wanted Boyington to try out the merchandise. Gregory eagerly mounted, and the adventure began. "The Indian didn't even hand me the reins," recalled Boyington. "He hit the horse and off the horse went. I tried to get the reins but they were dangling out of reach. There was nothing I could do but hold on." A string of shouted "Whoas!" did nothing to slow the stubborn animal. As the horse approached a group of lumberjacks intent on stopping him, the animal swerved to avoid them and ran directly into a building. The collision flipped the hapless Boyington out of the saddle and onto the ground, knocking him senseless. By the time Boyington reached school after regaining consciousness, a lump the size of a giant egg adorned his forehead and temple.

Another encounter taught him a lesson that proved useful later in his life. "I'll never forget my fourth-grade teacher—in those days you didn't treat the children quite as gently as you do now. She was a tough old gal, and I knew she was going to belt me one. I thought everybody was a right-hander, and I was waiting to duck her right hand when doggone if she didn't come around with her left hand and whack me smack on my jaw and right on my fanny. From then on, I observed whether people were right-handed or left-handed before I tangled with them."[11]

Boyington developed such a reputation for spectacular stunts that he earned the nickname "Deeds" from his mother. Neighborhood friends like Johnny Theriault and Reed Elwell knew better than to challenge him. He seemed driven to prove himself whenever the opportunity arose, as if trying to show that he was the equal of anyone else. Of course, being noticed never hurt, either. Boyington loved being the center of attention.

Part of that proof, of course, consisted of fighting. Boyington "was always coming home with a bloody nose," his mother recalled.[12] He absorbed the best that any schoolmate pugilist could offer, and stood his ground even in the face of severe thrashings. Persistence, to the verge of excessive stubbornness, became a Boyington trademark. Kenneth Fisher attested to that. A neighbor who lived three doors down from the Hallenbecks, Fisher outweighed Boyington by forty pounds. During one brutal altercation he pounded his smaller opponent into a bloody mess. Boyington headed home, clothes torn and bloody, and his mother cleaned him up. Twenty minutes later he knocked on Fisher's door and issued another challenge. His foe emerged and delivered another beating as severe as the first.

When he returned home, in even worse shape than before, Boyington's mother washed off the grime and warned, "Now this is the last time. You stay away from Kenneth."[13] But the budding warrior had other thoughts. Never one to take anyone's advice, especially when a fight loomed, Boyington grappled with the much larger Kenneth Fisher a third time, again meeting with similar results. Though he had lost the battles, Boyington's refusal to concede won the admiration of both his antagonist and his classmates.

"There's an airplane gonna land!"

Boyington admitted to an "early daydream since the first grade of becoming an aviator and flying high in the sky like a bird."[14] When he was not injuring himself through accidental falls or premeditated bouts with schoolmates, he thrilled to the exploits of famed aviators from the Great War. The feats of Raoul Lufbery, Manfred von Richthofen—the famous "Red Baron"—Frank Luke, and Eddie Rickenbacker, courageous fliers who manned rickety aircraft in the skies above Europe and engaged in death-defying antics, enthralled the young Boyington. Far more than mere pilots to the fascinated youth, these men were medieval warriors who charged into combat in metallic horses, scouring the horizon for the next foe.

One stood above the rest as knight exemplar—Rickenbacker, the American flier who gained the appellation "Ace of Aces" for shooting down more enemy aircraft than any other American aviator. Rickenbacker was an automobile devotee who had driven in four Indianapolis 500 races, but he gained far more fame as a pilot. He engaged in epic aerial contests against Richthofen's

"Flying Circus," German aviators feared for their tenacity and deadliness. Rickenbacker's exploits brought him the Medal of Honor and the adulation of young Gregory Boyington, who dreamed of one day matching the ace's extraordinary feats.

The fact that aviation during and after the war was a perilous endeavor only made it more intriguing. "Young man, I know of no better way for a person to commit suicide," retorted one Army officer to 2nd Lt. Henry Arnold—who would rise to become the head of the Army Air Corps during World War II —when he requested duty in aviation in 1911.[15] Flight could be exhilarating for a young man in those days, but it had to be strongly tempered with caution. A pilot could lift into the skies as easily as a lark, but he could also plunge frighteningly to the ground from a midflight malfunction. The flimsy planes often proved to be death traps, and the weather was an unknown element that could start out as a supportive friend but quickly morph into a deadly foe. Early aviators gave few thoughts to retirement. "Everybody expected to be killed," said one Army pilot. "Good Lord, I don't know of anybody who didn't figure he'd be killed before he got through."[16]

Even after the thrilling heroics of the war, aviation had its detractors. In 1919, for example, Chief of Naval Operations Adm. William S. Benson claimed that "aviation is just a lot of noise." President Calvin Coolidge drawled that fliers "just like to run around and burn a lot of gasoline."[17] Those statements and others like them failed to deter Boyington. A young man who could not be intimidated by falls and school bullies would not allow such negative thoughts about aviation to affect his dream, especially when he had a local hero—St. Maries' own Clyde Pangborn—to toss back as a rebuttal.

In the years following the Great War, Pangborn flew stunts as part of the Gates Flying Circus, which toured the nation thrilling spectators with dazzling aerobatics. "The Silent Reaper of Souls and I shook hands," proclaimed one advertising brochure for an aerial exhibition. "Thousands of times we have engaged in a race among the clouds—plunging headlong in breathless flight— diving and circling with awful speed through ethereal space."[18] These men, as hardy a group as ever was, willingly accepted the possibility of death or maiming in an air accident for one reason: the risks were a part of what they wanted to do. It was a package deal; if a man yearned to race through the sky, he had to accept the hazards. They did so willingly, for only one thing mattered—the compelling need to fly.

Lincoln Beachey, one of the most renowned daredevils in the early days of aviation, perished during a 1915 air show crash. In a newspaper interview given shortly before he died, he said something that struck a chord in every flier. In many ways the statement became his epitaph. "If it came my time to bow to the scythe-wielder, I wanted to drop from thousands of feet. I wanted the grand-stands and the grounds to be packed with a huge, cheering mob, and the band must be crashing out the latest rag. And when the ambulance, or worse, hauled me away, I wanted them all to say as they filed out the gates, 'Well, Beachey was certainly flying some!'"[19]

Pangborn knew the risks—and took them. He had been injured once when he fell out of a speeding car as he attempted to jump onto a flying plane. On another occasion he had to rescue a stuntwoman—in midair—who had become entangled on his landing gear during an exhibition. Years later, Boyington fondly recalled September 17, 1919, the day his hero, Clyde Pangborn, came back to St. Maries and offered residents—for five dollars—a ride in his shiny airplane. Pangborn had the whole town talking. His first sight of an aircraft and of a flier who seemed to possess supernatural skills was a magical experience for the five-year-old Boyington. Nothing, certainly not school, was going to keep him away.

"I believe I was five when I saw my first airplane," Boyington reminisced in 1977. He was outside, enjoying recess with the rest of his classmates, when he spotted a World War I aircraft circling lower and lower. He could barely contain his excitement. "I knew the plane was going to land, and so I started running toward this little field from school, and the school teacher yelled at me, 'Gregory, come back here, recess is over!' I shouted over my shoulder, 'I can't, teacher! There's an airplane gonna land down on the field and I got to be there when it lands!'"

Boyington raced as fast as he could, hoping to arrive in time to watch the pilot climb out so that he could find out who he was. "The pilot was a freckle-faced nineteen-year-old teenager. He never got overseas during the war. He turned out to be Clyde Pangborn. The name didn't mean anything to me then, but later he was one of the great pioneers of the early days. His mother lived in St. Maries, a widow." Boyington begged Pangborn for a ride. The pilot laughed at him but was impressed that such a young boy was so eager to hop into an airplane. He told Boyington that he would be delighted to take him into the air—as soon as he came up with five dollars.

Where Boyington got the money is not clear. He said in 1977 that Ellsworth gave it to him.

> I remember my father only made a hundred dollars a month, and he was supposed to be well paid. . . . I tore off and ran all the way to my father's office and told him I had to have five dollars for a ride in this airplane. I guess my father was as excited as I was. He couldn't leave the office, but he put his hands in his pockets, but he didn't have five dollars there so he just punched the keys on the register and fished five dollars out of the register. I don't remember if I said thanks or anything, but I grabbed that five and ran back to the airplane.[20]

Grace claimed in a 1945 radio interview that she had given him the five dollars—that her son had raced home and begged *her* for the money to fly with Pangborn. When she objected, he had moaned, "But, Mother, how will I ever learn to be a flier if I don't go up?"[21] Outargued, Grace scraped together the money and handed it to her determined son. Whichever parent had delivered, a jubilant Boyington returned to Pangborn's meadow, money in hand. But by then it was too late in the day for a ride. Pangborn promised to take Boyington up the next morning.

After a long night of sporadic sleep, the excited boy raced back to the aircraft. The daredevil pilot lifted the child into his airplane, and Boyington embarked on the initial ride in a career in aviation that lasted for almost seventy years. Pangborn circled the town so that his exuberant passenger could survey the trees, fields, and buildings below, then handed him some advertising handbills and told him to toss them over the side of the open cockpit. "On my ride, I had no helmet or goggles, and I wasn't even strapped in the cockpit, and I remember the slipstream blowing wind in my face, and I would reach down—I was standing up most of the time in the cockpit—and letting these handbills float down over the tiny city of St. Maries, Idaho. That's when the bug really hit me. I was bound and determined that I was going to be an aviator like Clyde when I grew up."[22]

Like Rickenbacker, Beachey, and Pangborn, Boyington had found his purpose in life. If he could only get into the air, he could explore the wonders of flight—and he would have an audience! From then on, Boyington was obsessed with everything about aviation. He and a friend constructed an aircraft out of old pieces of wood and some battered wagon wheels, then hustled to a local hill to test it. The adventure, predictably, ended in disaster. "I recall going down this hill pell-mell getting plenty of speed. By the time I got to where the downtown buildings were, just before I got to this store, the front wheels of this airplane got off the ground. The wing was up about two feet off the ground, just enough so there was no more control of the wheels on the airplane. It was just high enough to go through one of the store's plate glass windows when it went out of control."[23]

Greg's love for flying merged with a desire to serve in the military on the day his second-grade teacher's husband visited the classroom. A Marine in dress uniform replete with medals, the man so impressed Boyington that the boy vowed to become a military pilot. His dream would alter and even disappear for brief periods as the years passed, but Boyington had found his avocation in the second grade.

His passion for the air strengthened in September 1925 when Boyington and a friend went to Spokane to watch an air show. They thrilled at the many different types of aircraft racing above their heads. All of a sudden, Boyington gained firsthand experience of the dangers inherent in aviation. "One of the pilots was doing a turn off the edge of the field," Boyington recalled, "and he happened to be over a rock quarry. The air coming up out of the rock's surface was very light, and when this Jenny hit that in this steep turn, there wasn't enough solid air to keep the plane up. It went off in a spin about five hundred feet high and into the quarry went the Jenny, and the pilot was killed."

Along with the rest of the crowd, Boyington and his friend hastened to the crash site. What most stunned Boyington was not the pilot's death but the macabre reaction of the spectators. "I was amazed then at that early age, and the amazement never ceased through the years, the spectators seemed to be going wild. Before they could remove the poor pilot's body, they were in there hacking away at different parts of that fabric and wood airplane, getting souvenirs. They were like wild animals, like wolves, the way they tore that airplane literally to shreds acquiring souvenirs, at that first air show."[24] His thoughts had been with the pilot's fate; the spectators worried only about retrieving a memento of the sad occasion. The youth departed with a far deeper understanding of what flying entailed.

"I wanted to unchain this little airplane"

High school offered a pleasant oasis for Boyington. He earned a varsity letter in wrestling, a sport in which he could employ his thickly muscled, powerful upper torso to pin opponents, and participated in swimming and yearbook. His B average in the classroom gained an invitation to join the Knights of Lincoln, an organization consisting of the school's most prominent students. When he graduated in 1930, the school yearbook, *Lincolnian,* used a mere four words to describe him: "He can't be beat."[25] Boyington loved both the brevity and the message.

Following high school, in the fall of 1930, Boyington entered the University of Washington at Seattle, where he planned to study architecture and engineering. He had briefly considered aviation as a career—he had, after all, spent much of his youth flying through the air—but lack of funds and opportunity seemed to block that path. Only rich men could afford airplanes. Because he also loved to draw, Boyington turned to architecture. He seems to have enjoyed his time at the university. He socialized with the members of Lambda Chi, although he lacked the money to join on a full-time basis, and he enrolled in the school's Army Reserve Officers' Training Corps, performing well enough to be named captain of the cadet corps. The combative Boyington, still going by the last name Hallenbeck because he as yet knew nothing of his birth father, had no intention of participating in varsity sports until Washington's wrestling coach watched him sail through an intramural wrestling tournament. Impressed with the young man's ability to pin opponents and with the incredible strength of his upper torso, the coach invited Boyington to wrestle with his squad.

During his university years, a solitary moment involving Boyington and a machine determined the course of his life, almost as if fate had chosen his path. As he recalled later of the occasion, "I had my mind made up for me." During a Sunday ride in his Model T Ford, Boyington wound up near the Boeing Aircraft Company's factory. Not a sound issued from inside the factory to disturb the peaceful afternoon, and Boyington halted to gaze at a single aircraft that rested beside one of the factory's hangars, one of the F4B fighters that Boeing produced for the Marines.

On closer inspection Boyington spotted the words "Marine Corps" stenciled on the plane's side. He studied the beautiful aircraft for a time, admiring the sleek exterior surrounding the potent 450-horsepower engine. Chains attached to each wingtip and the tail locked the plane to the ground, an irony Boyington appreciated. The polished machine had been constructed to soar to the heavens, not remain chained to the ground beside a silent factory. An occasional gust of wind rattled the plane, momentarily breathing life into the still aircraft.

Boyington felt an immediate rapport with the metallic object. "It seemed to me like it was a chained animal just striding to get loose from its chains and take off into its natural habitat in the sky," he said in 1977. "I had an emotional feeling run through my body that I wanted to unchain this little airplane and take it on up to wherever it would be happy. I had always had a great love for animals of all types, especially birds that fly. To me, this little chained-up fighter plane was very, very similar. . . . I knew that it breathed, as an engine has to have air in order to run. I knew it had to have food, or fuel, to run its engine."[26] When recalling that moment years later, though speaking of the aircraft Boyington was actually referring to himself. The zest of the little boy who had raced from school to watch Clyde Pangborn perform his aerial acrobatics, and whose love for the air had lain dormant through high school and into college, now reappeared. Boyington felt as if he and that fighter inhaled and exhaled in unison. As the machine was meant to be in the air, so too was he. Rather than staring at an aircraft, Boyington was staring into a magical mirror, seeing himself and his future. Like the fighter, Boyington's intended realm existed with the clouds and wind and speed. Like the fighter, which was productive only when it lifted into the skies, Boyington had known little happiness on the ground. In the air, however, alone with his thoughts and with his aircraft, he sparkled with vitality, free of the quandaries that plagued his life.

Boyington had been thinking of switching his major even before that Sunday drive. With the nation mired in the depths of the Great Depression, architects struggled to earn a living. Few new prospects beckoned, and many architects had to fall back on remodeling work. Alarmed at the situation, Boyington debated the pros and cons of other fields. Now, during a single Sunday, he knew his future. Boyington switched his major to aeronautical engineering.

By the time Boyington graduated with his bachelor's degree on December 20, 1934, he had the added responsibilities of a family to look after. He had met Helene Clark at an ROTC dance in 1933 and married her the following July. Pregnant within a month, Helene gave birth to a son, Gregory, on May 24, 1935, only five months after Boyington graduated. Having already completed his mandatory active duty with the U.S. Army the summer before, serving at Fort Warden along Puget Sound, he was free to explore opportunities in the private sector. To help pay the bills Boyington accepted a position with the Boeing Aircraft Factory. It was not the same as being in the air, but he was at least working in the field of aviation, and he felt fortunate not only that he had a job in the midst of the Depression, but that out of the numerous applicants, Boeing had selected only Boyington and one other University of Washington graduate.

"To fly the best aircraft that were available"

Boyington soon realized that working with aviation blueprints held little excitement for him. He wanted to fly planes, not draw them, and the finished aircraft parked just outside his window seemed to taunt him with their sleek good looks and shiny exteriors. "As fortunate as I could have considered myself, I was not happy at all," he later explained. "I sat there at my desk in the plant . . . at the Boeing Aircraft Company, and I would be looking out the window whenever a plane came by. Actually, I was of very little use to the company. I don't think they really knew it, or maybe they did. In any event, I was not happy."[27]

The Marines came to the rescue. Boyington read in the newspaper about a new government program designed to increase the number of Navy and Marine pilots. On April 15, 1935, Congress approved the Aviation Cadet Act, which gave men a year of training at a Navy flight school along with a salary. Following that year, the individual would have to serve three additional years of active duty at cadet's pay before being commissioned, at which time he would receive a $1,500 bonus.

Boyington considered it a can't-miss opportunity. Not only would he learn to fly, he would earn a tidy bonus for doing it. He recalled that sparkling aircraft with "Marine Corps" stenciled on its side and decided he would enter that branch of service rather than the Navy. He had seen Marine recruiting posters with their lustrous Marine in a crisp uniform and shiny shoes, but the spit-and-polish aspect held no attraction for him. "I didn't join the service to shine shoes and polish brass, and do a lot of things that I had to do," he later stated. "I did them because that was the only way I could do what I really wanted to do and that was to fly the best aircraft that were available at the time."[28]

Boyington received the shock of his life while going through the application process. On obtaining a copy of his birth certificate, he learned to his consternation that his father was Charles Boyington rather than Ellsworth Hallenbeck. That information unnerved the young man, who had suddenly gone from being Gregory Hallenbeck to being Gregory Boyington, but he saw a silver lining in this particular cloud. He had been trying to figure out how to evade a provision in the Cadet Act precluding married applicants. His marriage certificate bore the name Gregory Hallenbeck, not Gregory Boyington, so from then on he took his father's surname. The "unmarried" Gregory Boyington joined the military. Boyington successfully navigated the application process, keeping his wife and child a secret from the Marines.

On entering the program, Boyington embarked on ten hours of preliminary training at Sand Point, Washington, that was designed to weed out obviously inept cadets. Boyington first took to the skies in a biplane with fixed landing gear and a 200-horsepower engine. It was painted bright yellow to make it easy to spot in the air in the hopes of reducing the number of accidents. The cadets dubbed these craft "Yellow Perils."[29] After completing the initial training flights, Boyington passed a check flight. An instructor observed as Boyington flew the aircraft and gave him a thumbs-up signal to indicate that he had passed that stage and could move on to what Boyington had been waiting for—his first solo flight.

July 3, 1935, was one of the greatest days of Boyington's life. Finally, like Clyde Pangborn, Eddie Rickenbacker, and the other aviators he longed to emulate, Boyington would lift from the runway and take his rightful place among the clouds and the air currents. He would be in charge; the tiny aircraft would veer to the right or left, dive down or rise upward at his command. More important, he would perform on his own, without interruption or interference from anybody. No angry parent to object; no authority figure to deny access.

The sky was his arena, and Boyington, for that moment at least, would be the sole entertainer. The excitement of that day still moved Boyington forty-two years later. "I will never forget this. This is one of my great thrills. I was so happy to have an instructor and a check pilot out of that plane and to have that plane all to myself that I just couldn't contain myself."

Boyington had only to take off, complete one circle around the airfield, and land, but in his mind he joined a fraternity whose members included those daredevils who astonished spectators with their aerobatics. "I know as I got the gun on and started down the field for takeoff, I just let out a whoop. I was so happy to be all alone with that plane, that I 'YAHOOED!' I don't know whether they could hear over the noise of the engine, but I said it so loud that I'm sure they could have."

Boyington waved to the people watching below on the ground. In the exhilaration of the moment, he did not even care that most of them were the crews of an ambulance and a fire truck parked at the end of the field, waiting to rush into action should Boyington crash. "We called the ambulance the 'gut wagon.' . . . I waved at these people. I took my hand right off the throttle and around I went and made a perfect landing."[30]

"He just loved to fly"

His stint as a cadet completed, Boyington was sworn into the service on January 27, 1936, and assigned to further flight training at Pensacola, Florida. The beach town in northwestern Florida offered plenty of excitement for the eager pilots. The base featured a library, bowling alley, and billiards room, and officers relaxed in the officers' club with .15 beer and .20 mixed drinks. Off base the men could enjoy fine dining at a number of superb restaurants or dancing at the San Carlos Hotel and B&B Casino. The beaches bordering the shimmering blue waters of the Gulf of Mexico made Pensacola a subtropical paradise. Boyington could not afford to let such amenities distract his attention from the business at hand. Almost half of the men attempting to earn their wings would wash out before the year ended, and a slip in concentration could mean the difference between advancing and winding up a mangled mess in a ruined aircraft.

The training commenced poorly for Boyington. Because many of the enrollees were civilians lacking any military knowledge, Boyington had to sit through classes in military methods, etiquette, close order drill, and other topics he already learned during ROTC. And because most of the men would wind up in the Navy, he also had to wade through manuals pertaining to ship recognition, naval engineering, and each department on board naval craft. Boyington was bored. He had entered the program to fly, but because he could not pilot an aircraft without passing this part of the course, he had to quietly tolerate the delay.

Boyington next moved into Squadron 1, the first of the five steps advancing a student toward his wings. As each man progressed through the various squadrons, he learned the intricacies of different types of aircraft and the different skills needed to fly them. Squadron 1 consisted of six weeks of classroom study in the morning followed by afternoon flight sessions. Boyington again flew the Yellow Perils, this time with floats attached so that they could take off and land in water, a far more forgiving "landing field" for the student pilots than a concrete runway.

Boyington struggled through morning classroom sessions on aerodynamics, aircraft construction and maintenance, and engine systems, but sparkled each afternoon when sitting behind the controls of his aircraft. John F. Kinney, an aviator with whom Boyington would later serve and who also earned his wings at Pensacola, described the flight classes. Each day before taking off, Boyington and the other students prepared two parachutes—one for themselves and one for the instructor—climbed into the front seat, and strapped on the harness and safety belt while the instructor taxied the craft down the runway. A tube called a gosport connected the two open cockpits so that the student could hear the instructor sitting behind him. The gosport attached to the student's ears, much like a stethoscope, and the instructor talked through a speaking tube.

Boyington first practiced takeoffs and landings in Pensacola Bay, then performed full-stall landings in which he brought the aircraft within a few feet of the water, cut power to the engine, and allowed the plane to settle gently on the surface. The trick was to cut the power at just the proper moment, else pilot and instructor experienced a harsh, bumpy landing.

Above all, the students hoped to avoid mistakes that earned a "down" from the instructor, a mark indicating the pilot had not performed adequately. Should an instructor hand out a down, the offending student received extra instruction, called "squadron time," after which he received another evaluation. If the trainee failed that as well, a board decided his fate. The board generally granted further instruction, called "board time," but a pilot who earned another down after this stage had sealed his fate. Only a rare intervention by the school's commandant could retain him in the program. Boyington failed his first flight check in Squadron 1 but bounced back to advance to the next phase.

Boyington loved the eighteen weeks in Squadron 2, which taught basic aerobatics in addition to cross-country and night flying. Like his boyhood idol, Clyde Pangborn, Boyington twisted and turned in the air as he practiced various maneuvers. He learned loops, in which he pushed the stick forward to gain airspeed, then pulled up into a vertical circle and wound up flying in the same direction as he started; the snap roll, in which he rotated the aircraft 360° about its longitudinal axis without changing direction; the Immelman, in which he combined the first half of the loop with the second half of the snap roll and wound up flying in the opposite direction; and the split S, the reverse of the Immelman.[31] Many students washed out during this arduous stage. Though Boyington failed another three check flights, each time he qualified in subsequent attempts and graduated to the next step.

In Squadron 3 Boyington handled more powerful aircraft, such as the Vought O2U biplane and the Vought SU-1 scout plane; learned how to use two-way radios; flew in nine-plane formations; and experienced the unique rush of a catapult launch. He most loved gunnery practice, however, mastering the complex mechanics of shooting at a target while speeding through the air. Boyington and the other pilots aimed at targets—huge fabric sleeves attached by cables to aircraft, which pulled them through the air—but soon realized that aircraft gunnery was far more difficult than peppering a cardboard box with a BB gun. Because the plane had fixed guns, the pilot had to aim the entire aircraft at the target. He also had to determine the distance to the target, the speed at which it was moving through the air, and the point at which his bullets would intercept it. "In that sense," Kinney wrote, "it is not unlike hunting birds with a shotgun or throwing a touchdown pass to a receiver running at full speed. You have to learn not to aim *at* the target but to aim at the point your target will reach when your bullets get there."[32]

Boyington met his nemesis in Squadron 3 in the form of one of the instructors, Capt. Joseph Smoak, who constantly berated the student pilots as they attempted to execute an Immelman or shred a sleeve. No one liked the officer, who seemed to enjoy handing out failing marks. He passed Boyington—barely—but had so often rebuked him during their flights that Boyington marked Smoak as a man to avoid in his career. Unfortunately, Boyington and Smoak would tangle again in the South Pacific.

Squadron 4 offered nine weeks of piloting twin-engine flying boats, learning how to launch torpedoes, and embarking on cross-country flights. That stint and the previous three squadrons, however, were only preludes for what Boyington had long awaited—fighters. "I was never really excited until I got to the fifth squadron, which happened to be a fighter quadrant, single seaters again. This happened to be my first love and little did I realize that I would be able to stay in fighters for the rest of my flying career."[33] Not only did he thrill to the prospect of piloting a fighter, but as he neared the end of his training and became a Marine aviator, he was eligible for an additional eighty dollars per month.

One-on-one combat in the heavens proved to be Boyington's arena; up there only he controlled his destiny. No one else could bother him; no officer could shout in his ear or nag him about mistakes or errors in judgment. He knew it was only mock combat and that the true test—aerial dogfighting with an enemy bent on killing him—awaited, but in Boyington's view, Squadron 5 was the supreme test. He even flew against Lt. Charles Crommelin, recognized as one of the Navy's top fighter pilots. Though Crommelin bested him, he gave Boyington a passing grade.

Boyington relied on an old college tactic to help him withstand the incredible physical force exerted on him when veering the fighter into a steep dive. "I had learned to tighten my neck muscles in my intercollegiate wrestling days," he later wrote, "retarding the blood from rushing out of my head."[34] His muscular chest and upper arms also helped him absorb the gravitational force that pinned pilots against their seats during steep dives.

In Squadron 5, every student at Pensacola faced one of the most frightening moments of his training—learning to fly the aircraft solely on instruments. Boyington started on a device called the Link Trainer. The instructor sat at one desk and relayed instructions to Boyington sitting at another in a flight simulator. The trainer gave Boyington and his squadronmates the opportunity to practice flying on instruments without facing the real danger of flying into the ground or a nearby hill.

Once finished with the trainer, Boyington faced the actual test of flying blind in an aircraft. A canvas hood shrouding the cockpit windows forced the pilot to rely on the information imparted by the instruments. Boyington had to stifle the natural urge to peek out and trust the dashboard when it indicated that he was flying at one thousand feet in a level approach. He had to climb and descend, and make turns and loops to fulfill this portion of his training. In separate sessions Boyington also learned how to land on an aircraft carrier. None stood ready to use in Pensacola Bay, so the students instead "skipped the rope," landing as close as possible to a rope stretched ten feet high across the runway to simulate the edge of a carrier flight deck.[35]

Boyington had little trouble adjusting to life in the air. As would be the case throughout his life, it was personal problems on the ground that nagged him. His superior officers entered negative comments in his file, most often referring to Boyington's failure to keep pace with his paperwork. Family problems bedeviled him. He sent Helene as much of his $105 monthly salary as he could, and even lived in a house with ten other aviators to cut expenses, but he could never satisfy his wife back in Seattle. The tumultuous relationship deteriorated when Boyington learned that Helene had moved in with another man. Rather than facing these issues head-on, Boyington turned to alcohol for relief. Drinking fueled his natural aggression—Boyington never backed down from an opponent, in or out of a bar—and before long he carried the reputation of being an outstanding aviator but a drunk prone to violence.

His friend 1st Lt. John Condon referred to Boyington's conflicting personalities in the air and on the ground. "I always liked him in many ways and there was never a question about his ability in the cockpit. He was fun to be around until he got too 'relaxed,' and then, 'Katie, bar the door!'"[36] Boyington possessed that Dr. Jekyll–Mr. Hyde complex that alcoholics often exhibit. At this stage of his life, no one accused Boyington of flying while impaired, but the issue would arise again in the early 1940s during his World War II combat and after the war, when alcohol offered tougher tests than Japanese aces.

Boyington emerged from his year at Pensacola by passing one of the hardest exams of all—proficiency in Morse code. He had to show that he could correctly receive twenty-five words per minute and send twenty words per minute without error. Fortunately, he and his classmates benefited from the kindliness of the Navy chief administering the test, whose willingness to issue satisfactory marks rose whenever a bottle of his favorite whiskey materialized.

Boyington earned an unflattering number of "downs" during the year-long program, yet always passed during subsequent attempts. The officer who completed Boyington's fitness report near the end of training succinctly stated, "A little slow to learn, but works hard."[37] Classmates who saw in Boyington a talented aviator besieged by problems on the ground were surprised when he earned his wings in 1937. "Flying for him was a pleasure," said friend and roommate William Millington, "but if he had to do any paperwork, forget it. He loved to live 'off base,' so to speak, as far as anything military was involved. It's a wonder to me that he passed inspections or could march in parades, because none of that meant anything to him. He just loved to fly."[38]

"Along came my answer"

The Marine Corps next sent Boyington to Quantico as part of Squadron VF-9M, a fighter squadron that became VMF-1 when the Corps changed its designations ("V" meant fixed-wing aircraft, "M" stood for Marine, and "F" indicated fight-er). Many considered the unit one of the Marines' top squadrons, and VMF-1 often performed at air shows around the country.

In hopes of calming his unstable family situation, Boyington brought his family, including a contrite Helene, to Virginia to be near him. The tribula-tions of supporting a family on a Marine aviator's pay overwhelmed Boyington, however, and he continued to seek comfort in a bottle. The birth of a daughter, Janet Sue, in January 1938 compounded the crisis, and when he was not look-ing into a bottle, Boyington stared at a huge stack of unpaid bills.

A change in assignment to the Philadelphia Navy Yard to attend a year of Basic School in July 1938 failed to help matters. The air, not a classroom, was where he wanted to be. Shorn of his sanctuary, the one place he felt free from his troubles, Boyington's strained relationship with his wife deteriorated. He sank further into debt, and his studies suffered. At the end of the year he gradu-ated from Basic School ranked seventy-first out of seventy-three students.

At least Boyington had something more exciting in the offing. Now that his year in Philadelphia had ended, he would be returning to his love—fighters. The Marines assigned him to the 2nd Marine Aircraft Group stationed in San

Diego, California. He joined VMF-2 in the first week of January 1940. Here he was surrounded by men who shared a similar love of flying and a willingness to plunge into the heat of battle. He mingled with fliers who would make a mark during the war against Japan, men such as John Kinney and Henry Elrod, who both gained fame at Wake Island during a stirring defense against numerically superior Japanese forces in December 1941. Everyone admired Elrod, who so loved to wait until the final moments before firing at a sleeve that Boyington and the others feared he would crash right into the target. Boyington chatted with and flew competitively against Harold "Indian Joe" Bauer and Bob Galer, two men who would be awarded Medals of Honor for their prowess in shooting down enemy aircraft. Captain Bauer, who later splashed eleven Japanese aircraft, was already known as one of the Marines' most talented aviators, and with VMF-2 he illustrated that he could also be a deft leader of men and an apt teacher. Galer, who was awarded his Medal of Honor for action against the Japanese in August–September 1942 over the Solomons, notched thirteen kills during the war, while Kinney survived the fighting at Wake Island only to be incarcerated for almost four years in Japanese prisoner-of-war camps. Bauer, killed in November 1942 off the Solomons, and Elrod, who perished in combat over Wake Island, received posthumous Medals of Honor.

In this last year before the war, these pilots relished the chance to participate in maneuvers off the California coast and the opportunities to show their prowess against a towed sleeve or, sometimes, in mock combat against each other. Boyington was in his element training with kindred spirits like Bauer, Elrod, Kinney, and Galer. Inferior pilots and stuffy officers whose authority rested on rank rather than ability were forgotten; Boyington pitted his skills against the big boys now. During their time with VMF-2 these men honed the skills they would so ably exhibit in Pacific aerial combat with Japan.

Boyington and his comrades faced a new challenge when they qualified in carrier landings. All had "skipped the rope" at Pensacola or another airfield, but as tricky as that maneuver was, it paled in comparison with landing on a carrier at sea. Before attempting the real thing, Boyington, Kinney, and the others practiced at an airfield with a flight deck outlined on the runway. Nothing quite prepared them for their first sight of a carrier from the sky. What had appeared mammoth from shore shrank to insignificance when seen from the air. "It is amazing how small something as large as an aircraft carrier can seem when you are trying to land an airplane on it," Kinney wrote after the war.[39] He admitted to having butterflies during his first run, and Galer had to ditch when his plane's engine quit.

In February 1940 Boyington qualified aboard the carrier *Yorktown*. A few months later he participated in Fleet Problem XXI, a massive naval exercise in Hawaiian waters that in some ways foreshadowed the events later to unfold at Pearl Harbor and included many of the operations that would be used in the Pacific fighting against Japan. In maneuvers involving Maroon forces against Purple forces, ships' crews and squadron members practiced screening and scouting, tracking opposing forces from the air, coordinating surface and air units, convoy protection, and large-fleet engagements. Air operations played a major role in Fleet Problem XXI, the last such operation before the war. Subsequent recommendations included the need for improved coordination between the Army and Navy in the defense schemes for Hawaii. The sense that deteriorating conditions in the Pacific were prodding the United States to take action grew ever stronger following this exercise when President Roosevelt ordered the fleet to remain at Pearl Harbor in hopes that its presence would deter Japan's moves in the East Indies. If Boyington hoped for wartime action, his wishes seemed about to materialize.

The thrill and excitement Boyington experienced in the air clashed with the emotions he felt at home. Another child joined the family—and added to the financial burden—when daughter Gloria was born in April 1940. Helene's drinking began to interfere with her family responsibilities, and rather than deal with that and his other problems, Boyington predictably turned to drink instead. Bob Galer once had to rescue Boyington when the inebriated officer, stuck at a party without a ride back, swam across San Diego Bay, shucking clothes as he went. The Shore Patrol picked up the exhausted, naked Marine and held him until Galer drove down to retrieve his drunken squadronmate.

Boyington's time in San Diego ended in October 1940 when he was promoted to first lieutenant—the last of his squadron to earn the advancement—and received orders sending him back to Pensacola to serve as a flight instructor. He hoped that a change of venue and the added pay that came with the promotion would smooth matters on the home front, but the situation had deteriorated beyond saving.

Both Helene and Gregory continued to find answers in the bottle and in a series of affairs. Boyington's indebtedness had so escalated that his creditors contacted the Marine Corps, who placed Boyington on a rigid schedule of payments to get him out of debt. A part of each paycheck went directly to his creditors rather than to the support of his family. Except when he was in the air, where the excitement of flying freed him and he alone was in command of his fate, Boyington felt trapped. Unless something grand came along to help him, he could see no way out of his dilemma. The worries led to more drinking, which in turn led to more problems. With each day, Boyington seemed to slip deeper into a morass.

"At that time," he recalled in 1977, "along came my answer. It seemed over my lifetime always when I was most troubled, something always seemed to come along to solve my problem."[40] To remedy his difficulties at home, Boyington turned to an organization offering lucrative bonuses to volunteer pilots. That the flying would occur in faraway Burma made the offer more enticing. In true fashion, Boyington fled to the far side of the world to evade his problems at home.

Chapter Two
"He Was Restless and Lonesome"

A history of the American Volunteer Group—the organization Boyington was about to join—describes "America in the winter of 1941 [as] emerging from behind the blindfold fastened on its eyes by years of peace, of wishful thinking, and isolationist oratory."[1] The book, written only months after the Japanese attacked Pearl Harbor, has an immediacy that later works lack, for the author viewed events through the shaded prism that only active participation in the events being described can produce.

The prewar world that Boyington inhabited offered a strange concoction of idealism and realism mixed with a touch of Alice in Wonderland. For much of the 1930s, while Adolf Hitler was threatening to drag Europe into war, the Japanese were quietly embarking on their quest to dominate the Pacific. Franklin Roosevelt, although not unaware of events in the Far East, was hamstrung by the need to wrest his nation out of the Great Depression and hampered by a vigorously isolationist Congress. Prior to December 7, 1941, his available courses of action were few.

Sources of friction between Japan and the United States existed long before the war between the two nations actually began. As early as the late 1800s, American politicians were proclaiming America's "manifest destiny" to expand beyond its continental borders into the Pacific. They viewed with greedy eyes the lucrative natural resources in the Orient, and intended to implant and maintain an economic presence in the region. American manufacturers longed to have a ready market for the vast amount of goods their factories churned out.

Japan's role in the Pacific and Far East was far more complex than that of the United States. Japan yearned to be the dominant nation in the region, but Great Britain and other colonial European countries controlled many of the area's natural resources. Only Japan stood as an Asian challenge to European mastery in the region. Many Japanese believed that achieving a leading position in the Orient would guarantee the nation's survival, while accepting an inferior status would relegate Japan to the world's backwaters.

Unlike the United States, which enjoyed spacious land into which its population could spread, Japan existed inside a tiny area about the size of Montana framed by enormous expanses of water. Approximately 80 million people lived in Japan in the 1920s. The more its population increased, the less space became available. Continued growth would have to occur at the expense of other nations. China, with its vast stretches of land, stood as the obvious choice.

"The people are filled with disquiet"

The initial aggression that culminated in World War II in the Pacific occurred on September 18, 1931, when a bomb exploded along the Japanese-controlled South Manchuria Railway near Mukden, Manchuria. Officers of the Kwantung Army, as the Japanese force in the region was called, immediately launched an invasion to overrun all of Manchuria, which they quickly seized and renamed Manchukuo. The Japanese threat to China's existence had taken stark and violent form.

Other nations, including the United States, condemned the move. When the League of Nations refused to recognize the puppet state of Manchukuo, Japan withdrew from the organization in 1933 and continued to exploit its new possession. Military force against Japan was not an option because many nations were battling the severe economic problems stemming from the 1929 Wall Street crash. The leaders in Japan, as well as Hitler and Mussolini in Europe, saw this refusal to take action as timidity and embarked on a bolder strategy as the decade unfolded.

A more serious incident occurred on the Asian mainland on July 7, 1937, when Japanese soldiers opened fire on Chinese troops at the Marco Polo Bridge near Peking, China. Who fired first is unclear, but the Japanese army used the incident as justification to unleash a huge offensive against Generalissimo Chiang Kai-shek's Chinese army. Chiang's army faced nearly insurmountable obstacles. Within weeks the Japanese army had pushed the poorly trained and underequipped forces toward the interior of China, leaving many key Chinese coastal cities open to Japanese invasion.

Relations between the United States and Japan worsened in December 1937 when a squadron of Japanese aircraft attacked the U.S. gunboat *Panay* as it was removing the last of the American embassy staff from the besieged town of Nanking. Though American flags clearly marked the sinking *Panay* as belonging to the United States, the Japanese pilots continued their assault. Two American sailors and one Italian journalist were killed in the attack, which a news reporter filmed as it was occurring.

Politicians and citizens in the United States reacted angrily to the incident, and for a while the two nations appeared on the verge of warfare. Franklin Roosevelt, knowing that he could do little to assert America's power in China, wanted to avoid engaging in hostilities over a single vessel. The Japanese government likewise hoped to avoid conflict with the United States for two reasons: Japan was already embroiled in China, and the United States might halt the shipment of valuable scrap iron and oil to Japan. With neither side looking for a scrape, a peaceful solution emerged. When Roosevelt demanded that Japan offer a public apology and pay more than $2 million in damages, Tokyo agreed, and Roosevelt diplomatically accepted the explanation that the Japanese pilots had incorrectly identified the *Panay* as a Chinese boat. Though both sides avoided war at this time, the affair soured relations between Japan and the United States.

Chiang Kai-shek steadfastly refused to negotiate surrender terms with the Japanese, even though his troops were faring poorly in the field. In October 1938 he withdrew farther into China's vast interior, moved the country's capital from Peking to Chungking, and created an alliance with his Communist opponent, Mao Tse-tung. The two bitter enemies—battling for control of their homeland—united in the common cause of repelling the invading Japanese. Despite being impeded by inferior weaponry and training, the Chinese fought admirably. The Japanese reacted to the resistance swiftly and brutally. Though they stalled at Shanghai, where Chinese forces fought for three months and inflicted 40,000 casualties, the Japanese army quickly overran other major cities. Bombers roamed the skies almost at will against the outnumbered Chinese air force. "Japanese bombing goes unchallenged," moaned Chiang Kai-shek, "and the people are filled with disquiet."[2]

The United States protested these criminal acts against a nation with whom it shared sentimental bonds developed by American missionaries who had long worked in China. Since no nation was willing or able to mount military action to deter the Japanese, however, the protest achieved nothing. The Japanese continued to plunder China at will.

By the late 1930s Roosevelt had almost irrefutable evidence that sooner or later the United States would be engaged in war with either Germany or Japan. Beset by economic problems and leading a nation whose citizens wanted to avoid overseas entanglements, Roosevelt had to adopt a cautious approach in which he could gradually awaken his fellow countrymen to the existing dangers and in which he could slowly build America's military might.

With Hitler's speedy defeat of France and the Netherlands in 1940 and his invasion of Great Britain imminent, Japan saw an opportunity to seize European possessions in the Pacific and gain control of their valuable resources. In September 1940 the Japanese signed the Tripartite Pact with Germany and Italy. The agreement bound each party to declare war on any nation not currently involved in a war against one of the three should it launch an attack against a signer of the pact. The trio hoped this alliance would deter the United States from entering the conflict.

Tokyo then pressured a weakened France into allowing the presence of Japanese troops in Indochina, ostensibly to protect their southern flank in China. In fact, Japan was hoping to gain possession of Indochina's vast natural resources and a base from which to push westward and southward against British-held Burma and Malaya. When Japanese troops moved into Indochina in July 1941, President Roosevelt cut off all trade with Japan, including the flow of oil, vowing to maintain the embargo until Japan withdrew from both China and Indochina and renounced the Tripartite Pact.

In the hope of acquiring more aid, China dispatched a delegation to the United States that included Claire Chennault, a former Army Air Corps captain who had resigned to become a colonel in the Chinese air force and air adviser to Chiang Kai-shek. Chiang knew that if he was to continue the fight against the Japanese, who by now had seized roughly one-third of China, he had to maintain the vital flow of supplies that entered the nation along the southern road that meandered through Burma and into China. Badly needing an air arm to protect the Burma Road, Chiang ordered his delegation to seek planes and pilots that might be employed in such an endeavor, certain that with modern bombers and fighters in his possession he could not only defend his homeland but launch strikes against Japan itself.

The Chinese believed they were, at least in part, fighting America's war. The U.S. public, however, was not prepared to accept Chennault's ardent arguments that current Chinese military strikes against the Japanese would preclude the need for future American action. Many civilians simply could not accept that the Japanese, whom they considered a nearsighted, short-statured, inferior Oriental people, could pose any significant risk to a Western power. Despite his most passionate statements against such stereotyping and extolling the superiority of the Japanese-made Mitsubishi A6M Zero fighter over anything the Allies had to offer, Claire Chennault could never overcome the prejudicial views that blinded his countrymen. In any event, Americans believed that the most serious threat to the United States came from the other side of the world, in Europe, where Hitler and his Nazis threatened to topple democratic governments.

Chennault's proposal for increased aid to China initially faced stern opposition from George Marshall and other top military officials, who felt that the United States would be best served by retaining every one of its trained aviators. America faced a potential war of its own, and sending aircraft and skilled pilots to the Far East would only weaken the nation's ability to respond. But with the support of Treasury Secretary Henry Morgenthau and Secretary of the Navy Frank Knox, who sided with Chennault, Roosevelt secretly agreed to send one hundred Curtiss-Wright P-40 fighter planes to China. In April 1941 he also signed an executive order that authorized officers and enlisted men to resign from the military to fly in Burma against the Japanese.

Roosevelt resorted to subterfuge to make the aid possible. Since the United States was not then at war with Japan, he could not openly support active programs helping one side. Instead of sending U.S. military personnel to run the operation, Roosevelt worked through an intermediary. William Pawley, an airplane salesman who owned an aircraft factory in China, suggested that the government secretly utilize his company as a way of shifting skilled pilots and planes to the Far East. The pilots would resign from the U.S. military and accept posts with the American Volunteer Group (AVG), a unit that would fly for a dummy corporation set up by Pawley. That way, should any pilot be captured in action against the Japanese, Roosevelt could deny all knowledge in the matter. Thus was born the Central Aircraft Manufacturing Company (CAMCO), a New York–based corporation outwardly involved in Far East trade but actually serving as a cover for American aid to China. To attract pilots, CAMCO offered an astounding salary plus a bonus for each Japanese aircraft destroyed.

Gen. Hap Arnold, head of the Army Air Corps, and Rear Adm. John Towers, chief of the Navy's Bureau of Aeronautics, still objected to the program, which removed one hundred top aviators from the military's rolls when they were most needed at home, but they could do little in light of President Roosevelt's support for the AVG. Some base commanders likewise protested when Chennault's recruiters suddenly showed up at their airfields and swiped their top pilots, but their objections were quickly shunted aside.

"I would be certainly free of debt"

The situation seemed ready-made for Boyington. He needed money and longed to escape the pressures of family and the military; the AVG offered both. The summer of 1941 had been one of the lowest periods of his life. With a touch of exaggeration and a large amount of self-pity, he later stated that the only friend he had left was his dog, Fella. "Many people wondered why the dog and I were so inseparable. As I look back on this, I realize that I was down to my last friend."[3]

That attitude would not work in Asia, though. He was about to join an organization that, while it handed him the means to ease his financial crisis, also placed him among a group of superb pilots to whom self-pity was anathema. Performance, not words or attitude, was all that mattered. The other AVG men knew nothing of Boyington. His time in the Marines and his love of aviation meant little to these experienced pilots. Boyington would gain their acceptance with what he did in the skies over Burma and China, or not at all.

During the spring and summer of 1941, Colonel Chennault dispatched recruiters to seventeen air bases throughout the country. He instructed his recruiters to accept only men with at least two years of flying experience, preferably in the military; between the ages of twenty-two and twenty-eight; who could display initiative and leadership within the restrictions of discipline; and who loved combat. Armed with the dual enticements of an ample salary and prospects for combat, the recruiters scoured air bases for individuals matching that description. To groups large and small the recruiters explained that the men they hired would embark on a mission shrouded in secrecy—they were, after all, Americans heading into battle for another nation while their own country remained neutral—but with the approval of top government officials. They described the fighting in China, where Japanese forces had pushed Chiang's military deep into the interior, seized most of the important cities along the coastline, and devastated the outmatched Chinese air force. With the aid of men like themselves, however, volunteers eager for aerial combat, the Chinese could halt the Japanese advance in China, ensure that vital supplies continued to pour into the nation along the Burma Road, and tie down Japanese forces that might otherwise be used elsewhere. In the process the men would gain valuable experience in combat flying that would be priceless when the United States entered the fighting. Not only would they form a cadre of experienced pilots, these men would be able share their talents and knowledge with other, less experienced aviators at a time when they would most be needed.

The lucrative financial inducements proffered by the recruiters gained everyone's attention. Pilots would receive the fantastic sum of $600 a month—double and triple what most of the men made—a stipend that rose to $750 for squadron commanders. In addition, travel expenses and living quarters would be provided, and each man would receive one month of paid leave. In what should have made Boyington and the other volunteers wary, recruiters added that pilots would receive an additional $500 for each Japanese aircraft they destroyed. The sole negative feature, besides the secrecy, was that Chennault could dismiss any man for insubordination or excessive use of alcohol or drugs.

Like Boyington, most of the men who joined the AVG signed on for the money and the adventure, although some volunteered out of a desire to help the Chinese or to take advantage of the opportunity to defend democracy. Joseph Alsop, a writer, thought he could find his next big story in Burma. Charles Bond jumped at the chance to gain combat experience that would help him acquire a regular commission when the time came to return to the U.S. military. Chuck Baisden wanted a crack at the Japanese. Though Baisden admitted to a lack of knowledge about world affairs in the book he later wrote about his adventures, he also noted, "I did have the feeling that the Japanese were the bad guys. I also knew this was a great opportunity to have an adventure and get paid for it, so I decided to sign up."[4] Recruiters even signed up four women—two nurses and two administrative assistants.

After listening to a presentation at Pensacola's San Carlos Hotel by Richard Aldworth, a veteran of the famed Lafayette Escadrille, a similar volunteer organization that operated during World War I, Boyington joined the AVG on August 4, 1941. Aldworth's sales pitch was not entirely accurate. He told Boyington and the other recruits, for instance, that "if we ran into any enemy military planes and fighters, that we would have better equipment than they had, much faster, and much more maneuverable, higher rates of climb, more speed, and that Japanese pilots were not mechanically inclined like the American pilots." What Aldworth said next was obviously based on the common stereotypes that then existed about the inadequate flying skills of Japanese aviators: "The Japs are flying antiquated junk over China. Many of your kills will be unarmed transports. I suppose you know that the Japanese are renowned for their inability to fly. And they all wear corrective glasses."

Boyington doubted the veracity of Aldworth's statements about the Japanese, but it did not matter to him whether he faced the best or the poorest pilots in the world. The nature of the competition paled in light of the true attraction for him—money. "It was about three times as much as I was making in the service as a monthly salary plus the fact that we would be rewarded with a $500 bonus for every plane that we shot down. I could mentally calculate in a very short time that I would be certainly free of debt and have a nice little nest egg." Boyington signed for no other reason than the dollar, a compelling motivation in light of "fatal gap between his income and accounts payable."

Boyington agreed to serve for one year, with the proviso that at the end of that time he could return to the Marines without loss in rank. Since the United States was not then at war with Japan, he and the other military personnel had to leave the service. "If we had not resigned, this would have been committing a war-like act on Japan to send military pilots over," he later said. He was told that his records and those of the other AVG members would be kept in a safe, and "that we would be reinstated without loss of [rank], meaning if there was an advance in rank while we were gone, that we would be put right back where we would have been had we not gone on such a mission. So, this all sounded good."[5]

Boyington officially tendered his resignation on August 8, then spent the next month making arrangements for his departure. On September 12, 1941, two and a half months before the bombing of Pearl Harbor stunned the nation into war, Boyington left for San Francisco, where he joined other AVG men for the long ocean voyage to Burma.

"Appointments of the ships are excellent"

Although the program was supposedly kept secret, few things pass through Washington, D.C., unnoticed—by domestic or foreign sources. *Time* magazine had already begun reporting on the AVG, and the day the first collection of pilots left California aboard a Dutch ship, Japanese radio reported the departure of American pilots for China. The radio commentator boasted that despite the dearest hopes of Chennault and Chiang Kai-shek, the Japanese navy would sink the ship long before it reached Burma's shores. As often occurred in the war, however, Tokyo's boasts failed to materialize, and the first and second groups safely found their way to the Far East.

Boyington settled his affairs at home and waited for word sending him and the third detachment west. In early September he received a telephone call explaining that an airplane ticket for San Francisco had been mailed to him. On arrival in that city, he was to register at the St. Francis Hotel. The caller instructed him to say nothing about the AVG. On the hotel's registration form he was to declare that he was embarking overseas for missionary work. Other AVG members, such as Charlie Bond, listed their occupations as clerks, artists, acrobats, and musicians in attempts to shield the true purpose for their travel.

The group Boyington joined in California formed the third and final collection of pilots and mechanics that CAMCO recruiters were bringing to the Far East. The initial unit had departed in June, with a second following the next month. Once Boyington and his companions arrived in Burma, Chennault would have his full complement on station in the Far East. Boyington and the other nineteen pilots of the third group luxuriated in the amenities of San Francisco until their September 24 departure, often in one of the hotel's bars or lounges. While they wasted no time enjoying the city as they waited, they looked forward to reaching Burma and joining their brethren, who had already begun learning to fly the fighters the AVG would use against the Japanese.

At 1:00 PM on September 24 Boyington stood on the deck of the Dutch ship SS *Boschfontein* and watched as the ocean liner steamed beneath San Francisco's famed Golden Gate Bridge, veered out into the Pacific, and set a course toward Hawaii. The Dutch crew and Javanese stewards and waiters made every effort to ensure that each passenger—AVG men made up only a portion of the ship's manifest—enjoyed the trip. Exquisite food and abundant alcohol probably did more to guarantee a pleasant voyage, although the large party of actual missionaries—not the fake one Boyington pretended to be—focused on the food rather than the liquor. Few warriors have ever headed into battle in so luxurious a style.

The conditions aboard the *Boschfontein* helped make the lengthy ocean voyage more appealing. "Appointments of the ships are excellent," wrote AVG member George Burgard in his diary, "but 35 days of this are in prospect, so there is much time ahead." Like Boyington and the others, Burgard relaxed aboard the ship, but with a sense of unease. "I'm ready to fly again—the sooner the better."[6]

Despite the opulent conditions, no member of the AVG could ignore the fact that the group was now steaming into open conflict. As soon as the *Boschfontein* left the United States, nightly blackouts from sunset to sunrise darkened the transport to shield it from prowling Axis submarines. Crew members extinguished all the lights on deck and stretched tarpaulins over the hatches. As a precaution against Japanese submarines, they refrained from dumping garbage overboard until sunset. Any submarine patrolling the area would not spot the trash floating on the surface until daybreak at the earliest, by which time the *Boschfontein* would have put twelve hours' steaming time between the ship and the refuse. Officers informed the passengers that ships from the American, Australian, and free Dutch navies were within two hours of the *Boschfontein* at any time, and the ship adopted a course—usually zigzagging to make it harder for a submarine to track its course—set by the consulates of those three nations. Though the United States had not yet taken an active role in the war, Boyington and the AVG traveled aboard a combatant vessel and had to take extra care.

Despite the wartime conditions, levity trumped gloom and doom aboard the *Boschfontein*. Boyington faced an uncomfortable, though comical, dilemma when he encountered the real missionaries early in the voyage. "We were out to sea I guess about two days, and one of the younger missionaries hailed me out on the deck as I was heading towards our headquarters for the pilots, which happened to be the bar. He said, 'Good morning, Reverend.' I didn't pay much attention. So, I went, 'Oh, oh, how are you?' I started on by again heading to the ultimate destination."

According to Boyington, a rather uncomfortable conversation ensued. "Well, just a minute. You weren't at our meeting last night," said the missionary.

"No, I wasn't," answered a flustered Boyington. "I hope you got everything solved and accounted for."

"Oh yes, we did. You know, we have to have Sunday services at sea."

"Oh, yes, yes, of course we do."

"Well, by the way, at the meeting, we decided you would be the one to give the first Sunday services."

"Oh, brother," Boyington later reminisced, "I hemmed and hawed, and did everything I could to get out of this assignment."[7] He successfully talked his way out of conducting the Sunday service, then took every measure to avoid the missionaries for the remainder of the voyage. The last thing he wanted was to stand in front of a crowd as a minister.

The other activity he planned to avoid—besides family and financial obligations—was military rigidity. He had hoped that as a member of a volunteer group fighting in an out-of-the-way spot for a different nation, he would not be subject to the military rules and strictures he found so annoying, but that paradise did not unfold on the trip across the Pacific. Curtis Smith, an ex-Marine captain who was in charge of the volunteers, insisted that the men maintain a military demeanor. "Smith had plotted the entire trip in minute military fashion, although we were no longer military men," Boyington later complained. Smith organized duties and watches and drew up a list of infractions deserving disciplinary action. He even gathered the men in formation and called roll. "Jesus, how I dreaded Smith's formations. I had counted on getting away from it all when I resigned, and hoped for something better instead of something worse."[8] Thus Boyington took his turn standing watch in the crow's nest, peering out to sea from his perch one hundred feet above the deck. At least it gave him a better view of the numerous flying fish and other aquatic life that amused the passengers.

For most of the six-day voyage to Hawaii, the men played deck tennis or sat around in informal bull sessions, sharing scuttlebutt and alcohol in equal amounts. They also discussed reports that the Japanese had sent additional troops to Indochina, which meant more risk for them when they finally arrived in Burma. On September 30 Hawaii's famed Diamond Head came into view. As soon as the ship docked in Honolulu, Boyington and the other AVG members rushed to the Royal Hawaiian Hotel and Waikiki Beach, in what George Burgard described as "the start of a wide open day."[9] Unfortunately, their time in tropical paradise was limited to a few hours. Everyone had to be back on board the vessel by 4:00 PM for another lengthy leg across the Pacific—this time to Java.

"He has ... been well oiled since the trip began"

Once the ship was beyond Hawaii, the war drew closer yet, at least in the minds of everyone on board. On October 1 the U.S. cruisers *Northampton* and *Salt Lake City* joined the *Boschfontein* to escort it across the Pacific. The passengers listened to an English-language broadcast from Tokyo that described the ship and its passengers, and explained why the men were headed to the Far East. The broadcast concluded with a stern warning that the *Boschfontein* would never reach its destination.

Facing a long stretch at sea, the American fliers relaxed into a routine of a few chores sprinkled amid much relaxation. Curtis Smith gave most of the men buzz cuts. According to Ed Overend's diary, Boyington's new haircut made him look like "a combination of Mussolini and Gargantua."[10]

The lightheartedness continued on October 6 when the ship crossed the International Date Line and jumped from Sunday to Tuesday. "Monday—This day's entry is a trifle hard to write—for today is a day that isn't," George Burgard scribbled in his diary. "Sunday night we went to bed, and then woke up Tuesday morning. The catch is that we crossed the International Date Line during the night. One bright feature is the fact that we still get $20 pay for the day even though it doesn't exist. I wish to goodness there could be about a half a dozen of these things each month." Despite the extra twenty dollars, Burgard also recorded feelings that he, Boyington, and the rest shared—boredom and eagerness to reach Burma. "The time seems to be passing so slowly as to be almost painful—but this will probably be corrected once we get to Rangoon and start flying. That can't be too soon to suit me. And so good bye to the day that never was."[11]

When the *Boschfontein* reached the Coral Sea off Australia's coast the following week, the old salts on board conducted the traditional King Neptune ceremony, an initiation rite for those crossing the Equator for the first time. Although the ceremony is normally held the day a ship crosses the line, poor weather delayed the celebration by a few days. With Lewis Bishop dressed as King Neptune, Charlie Bond as his queen, and Dick Rossi serving as the barber, everyone from CAMCO, including Boyington, suffered through a series of humiliating activities. Enjoying the festivities as much as anyone, Boyington had to approach and kneel before Neptune's Court; avoid gagging from the rotten fish stuffed in his mouth; drink salt water; remain still as men who had already crossed the Equator covered him with a mixture of flour, water, and rotten fish soup—described by Charlie Bond as a "horrid-smelling goo"—and then sit in the barber's chair while Rossi shaved off the paste with a wooden sword.[12] Afterward, the old salts tossed each initiate into the swimming pool and held him under water until the hapless target thought he would drown.

Some of the men became ill during the procedure, either from the foul-tasting mixture and rotten fish, too much alcohol, or both. Boyington, as drunk as anyone, somehow managed to remain on his feet, but his natural belligerence, fueled by liquor, almost ignited a fight with another AVG member, Robert Keeton. Despite a few scrapes and bruises, everyone had fun. Burgard recorded it as "a shindig that will long be remembered."[13] Few members of the AVG made it to breakfast the next morning.

The levity of October 13 proved to be but a break in the tedium that marked a Pacific voyage that was straining already frayed nerves as each day brought the men closer to combat. "Same old routine," wrote Charlie Bond; "breakfast, reading, Chinese lesson, bull sessions, rolling dice for drinks, lunch, nap, shooting dice with Jim and George for a dime, deck tennis, sun bathing, shower, reading, evening formation, dinner, lounge, discussions, and watching the setting sun."[14] Bond ate so much that he gained twelve pounds. Other bored AVG members engaged in fights over card games and other trivial matters. Boyington believed that the short tempers were partly due to the fact that the American cruisers were no longer escorting the ship. "Four weeks out the tension mounted still higher," he later wrote, "as we were unescorted and zigzagging all over the Pacific Ocean, it seemed. The pilots had begun to snarl at each other in earnest. A few had lost too much in card games."[15]

Inevitably, the drinking gained steam, with Boyington leading the way. With time on his hands, an available bar, and facing nothing but endless days on a universe of water, Boyington could frequently be found with a glass in his hand. Though the other AVG men freely participated, Boyington's drinking astonished his compatriots. "He has, incidentally been well oiled since the trip began and only stays sober long enough to apologize to the missionaries whom he has insulted," remarked Ed Overend in his diary. "He is strong as an ox and when he is three sheets to the wind, insists on wrestling—with the result that the surrounding territory often resembles Coventry after a blitz. He is a good fellow with all that, and a red hot flyer."[16]

The lengthy trip also gave the men time to reflect on their situation. They often gathered in clusters to chat about aviation, why they had joined the AVG, and what they expected conditions to be like in Burma. Some of the pilots, undoubtedly including Boyington, boasted of their past accomplishments, but most remained silent on that point, preferring to let their flying speak for them.

At last, on October 19, the *Boschfontein* reached Surabaja, Java, an important Dutch navy port. Delighted finally to reach land, the disembarking pilots exchanged tales with a group of CAMCO men who, frustrated with the poor conditions in Burma, had given up and were returning to the United States. They told Boyington and the rest that Chennault's setup lacked organization and equipment and that the AVG would never pose a significant threat to the Japanese. Most of the new arrivals dismissed the information as nothing more than the bitter exaggerations of disgruntled men, but the angry chatter put doubts into Boyington's mind and doubtless caused others to wonder if they had made the right decision.

During the time in Java, Boyington joined a group of men for a two-day visit to legendary Bali, a lush island two miles off Java's eastern coast. On October 21 they drove to the port through native villages and around perilous hill roads at such reckless speed that they ran over two goats and a handful of chickens. Finally arriving at their destination without further carnage, the men hopped into a fifteen-foot sailboat for the jaunt across to Bali and a stay at the luxurious Kuta Beach Hotel on one of Bali's most stunning beaches. "After a good drink we buzzed off to bed," wrote George Burgard. "I was so worn out after the wild ride that I could hardly stand."[17]

The next day offered both repulsion and delight for Boyington. He could not deny the island's beauty, he later said, but he "got a little sick" when he saw a beautiful young Balinese girl in one of the villages being held on the ground "while a priest was filing off her teeth. And even now, today, I can still hear the sound of that file. I had to hurry away." Whether it was a religious ceremony or some other rite, Boyington knew he preferred the indignities of King Neptune to that tooth-filing ceremony. Fortunately, the island's other abundant pleasures helped him to forget the sight. The men rode bicycles for much of the morning, swam in the warm waters off the beaches, attended a cockfight, observed a native dance, and stared at the gorgeous females—"No brassieres and so forth,"[18] Boyington explained—who seemed to be everywhere.

Their sojourn in paradise ended much sooner than they would have preferred, but the *Boschfontein* was scheduled to depart Java on October 23. The group started out on the return to Surabaja, but a delay at a ferry crossing caused them to arrive after the ship had left. The men pooled their money, checked in at a local hotel for the night, and then boarded a train the next morning to meet the *Boschfontein* at Samarang.

The war that had once seemed so distant suddenly drew near. While the AVG men frolicked about Java, crew members installed 3-inch guns on the bow of the *Boschfontein*. Once the ship had steamed beyond Java and headed toward Indochina, the prospect of encountering the Japanese multiplied exponentially. The time for celebrating had ended; the time to prepare for action had commenced. "I guess these people are getting serious about the Japanese," wrote Charlie Bond in his diary. "It made me feel closer to war."[19]

"An entomologist's paradise"

On November 4 the *Boschfontein* arrived at Singapore, the powerful base for the British Far Eastern fleet and the final stop before Burma. Boyington and the rest of the AVG headed for the Raffles Hotel, a five-star institution famed for pampering its customers but now on the lookout for American pilots. It seemed that an earlier group of raucous AVG pilots had done substantial damage to their rooms, and management was in no mood to endure further mayhem from Boyington's crowd. The men were allowed to check in nevertheless, and the accommodations far surpassed their expectations.

In his five days in Singapore Boyington was struck by how the residents maintained a balance between their daily lives and a war that was conspicuously absent in the United States. On the one hand, pilot Dick Rossi arranged an invitation for the men to visit one of the world's most sumptuous places, the palace of the sultan of Jahore, where Boyington marveled at the banquet hall that seated four hundred people while the sultan's lush green golf course awaited the group's enjoyment. On the other hand, signs of war were everywhere. Camouflaged gun fortifications blanketed the nearby hills, concrete walls shielded building doors and windows, air raid shelter signs were everywhere, and war bulletins covered walls and poles. The men read in English-language newspapers that the Japanese had warned the U.S. State Department that any American pilot captured while flying for China would lose all rights and be shot without delay. "Some of the boys are worried," George Burgard noted; "others getting a trifle scared." He added later, however, "Soon, very soon, we'll be flying and probably fighting. Suits me 100 percent." He ended with a feeling Boyington shared. "Let's get going."[20]

On November 9 the *Boschfontein* pulled out of Singapore and set a northwesterly course for the Bay of Bengal. At 11:00 AM on November 11, Armistice Day, everyone paused to honor the Great War's end, a moment that undoubtedly focused their attention on what lay ahead for them. Later that night the AVG men shifted gears and hoisted glasses of champagne to mark their final stint of sea travel.

After fifty days at sea the ship steamed up the Irrawaddy River and docked at Rangoon. Ed Pawley, representing CAMCO, greeted the men and arranged for them to receive their first payment, which many used to pay the enormous bar tabs they had amassed on board the ship during the trip. A 4:00 PM train whistled the men to their final destination, 170 miles north to the airfield at Toungoo, Burma. Boyington at long last had reached the war front.

Russell Whelan's book about the Flying Tigers calls Toungoo "Burma at its worst."[21] To block out the stench wafting about the town from refuse and rotting vegetation, Boyington walked with his mouth tightly closed lest the smell make him ill. The suffocating heat and humidity bathed the men in sweat around the clock. Depending on the rains, which could be torrential, they either walked through irritating clouds of dust or tried to pull their shoes free of sucking mud that stained their clothing. The continuous stream of cargo trucks that bounced through the town's main street ferrying valuable supplies to the city of Lashio and the Burma Road into China either kicked up dust or splattered mud. A bustling marketplace offered shops on one side of the road and open market stalls on the other.

Swarms of insects blanketed plates of food, flew up noses, and assaulted mouths and ears. Centipedes, scorpions, and cobras made it necessary for the men to take flashlights with them in their nighttime visits to the latrine, and they quickly learned to check their socks and shoes in the morning before putting them on lest an unwelcome visitor sting or bite them. When Boyington forgot to shake out his shirt one morning before donning the garment, a hidden scorpion stung him and caused a lump the size of a cantaloupe to swell up on his back.

"I can brush Toungoo aside with a few well-chosen expletives," Olga Greenlaw, the wife of AVG executive officer Harvey Greenlaw, wrote in her memoirs. She explained that Toungoo and the surrounding region offered "all the bugs God created to fly through the air or crawl on the ground, floors, walls, ceilings, into your food, down your back, up your legs and in your hair—beetles, lice, spiders, flies and fleas, moths, mosquitos [sic], centipedes, bedbugs, ticks and a lot more you never heard of. The place was an entomologist's paradise."[22]

None of the men with Boyington had expected to live in the lap of luxury, but these harsh conditions taxed even the sturdiest among them. The airfield at which they were based, Kyedaw Aerodrome, sat seven miles from Toungoo in a valley ringed by thick jungle. Heavy rains gave momentary relief from the sweltering heat, but as soon as the rain stopped, the humidity returned sevenfold. Claire Chennault said that the nearby jungle produced "a sour, sickening smell," and the humidity gave "the atmosphere the texture of a Turkish bath."[23] The mold that covered everything did not help to make the atrocious food provided by a Burmese mess contractor any more palatable.

Nor did the barracks offer much relief. The teakwood structures featured thatched roofs, screenless windows, and woven rattan walls. Men slept on beds made from rope springs and thin mattresses. Netting provided some relief from the insects, but no matter what precautions Boyington and the others took, lizards still managed to plop onto the sleeping men from above. "Breeze was more important than anything else," Boyington recalled, and "there were nightly attacks of millions of squadrons of mosquitoes."[24] Mosquitoes hardly confined themselves to the nighttime, however. So many swarmed through the windows and doors that Charlie Bond complained that "eating proved to be something of a challenge; the insects fought us for dinner and sometimes won."[25] The latrines were little more than holes dug outside the shacks.

Despite a few luxuries, such as native housekeepers and a nine-hole golf course constructed by the British, life at Toungoo could in no way be considered a pleasure. The lack of mail from home and female companionship did nothing to ease the situation.

"Two strikes against him"

Boyington had not traveled around the world to sightsee and relax, though. He would have appreciated better conditions, but he was there to fight, not on vacation. More than anything he looked forward to his first combat mission against the Japanese.

The United States had to agree to certain stipulations before the British allowed them to use their airfield at Kyedaw. Fighting its own war of survival with Nazi Germany but not yet involved in combat in the Pacific, Great Britain did not want to anger Japan by openly aiding China. The British let Chennault train his pilots at Kyedaw with the stipulation that he would move his base of operations to China as soon as the men were adequately prepared in the P-40 fighters. By taking that precaution Great Britain hoped to avoid an open clash with the Japanese, but events quickly dashed those aspirations. "Little did they realize that within weeks they would be clamoring for the AVG to remain in Burma," wrote Charlie Bond.[26]

Kyedaw was only one of the airfields the British maintained in Burma. Three others were positioned at Mingaladon near Rangoon, and a fourth was northwest of Toungoo at Magwe, 250 miles north of Rangoon. In addition to these bases Chennault and CAMCO arranged for facilities inside China, including an aircraft factory at Loiwing and airfields at Paoshan, Yunnanyi, and Kunming. Chennault intended to deploy his forces from each of these spots.

Kyedaw impressed Boyington, although after Toungoo anything would have been an improvement. One hundred pilots trained in the P-40s while two hundred support personnel battled a shortage of parts and the weather—the humidity rotted tires and caused radio equipment to deteriorate—to keep every available aircraft in the sky. One large hangar and additional maintenance and supply buildings stood beside a macadamized four-thousand-foot runway with a shorter runway close by. As a control tower Chennault used an open-sided hut eight feet square that rested on five-foot-high poles. The facility lacked a hospital, but a small infirmary with two doctors and two nurses took care of their health needs.

Boyington loved the lack of military rigidity that greeted him. Since each man had resigned from the service, no one walked around with signs of rank adorning his shoulders, although everyone knew what rank each man had previously held. Discipline largely depended on the individual. If a man treated the others with respect, he received respect in return. If not, the men had their own ways of dealing with an offender.

The pilots in the first two groups had eagerly awaited Boyington's arrival. They knew he had been a good pilot for the Marines but wondered why a man of his advanced age—in comparison with their own, anyway—would wind up in such a godforsaken spot as Burma. Had he been forced out of the Marines? Had money trouble or an angry spouse driven him away? Above all, why would a man relinquish an officer's commission with the Marines to fly as a volunteer for Chennault? Most concluded that Boyington was fleeing from some personal problem and decided they had best keep a close watch on the new arrival. Olga Greenlaw thought that "the boys placed two strikes against him before they ever saw him."[27] Boyington reacted to this guarded reception as he had always handled awkward relationships—he shut himself off from the other pilots and used anger and rage to maintain a safe distance from them.

Olga, with whom Boyington would develop what other AVG members diplomatically recalled as a close relationship, would come to understand Boyington's complex makeup far better than Chennault or any other AVG member. Boyington first met Olga at a bridge game at her home on the outskirts of Toungoo to which Olga's husband, Harvey, had invited him. Boyington made an instant impression on Olga when he strutted arrogantly up to the house whistling "The Halls of Montezuma." Olga later described the cocky Marine she saw that night as "not too tall, dressed in rain-soaked khaki shorts and unbuttoned shirt which exposed a barrel chest and bull neck supporting a square-cut face with powerful jaws, thick lips, flattish nose, broad forehead and protruding, heavy-lidded eyes. His waist and hips seemed much too slender for his massive torso and shoulders and his curly hair was wet." She added, "There was life and vitality in every line of his face; tenderness and humor too, and his eyes sparkled alertly." She claimed that Boyington "was the toughest of the lot and most of them were a little afraid of him."

The beautiful and charming Mrs. Greenlaw was instantly captivated. She sensed Boyington's unhappiness and frustration and astutely divined that what he most sought was acceptance. That understanding—especially when combined with ardor—allowed Boyington to relax in her presence over the coming weeks. He sensed that she understood him. "He became a frequent caller after that first visit," she explained, "popping in at odd times for coffee or whatever. He was restless and lonesome."

After many conversations Olga realized that Boyington was upset because he had not been named a squadron commander, a post commensurate with his former rank. By the time he arrived with the final group, all the top spots had been taken, thereby shutting off Boyington from a command. "I think this ruffled him," Greenlaw wrote. "His rank and experience entitled him to something better." Olga sensed, though, that something more was contributing to Boyington's misery. One day she noticed Boyington staring somberly at a photograph of Olga's nieces. "You didn't know I had three youngsters, did you?" he asked Greenlaw. He then explained that his wife had divorced him, and that he couldn't bring her and the children the happiness he felt they deserved. Though his ex-wife certainly had her faults, Boyington placed much of the blame on himself. "I'm no bargain to get along with, anyway," he confided to Greenlaw.

Despite his apparent scorn for the military—many AVG members remarked that Boyington was the most unmilitary man in the group—when he was with Olga he often spoke of the Marine Corps and displayed the pride he took in being a Marine. "He'd talk by the hour about the Marines and what a great outfit it was," she remembered. He frequently whistled the Marine Corps Hymn as he walked to his aircraft. She saw through the surface mask that Boyington wore for everyone else and realized that what he said and did often conflicted with his inner feelings, and that he loved those very things he outwardly treated with disdain.

Above all else, though, Olga understood that to be at his best, Boyington had to be in a cockpit, where only he and the plane mattered—no superiors, no debts, no unhappy wife—just Boyington alone in the skies, flying free as a bird. Without the sense of self-value he gained whenever he took to the skies, without the feeling of being needed and of contributing to something larger than himself, Boyington was a man adrift, a lost soul searching for meaning. "For quite a time he was tempestuous and unruly," Greenlaw recalled, "and for a brief period he was nothing more than a bad boy who had to hit bottom before he could zoom back into the skies where he wanted to be—and where he belonged."[28]

"A person who commanded respect"

Boyington could hardly have selected a worse location than Burma to straighten out his life, or a sterner commander than Chennault. In between what would be for Boyington too few moments of aerial excitement, Burma offered mostly boredom. Claire Chennault's stubbornness matched Boyington's, but he was at least guided by a determination and focus the Marine aviator lacked. A gifted pilot who had once performed daring feats with a popular aerobatics team called Three Men on a Flying Trapeze, Chennault's crusty demeanor and weathered face had earned him the appellation "Old Leatherface" from the press.

"The lean, heavily lined cheeks and forehead, tanned, sunburned, speckled, seemed to be made of worn-out leather," wrote Eve Curie, the daughter of famed scientists Marie and Pierre Curie, of her encounter with Chennault during her world travels. "His could have been the face of a buccaneer, of a great *condottiere* of centuries past, or that of a sailor having spent all his life on the high seas, between the sky and the water." Chennault was not unlike Boyington in possessing a love of adventure tinged by a pinch of the outlaw—but he differed in crucial ways. Curie noted that Chennault "hardly moved at all—but in his black, sparkling eyes, there was enough will power and enthusiasm to lift the world. What was spellbinding about him was his entire concentration on his task—on what he wanted, on what he planned."[29] Curie could not have said the same of the undisciplined Boyington.

Boyington fashioned a favorable opinion when he first met Chennault, who "looked as though he had been chiseled out of granite" and "seemed to be a person who commanded respect."[30] The good feelings would soon subside, though, as the two obstinate individuals butted heads. A bit of a maverick himself, Chennault realized that he commanded an unusual group of men who required a method different from military formality. While he insisted on tight discipline in the air, he took a more democratic approach when dealing with conditions on the ground and potential disciplinary issues. Thus he permitted the men to wear almost anything they preferred as opposed to requiring a common uniform. A visitor to Kyedaw might glimpse pilots and mechanics in cowboy hats and boots, silk scarves, or Russian astrakhans. Chennault often wore shorts, a sports shirt, and a mangy hat as he moved from man to man, offering advice or listening to suggestions.

He had not counted on encountering anyone as stubborn as Boyington, however, who arrived in China burdened by the heavy baggage of personal problems. Chennault could be a fair man, but he bristled at blustery, impetuous men who failed to take their duties seriously. As soon as the headstrong, independent Boyington stepped foot in Burma, a clash with Chennault was inevitable.

Boyington would be small potatoes for the former Army captain who had taken on the military establishment in the 1930s. At a time when many aviation experts believed that fighter planes should do little more than provide support for ground troops, Chennault promoted fighters as an effective air arm. Breaking with prevailing doctrine holding that bombers flying in tight formation could handily repel attacks by fighters, Chennault argued that when trained and used properly, fighters could attack and disrupt bomber formations. Chennault intended to employ fighters in groups, as opposed to the romantic World War I image of a solitary flier scouring the air for an opponent. He believed that formation tactics, in which fighters worked in pairs or teams, would be far more effective than individual dogfighting. Fighter pilots enjoyed greater firepower and maneuverability when working together, a tactic that would better enable them to swoop down on the larger, slower bombers as they lumbered toward their targets.

Top commanders in the Army Air Corps dismissed his notions, countering that the diminutive fighters had little chance against a formation of bombers. Chennault's strategy relied on disrupting those formations. He argued that if fighters received speedy notice of approaching aircraft through radio intelligence or an advance warning system, they would have time to intercept and disrupt the enemy formations. Chennault even proved his assertions during a 1933 war game in which his fighters "destroyed" an opposing bomber formation. He gained the praise of a few air proponents, but most air generals continued to spurn his ideas.

Chennault resigned from the Army in April 1937 to accept a three-month mission to study the Chinese air force. While he was visiting Chinese airfields and factories in July, the Japanese struck Chinese forces near the Marco Polo Bridge. Soon thousands of Japanese soldiers streamed into China. Chennault, sensing an opportunity to prove his theories in actual wartime conditions, and believing that the United States would one day be pulled into the war, quickly offered his services to Chiang Kai-shek.

"My postgraduate school of fighter tactics"

Boyington's rude awakening to the realities at Kyedaw began on his first day when the Burmese barracks servant, Joseph, awakened the new arrivals at 5:30 AM by beating loudly on a gong. Chennault had a long day planned and wanted to get the men started early. He realized that he had to work faster with Boyington's group to bring them up to speed with the earlier arrivals, who had already enjoyed weeks of lectures and flight training in the P-40s. Upset that the new group arrived in such poor physical condition after their long, alcohol-fueled ocean voyage, Chennault intended to pound them into peak shape, in part by banning car or truck travel from Kyedaw to Toungoo and forcing the men to either walk or bicycle the seven miles. He scheduled calisthenics, baseball, and volleyball for the flabby pilots. Five men quit and returned to the United States rather than abide by the regimen. Boyington, who loved to show off his muscular physique, relished the intense activity.

Chennault had expected CAMCO to recruit more experienced pilots, but when he realized that only half had flown a fighter, and almost none a P-40, he decided to install what he called his "pilot kindergarten." He considered it foolhardy, almost criminal, to send his men into the air against experienced Japanese pilots until they had exhibited proficiency with the P-40 and familiarity with the tactics and machines of the men they would face. During seventy-two hours of ground instruction and sixty hours in the air, Chennault and his instructors hammered the basics of flying the P-40 into his men. Boyington and his fellow arrivals sat in classrooms each morning and then climbed into P-40s in the afternoon for training flights. Chennault held his breath each time a plane lifted off. Stuck in faraway Burma, distant from supply lines, Chennault could not afford to lose a single P-40 or pilot.

Chennault's emphasis on the basics irritated some of the pilots, especially those like Boyington who came with a solid air résumé. A few bristled because Chennault thought he knew more than they did about aviation and considered them so deficient that they had to attend "kindergarten." Boyington, fresh from his duty as an air instructor at Pensacola, chafed at being treated like a schoolboy.

"It was a rude shock to some of the A.V.G. pilots when they matriculated in my postgraduate school of fighter tactics at Toungoo," Chennault wrote later. "Most of them considered themselves extremely hot pilots. After a long sea voyage bragging to fellow passengers about their prowess as fighter pilots, many of them were convinced they were ready to walk down the gangplank at Rangoon and begin decimating the Japanese Air Force. Some were highly skeptical of what a 'beat-up old Army captain' who had been 'buried in China' for years could teach youths fresh from official fonts of military knowledge."[31] His words aptly depicted Boyington, who dismissed his new commander as an oppressive tyrant. After sitting through some of Chennault's lectures, though, the men began to realize that he knew what he was talking about and based his information on facts rather than supposition. Chennault handed out copies of captured Japanese flying manuals, sheets of tactical doctrine, information collected from interviews of seized Japanese pilots, and notes on Japanese aircraft that had crashed in China and been repaired and tested.

Charlie Bond, recognizing both Chennault's intellect and his value to his own survival, immediately warmed to his superior. "Our key advantage was Chennault's knowledge of Japanese Zeros and Japanese tactics, as a result of being in China for so long. He personally taught the first contingent that was sent over and then he used them to teach us. Yet at times he would come in and give us talks. Chennault was the 'father of fighting in pairs.'"[32]

Chennault's first major obstacle was overcoming the vaunted superiority of the Mitsubishi A6M, the Japanese Zero that had performed so spectacularly in the Chinese conflict. He assured the men that each aircraft, including the Zero, possessed strengths and weaknesses. He emphasized that it was their duty to understand not only their own aircraft, but also the planes they would face in combat, so that they could utilize the P-40's strengths and take advantage of the Zero's weaknesses.

Chennault admitted the Zero's obvious advantages—it could outfly and outrace almost anything then available to Chennault's men. It could climb faster, fly higher, turn more sharply, and featured superior maneuverability. Its two 20-mm cannon and other machine guns gave the Zero a potent punch, and a Japanese pilot had boasted of the aircraft's speed, "When we chase the enemy, we must be very careful not to get in front of him!"[33]

Chennault pointed out, though, that the Zero and the Japanese aviators also had weaknesses that his pilots could exploit. He stressed that while Japanese pilots exhibited courage aplenty, they lacked initiative. The Japanese always seemed to enter battle with a set plan, and never diverted from it even when it appeared to be working to their detriment. Bombers always remained in formation, no matter how many enemy fighters descended on them, and fighter pilots invariably employed the same tactics. Chennault explained how his pilots could use these shortcomings in their favor. He emphasized that they should always attempt to throw approaching Japanese pilots into confusion, break up their formations, and make them fly by American tactics instead of their own. Once outside their comfort zone, Japanese pilots were vulnerable. Chennault also pointed out that the same lack of armor plating that made the Zero faster and more maneuverable than the P-40 made it more susceptible to bullets. The AVG pilots simply had to learn how to get close enough to inflict damage.

The unit's chaplain, Paul Frillmann, claimed that a few volunteers left the AVG and returned home after listening to Chennault outline the Zero's superiority, but most, including Boyington, were only more intrigued. Chennault presented a challenge; if they were the skilled aviators they claimed to be, they would not shrink from it. Besides, Chennault offered ways they could defeat the Zero. "One great service the A.V.G. did for all Allied fliers was to explode the myth of the great superiority of the highly touted Japanese Navy Zero," noted Olga Greenlaw. "Japanese tactical weaknesses were drilled into them constantly —and then drilled into them again."[34] In Chennault's hands, the Zero's vaunted invulnerability diminished.

Time magazine recognized Chennault's genius in an early article about him. Titled "Magic from Waterproof," the piece described how Chennault

carried model airplanes with him. At mess, at recreation, on the field, he fished them out, put them through fighting maneuvers, figured out play after mass play to outsmart the Jap. He analyzed the enemy's crack Zero fighter, reduced its performance to ten or eleven categories (climb, speed, firepower, etc.). Beside that record he set the performance of the old P-40, decided the P-40 was superior in two or three categories. He concentrated on these categories, and no A.V.G. man thenceforth tried to compete with the Zero except in power plays Chennault laid out for his ships.[35]

"What's the matter, Captain?"

In his classes Chennault focused on the advantages offered by the P-40 while never downplaying its weak points. The plane's lengthy nose, for instance, obstructed the pilot's vision on takeoffs and landing, and that led to rough landings and minor accidents during aerial training. He taught the men to weave from side to side while taxiing down the runway so they could look for other aircraft. The P-40's heavier armor plating and greater array of gun power meant that the plane could not climb and maneuver as well as a Zero, but Chennault reminded his pilots that the armor plating provided protection superior to the lighter Zero's armor, and the additional firepower made the P-40 a lethal machine. Two .50-caliber and four .30-caliber machine guns rattled bullets at a rate the Zero's two 7.7-mm machine guns and two 20-mm cannons could not equal. The heavier weight also enabled the P-40 to execute significantly faster dives than the Zero could make. Chennault urged his pilots to use their higher diving speed to make fast passes on the enemy, fire quick bursts, and get away. He instructed them to start their attack from a higher altitude than their quarry, dive quickly on the Japanese formation to break it up, single out one target, and shoot in short bursts. After executing the attack, the flier should then dive away, quickly regain altitude, and repeat the process.

If an enemy appeared on his tail, the pilot should immediately veer into a split S power dive, utilize the greater dive speed to elude the Zero, then regain altitude for another attack. Chennault admonished the men never to engage a Zero in a horizontal dogfight, where the Zero's superior maneuverability gave it the upper hand. "Hit and run!" emphasized Chennault. "Hit and run, dive, and then come back to altitude."[36] Above all else, Chennault told his men to fly in pairs, so that one pilot could look out for the other. If he found himself alone, which frequently happens in the mad scramble that is dogfighting, the pilot should immediately search for another flier to team with.

Chennault also cautioned his fliers against wasting their ammunition. They were to hold off firing until close in, where short bursts at vulnerable points brought down an opponent faster. "Your plane carries a limited number of bullets," he warned. "There is nothing worse than finding yourself in a fight with empty guns."[37] He added that while he recognized and valued the talents of his own pilots, "I want to pass along one warning. Do not underrate the Jap pilots. They have had four years of combat experience." Pilot James H. Howard noted that Chennault's early training immediately won over most of the AVG fliers, who recognized a skilled commander when they saw one.[38] Chennault's tactics, which he saw as a novel way of negating superior numbers, did not gain universal acceptance from his allies, however. An officer in the Royal Air Force, which considered diving from an opponent an act of cowardice, placed an announcement on a bulletin board stating that any pilot carrying out such a tactic would be court-martialed. Likewise, a Chinese pilot risked being executed for diving away from his opponent.

Boyington largely sided with Chennault's detractors. During a lecture in which Chennault explained his method of having three P-40s attack a single bomber, for instance, Boyington openly disagreed. "We had almost a daily lecture on tactics for the enemy if and when we got in contact with them or if they came over and attacked us," reminisced Boyington of his first days in Toungoo. "This particular lecture was on flying in formation by three. . . . We had a leader and a plane on each wing. He [Chennault] gave the advantages of fire power and his lesson that day was how the three planes fly in formation and pass on a Japanese bomber and what the advantages of mobile fire power would happen to be." Boyington believed that the three-plane formation bunched the planes too close together, lessened the effectiveness of their fire, and restricted his ability to operate. True to form, he added his two cents' worth.

"On the way over here," he said to Chennault, "I dropped by the line out there where they were bullet-sighting the P-40, and they told me they will be bullet-sighted to 250 yards. Is that correct, sir?" Chennault indicated the information was true. "Well then," replied Boyington, "the thing that bothers me is if you fly in a formation with a distance of 250 yards, and you open up on a bomber, how in the world if I am flying in formation do I keep the wingman's wing tips out of my cockpit?" According to Boyington, Chennault turned livid at this challenge to his authority. He brushed off the remark, but he never forgot what Boyington had done in front of the assembled pilots. "I never got to really officially ever ask a question of the gentleman again," Boyington claimed.[39] Boyington's departure from the AVG was only a matter of time now, as the headstrong Marine aviator would never be able to avoid a clash with his superior, a man who could match Boyington's stubbornness with obstinacy of his own.

Despite the harsh feelings between the two, Boyington absorbed more than he let on. That cavalier attitude and nonchalance masked an intense intellect, especially when it came to matters pertaining to flying. Boyington might not have liked the man who propounded the notions, but he recognized good ideas when he saw them, and he intended to find out how they worked in combat. He had plenty of opportunity, as Chennault had his men in the air as often as possible. "We practiced these tactics for weeks over the skies of Burma," recalled Charlie Bond, who practiced landings and takeoffs, loops, and air tactics with the other AVG fliers.[40] The men gradually learned the P-40's characteristics. Bond noticed that the plane tended to yaw to the left during dives, and the men discovered that the heavy P-40 was difficult to land because of its tendency to loop.

Much to the chagrin of Chennault, who carefully nurtured his tiny collection of planes and had few replacements, accidents marred the training sessions. One afternoon six pilots overran the runway and damaged their aircraft. Jack Armstrong died when he collided with another aircraft, and Peter Atkinson perished when he failed to pull out of a power dive. Even the cocky Boyington failed to impress Chennault or his companions. During his initial landing attempt his aircraft bounced along the runway and he had to hastily regain altitude for a second try. He subsequently succeeded, but then ignored Chennault's advice to land on the main gear only by trying a three-point landing. The plane swerved off the runway and spun in circles until the engine died. The younger pilots, who had been eager to see if Boyington was as good as he claimed to be, observed his trouble with glee. After Boyington jumped out of his P-40, one pilot ambled up and sarcastically remarked, "What's the matter, Captain? Lil old shark get away from you?"[41] Boyington seethed over this rebuke, but with a crowd of witnesses could do nothing but give the heckler a dirty look.

It did not take long for Boyington to gather enemies. He had irritated Chennault by openly questioning him at a lecture, and now the other pilots mocked his flying skills, the one area of his life in which he had previously felt confident. Chennault's anger and his fellow pilots' taunts shredded that confidence, and Boyington's feeling of isolation from the group grew even stronger. He yearned for combat, where he could prove his talents to everyone. For much of his life Boyington would wage a mental battle with himself—a vicious cycle in which he yearned for acceptance to boost his self-confidence but created tension with his words and deeds, which thereby further diminished his confidence. "I was forever going somewhere," he would write in his autobiography, "but never getting anywhere."[42] He would not enjoy the respect he craved until he flew with the Black Sheep. For now, however, he had to make the best of a bad situation in Burma.

"Don't become too attached to any of these kids"

After the arrival of the third group of pilots and mechanics, Chennault split the unit into three squadrons of eighteen aircraft each. Boyington flew with the 1st Squadron, nicknamed the Adam & Eves and commanded by squadron leader Robert "Sandy" Sandell. John Newkirk commanded the 2nd Squadron, called the Panda Bears, and Arvid Olson led the Hell's Angels of the 3rd Squadron. The move bolstered morale, as each man now enjoyed a shared identity with a smaller group. At the same time Chennault announced plans to move soon from Toungoo, the British base they had been using during training, to more permanent facilities at Kunming, China.

Another morale booster came in mid-November. At the local Baptist mission, where some of the men had been invited for dinner, Charlie Bond picked up a British magazine containing an article on the war and spotted a photograph of an Australian aircraft with the mouth of a tiger shark painted on its nose. Bond liked the image, and when he returned to Toungoo asked Chennault if the AVG could paint their P-40s with the same menacing teeth. What better way to intimidate the enemy than by flying into combat looking like a shark? Besides, the logo would create an esprit de corps and fashion a unit individuality with which each man could identify.

AVG support personnel painted each fighter with the fierce-looking shark mouth, and CAMCO representatives asked Walt Disney if his artists could create a design for an accompanying insignia. Rather than a tiger shark, Disney produced a winged tiger leaping forward from the base of a large V, standing for victory. These two images—the tiger shark's mouth and the leaping tiger—

became the AVG's symbols, and before long the press back home was calling Chennault's pilots the Flying Tigers.

Accidents continued to mar the practice sessions, further enraging Chennault. "We just cannot afford aircraft losses from accidents," he admonished the pilots, "since we do not have all the P-40s on hand yet."[43] Lack of spare parts added to their woes. Mechanics stripped parts from disabled planes to enable other machines to operate, but when its tires went, the plane was grounded. The frequent accidents caused some of the AVG pilots to doubt the P-40's capabilities. "Many of the pilots had never flown a P-40," Boyington later said. "In fact, most of them had not. None of the ex–Marine Corps or Navy pilots had ever been in one. We had to all check out new planes, fly them around, and some of the boys had never even had any formation flying to speak of. It was kind of a crash training program, and we did not know at the time but we just had a little over a month or so before World War II would start."[44] Chennault arranged a November 20 mock dogfight with a British Brewster Buffalo to eliminate their qualms. The P-40 handily outperformed the Buffalo, and that quieted some of the negative comments.

Chennault considered training so important that he scheduled practice flights long after the men had entered combat. Even as late as March 1942 he was working with his pilots to make them more proficient. "No matter how pressing the immediate needs of combat," Chennault wrote, "I refused to throw a pilot into the fray until I was personally satisfied that he was properly trained. That is probably one of the main reasons Japanese pilots were able to kill only four A.V.G. pilots in six months of air combat."[45]

The men found plenty of opportunities to enjoy themselves when they were not training. They yelled and whistled so loudly during an undressing scene in *Ghost Breakers,* starring Paulette Goddard, that they could be heard outside the building where the film was being shown. Frequent softball games pitted squadrons against each other, and men rode their bicycles to Toungoo—where bars and women awaited—to stay in shape.

Separated from home by thousands of miles, the men observed Thanksgiving with extra fervor. "Thursday—We had a partial holiday today as it is Thanksgiving in the States," George Burgard wrote in his diary. "This afternoon was set aside for an all-state softball game between the pilots and the enlisted men. They picked me to catch the first five innings with Col. Chennault pitching. The enlisted men beat us 8–5, and I did a poor job of hitting. The prize was two cases of Java Beer, but the winners cut us in on that too."[46]

An alcohol-fueled Boyington generally made a fool of himself at such outings. On one occasion pilot Tex Hill was on his way to Toungoo when he saw something amiss on the road ahead. When he pulled near, he saw an obviously drunk Boyington pulling a rickshaw while the Burmese driver sat in the seat normally occupied by the customer. Hill, who had not yet met Boyington, asked his companion who the man was. "Oh, that's 'Pappy' Boyington. He's one of the new pilots, a Marine."[47] Hill wondered if the AVG had scraped the bottom of the barrel to fill its allotment of pilots.

When Olga Greenlaw told Boyington that his stunt had offended their proper British associates, who believed that a person lost face if he showed such familiarity with natives, Boyington explained. "You see, I missed the last station wagon and hired the rickshaw, and halfway out to the field I began to feel like a heel letting that poor, scrawny, underfed native pull a big husky guy like myself, so I changed places with him. I'm getting too fat, anyway."[48]

On the way back to Toungoo following a November 29 picnic in the mountains east of the town, Boyington spotted a stray cow wandering in the street. Bolstered with a copious amount of booze, Boyington decided to wrestle it to the ground, and he and the cow engaged in an impromptu match while other drunken AVG men acted as announcers. The University of Washington wrestler won, to the delight of natives and AVG men alike.

These were only two of a long series of outrageous actions Boyington engaged in, mostly to draw attention to himself, and neither involved one of the too-frequent battles he waged with anyone who doubted his talent or questioned his remarks. James Howard remembered that Boyington "was built solid like a wrestler and wasn't averse to using his fists in an argument. He reminded me of a man just asking for someone to knock the chip off his shoulder." Subsequent stunts and debacles earned additional contempt from the men in the AVG. Howard dismissed Boyington's actions as those of a man angry at being passed over for squadron commander. "He became a sorehead from then on and exhibited a high state of cantankerousness for as long as he stayed with the AVG."[49]

Boyington's frequent escapes into the bottle also drove away his colleagues. Although he was likeable enough when sober, once alcohol entered the equation a demon appeared from the man. "Pappy's biggest handicap at that time was the bottle," said Charlie Bond. "He was a terrific pilot. He just never did get off on the right foot in the Flying Tigers because he arrived drinking and kept on drinking."[50]

At least combat could not be far away. Swift Japanese advances in China had already placed Kunming, their next destination, within range of Tokyo's bombers, and events elsewhere indicated that the United States itself was not far from an open conflict in the Far East. Harvey Greenlaw, correctly assessing the situation, warned his wife not to become too fond of the men. "Look, Olga, I'm going to warn you," Harvey said. "Don't become too attached to any of these kids. Some of them are going to get killed. We even have a part-time embalmer on the staff."[51]

Chapter Three
"This Was Real. This Was War"

As December 1941 opened, the cluster of Americans in Burma could not fail to notice that the war was drawing closer to their tiny airfield. The onrushing Japanese continued to batter Chiang Kai-shek's forces, and on the final day of November other Japanese units seized Bangkok, Thailand, only 350 miles from Rangoon. No one doubted that the victorious legions would soon close in on the Thailand-Burma border, thereby placing the military juggernaut within easy range of overrunning Rangoon. Fighting with the Japanese could not be far away.

With danger looming, Chennault took precautions to guard his valuable aircraft. Rather than collect them in one spot where a single bomb could wreak extensive damage, he dispersed the planes to different locations. Smaller airstrips each housed a handful of P-40s so that if the Japanese struck any location, they could not wipe out the entire AVG in one disastrous attack.

A few of the men grumbled that the Old Man and the AVG recruiters had lied to them about the dangers they would face. Combat did not intimidate any of the volunteers, but some argued that they had no idea the Japanese would so outnumber the AVG. How long, they wondered, could the small collection of Americans last against Japan's top aviators?

Boyington, eager to see what he could do in aerial combat, dismissed the long odds and trained diligently for the storm ahead. On December 2 he engaged in a mock dogfight with Charlie Bond, winning one round but losing the other when he attempted to turn too violently and snap-rolled the P-40, allowing Bond to approach Boyington's tail and even the score. In the rest of the week before war came, Boyington trained with the other pilots, kept in shape, and visited Toungoo's bars.

"Things are really popping"

As it did for Americans in Hawaii and on the mainland, war arrived suddenly and in startling fashion for Boyington. At about 7 AM on December 8—December 7 at Pearl Harbor, which was on the other side of the International Date Line—someone rushed into the ready room to alert the pilots that the Japanese had just bombed the Pacific Fleet's bastion in Hawaii and that the United States was now at war with Japan. At first speechless, the men discounted the information. How could any foreign power strike unannounced so deep into the heart of America's Pacific defenses? "Today will go down in history!" wrote Charlie Bond in his diary. "Last night the Japs hit Pearl Harbor, also Manila. The reports are unbelievable; we are stunned."[1]

George Burgard, who shared Boyington's eagerness for combat, looked forward to exacting revenge for the Americans killed in Hawaii. Olga Greenlaw took a less military view of the situation. "I suddenly felt very far away from home—and alarmingly unsafe," she later wrote. She found a beehive of activity at the aerodrome when she arrived around 10 AM. The men were cursing "those God-damn Japs" and muttering derogatory sentiments about the "monkey-faced little bastards."[2] To a man they swore that they would quickly teach the hated Japanese a lesson. Chennault, who expected an attack within the hour, placed every pilot on alert and instituted a twenty-four-hour duty schedule.

Boyington empathized with the men suffering at Pearl Harbor and in the Philippines, but nothing could mask his delight at the prospects for combat. He had held his own in mock combat against Charlie Bond a few days earlier, and now he was about to pit his skills against a man trying to kill him. Finally, above Burma in his P-40, he would have the opportunity to prove his worth and show detractors that Pappy Boyington was not a man to be dismissed. Boyington had been a battler his entire life, from schoolyard bouts and college wrestling matches to drunken challenges in the military. War handed him the opportunity to harness those attributes and direct them at a clear objective. Aerial combat would ignite the spark that had lain dormant all those turbulent years. Boyington's talents had always been present, but misguided, undirected, and unfocused. War, here in Burma but especially later in the South Pacific with the Black Sheep, would bring clarity of purpose to a man foundering on the rocks of self-inflicted problems.

Well aware that a Japanese airfield sat less than two hundred miles from Toungoo, men scanned the eastern skies for signs of an attack. Their lack of radar placed the AVG at a distinct disadvantage and forced them to keep aircraft warming up on airstrips at all times. Having to wait until they had visually sighted the Japanese put the AVG at a disadvantage, but in the war's first moments they could do little else.

Most grasped the predicament they now faced. Untested in battle themselves, they were about to grapple with skilled Japanese airmen whose cohorts had devastated the U.S. Navy at Pearl Harbor and sent Chiang's armies reeling in China. They had no way of knowing what the future held, but they were ready. "This was real. This was war," Boyington later wrote of December 8.[3] The day passed without incident, however, and members of the AVG settled into their war routine—a few hours on duty, a few off. Pilots on a scouting mission thought they might encounter the enemy on December 9 when they flew their first war patrol, a three-hour outing to inspect the Thailand-Burma border, but they turned back without sighting a single Japanese aircraft.

The next day proved equally unsatisfactory. In the early morning hours of December 10, an air raid siren woke Boyington from a deep sleep. He rushed outside with the other pilots and support personnel to prepare the aircraft and was in the air within twenty minutes, but found nothing but an empty sky. Disappointed but confident that combat could be only a few hours or days away, he returned to the airfield. He would not have long to wait. Later that day opposition collapsed in Thailand along Burma's eastern border. The Japanese speedily moved men and equipment into Bangkok in preparation for a thrust into Burma. That same day the British, desperate for aid, asked Chennault to dispatch one of his three squadrons to Rangoon to support the beleaguered Royal Air Force (RAF). Chennault sent the 3rd Squadron to Mingaladon Aerodrome outside Rangoon to help defend the Burmese capital and dispatched the 1st and 2nd Squadrons to the Chinese airfield at Kunming, a quieter war zone that had yet to face the bulk of Tokyo's divisions. Chennault intended to rotate the three squadrons between Rangoon and Kunming to keep a fresh unit in combat while giving weary pilots a chance to rest in the comparative safety of Kunming.

The 3rd Squadron left Toungoo for Rangoon on December 12 while Boyington and the rest of the 1st Squadron remained behind and waited for the order to head to Kunming. In the meantime they maintained a heightened vigilance as enemy troops threatened to invest Thailand. Cooks brought food out to the airstrips so that pilots would always be ready to take off. "Things are really popping here," wrote Frank Losonsky in his diary. "The Japanese are only 60 miles from us in Thailand."[4]

"Damn, but we wanted to be with them"

The city of Kunming served as the northern terminus of the seven-hundred-mile-long Burma Road, Chiang Kai-shek's sole remaining supply line. Now that the Japanese controlled China's entire eastern coastline, guns and equipment heading for Chiang's troops had to come in through the port of Rangoon and then go north through Lashio and on into China. Once the supplies reached Kunming, officials diverted them to Chiang's armies. The Burma Road had to be protected from Japanese air power. Boyington and his comrades of the AVG were given that important assignment.

On December 18 Boyington climbed into his aircraft for the treacherous 670-mile flight across the mountains to Kunming. Atrocious weather and buffeting winds combined with lofty mountain peaks to offer flight challenges that Boyington had never before experienced. Poorly drawn maps offered meager guidance through the treacherous route. Storm clouds frequently hid reference points. When he examined the maps, Boyington discovered that they showed reference points miles from where they actually stood. He later said that his flight to Kunming "was by far the most rugged I had ever witnessed."[5] Charlie Bond and George Burgard, who served in the 1st Squadron with Boyington, agreed. Bond wrote that they flew "over some awful-looking terrain" that was "impossible in case of a forced landing," and Burgard added that "it was the roughest country I've ever flown over. Not a place to land, even in a parachute[,] for more than 500 miles."[6]

The eighteen aircraft flew in formation at 18,000 feet. Two planes flew 1,000 feet above them as weavers, crisscrossing the formation at an angle to the flight path to ensure that no Japanese planes had drawn in on their rear and flanks.

As he approached the field, Boyington received his first glimpse of his new home. The airfield at Kunming sat at the edge of a shimmering lake surrounded by towering mountains that formed a cradle around it. The pilots had learned shortly before leaving Toungoo that the Japanese had bombed Kunming, so they had no idea what to expect. The incomplete runway sported bomb craters from the attack, but all of the AVG aircraft landed safely.

The new arrivals were pleasantly surprised with their accommodations. Kunming enjoyed a warning system that, while crude by modern methods, worked well. Lookouts posted in Chinese cities along probable Japanese air routes alerted Kunming whenever they sighted Japanese planes. This information was then posted on large wall maps in Kunming, giving the AVG time to rush to their aircraft and meet the enemy before they arrived. The modernized airfield contained a library, a small hospital, a baseball diamond, tennis courts, and the feature that most pleased everyone—hot showers. Servants cleaned their rooms, cooked tastier food than the fare at Toungoo, washed their clothes, and for two cents would cut their hair.

The pilots of the two squadrons headed to different barracks. The 2nd Squadron occupied Hostel 1, an old university dormitory in the northern portion of the city. The 1st Squadron, the Adam & Eves, went to Hostel 2, a building constructed of sun-dried bricks with porous wooden floors. Though it had the advantage of being closer to the airfield, Hostel 2 was not as comfortable as Hostel 1.

"Kunming itself, the field, our quarters, the Chinese, everything—are heaven compared to Burma," wrote George Burgard in his diary the day they arrived. His opinion solidified after a day of inspection. "With every passing hour I find it harder and harder to believe that Kunming is such a tremendous improvement over Burma. This is really great. The quarters are splendid, soft cots, furniture, showers, good food, a nice bar, excellent reception at the hands of the Chinese, and a good field to operate out of for a change. This is good old Pennsylvania winter weather. Cold and clear. We have been issued good equipment, jackets and the like, and things are really nice."[7]

On their first night in Kunming, Boyington and a group of other pilots visited the town. The normally loquacious aviator lapsed into silence as he walked the city's streets and observed the damage done to the homes and buildings. Hundreds of dead bodies along roadsides and inside vacant structures bore stark testimony to the destruction the Chinese had endured in their battle with the Japanese. Dismayed by the sight, Boyington muttered, "I can't wait until I get my gunsights on those dirty little bastards!"[8]

In an effort to avoid wearing down aircraft and pilots, the squadrons adopted a day-on, day-off schedule. Those on duty idled away their time waiting for word from the advance warning system to send them into the air. Boyington missed the squadron's initial action because of that schedule. On the morning of December 20, squadron commander Sandy Sandell broke up a card game when he charged in and said, "OK, men, this is it. Jap planes have crossed the Indochina border and are headed this way. Stay in your planes and wait for the signal to take off."[9]

AVF personnel pinned flags on a map as successive reports poured in from different Chinese villages, and soon a string of flags pointed directly toward Kunming. Sandell scrambled his pilots when the bombers drew within two hundred miles, ordering them to ascend to 20,000 feet and attack the enemy when sighted. As the Flying Tigers lifted from the runway, Capt. Fujii Tatsujiro's bombers of the 21st Hikotai from Hanoi flew in three sections toward Kunming. Four bombers approached in a diamond-shaped formation, with three more following on their starboard side and three on their port side.

As luck would have it, Boyington and Burgard, not being on duty, were sound asleep in their barracks when the alert arrived that the Chinese had spotted ten Japanese bombers. The increased activity and shouts interrupted Boyington's sleep. He and Burgard raced to the airfield wearing only trousers, undershirts, and slippers, but by the time they reached the strip, Sandell and seventeen pilots had already departed, taking every available aircraft. Frustrated because they could do nothing but wait out the bombings, the two men rushed over to the operations building and listened to the radio exchanges as their buddies grappled with the Japanese. Being able to hear their voices made the situation even more frustrating for Boyington, who longed to be pursuing the Japanese with his squadronmates. Missing what he described as "the real McCoy," was excruciating for Boyington. "Some of us had to just listen while we heard Sandell, over the radio in operations, making contact with the enemy," he later wrote. "How eagerly I listened to the accounts of this first AVG action."[10] His intense desire to show the other pilots his extraordinary talent in aerial combat would have to wait at least one more day.

As Boyington eavesdropped, Sandell led his fighters against the ten badly outnumbered bombers. Japanese pilot Gouichi Suzuki took one look at the swarm of descending planes, which he correctly identified as American, and assumed that he would soon be going down in flames.[11] A frantic thirty-minute melee ensued, with Sandell's squadron trying to recall the tactics Chennault had hammered into them during their training in Burma. The AVG dove into the enemy formation as instructed, and sometimes drew so close to their targets that the Japanese pilots could see their faces. The Japanese pulled away without dropping a single bomb on the airfield, losing four bombers versus no losses for Sandell. The AVG had so badly battered the enemy that Captain Tatsujiro never again led his bombers of the 21st Hikotai against Kunming. The Japanese, at least over Kunming, had ceded air superiority to the American volunteers.

Sandell and his companions returned to Kunming and a robust victory celebration. Local Chinese citizens paraded to the field to fête the warriors. After town dignitaries delivered rousing speeches, girls draped a purple silk scarf around each pilot's neck and placed flowers in his hand. The crowd erupted in joyous singing and chanting, first the Chinese anthem, then the U.S. national anthem. In town, grateful Chinese civilians mobbed the men wherever they went, and Chiang Kai-shek sent a personal commendation the next day. "What we had done seemed small to us," Joseph Rosbert wrote, "but, to them it meant a feeling of security in place of one of fear."[12]

Boyington shared the jubilation of the returning pilots but inwardly seethed with jealousy that he had not been part of it. Fate seemed to have stacked the cards against him. He had traveled halfway around the world to see combat in Burma and had been stuck at the airfield during his first opportunity. Furious that he already lagged behind Charlie Bond, Sandy Sandell, and the others, he took consolation in the fact that other opportunities would undoubtedly come his way.

George Burgard vented his aggravation to his diary. "Saturday—This was one of the most miserable days I have ever spent. The Japs came over at 10:00 with 10 airplanes. Boyington and myself enjoying a day off, damn it—rushed over to the field but couldn't find a spare airplane so had to stay on the ground." "It was a great day for the 1st Squadron, but a hell of a day for me," he continued. "Damn, but we wanted to be with them."[13] Boyington certainly shared those sentiments.

"The hottest of hot stuff"

The AVG quickly became villains in Japan and heroes in the United States and China. According to AVG chaplain Paul Frillmann, Radio Tokyo labeled the men "unprincipled American bandits" while Madame Chiang Kai-shek referred to them as "my little angels."[14] The U.S. press, desperately searching for a morsel of good news amid the gloom following Pearl Harbor, found it in Chennault's volunteers. Claire Chennault claimed that his men performed so capably because "when the Pacific war broke out, my boys already had four months training adapted to the peculiar flying conditions [that] obtained in Burma and South China and so went immediately into high gear."[15]

Time magazine, which had in its December 15 issue reported that the AVG called themselves the Flying Tigers and had adopted a Disney-designed insignia of a "ferocious, striped tiger leaping through the point of a victory V," heaped praise on Chennault and his pilots. In an article titled "Tigers Prove It" accompanied by a picture of the squadron insignia, the magazine asserted, with more than a touch of national pride, that the AVG's "P-40s were of an early model, far from tops. They knew . . . they would be outnumbered: but it was up to them to prove a thesis that once had seemed beyond question: that man for man, plane for plane, anything labeled U.S.A. could whip anything labeled Made-in-Japan."[16]

Olga Greenlaw described the scene from her unique vantage point: "The Flying Tigers, as captivated war correspondents insisted on calling them, were the hottest of hot stuff and held the center of the martial stage longer and more completely than any single fighting unit has ever held in this or any other war." Victorious dictators held sway over the Allies in Europe, and in the early days of the Pacific war "the runty little brown men of Nippon were making our handsome white soldiers look ridiculous, stupid and futile." Then the Flying Tigers "slashed through the blue Burmese skies and not only kicked the daylights out of all the Japs in sight but proved, mathematically, that one good American is a match for any twenty Japanese—and thereby saved the white man's ego from a total breakdown."[17]

The AVG, now simply called the Flying Tigers at home and in China, had lifted home-front morale with their exploits and regained bragging rights over their Asian foes. In the coming weeks they would meet the enemy in repeated forays, and would usually fly away with another victory.

"Damn it to hell. Stuck here"

The triumphs did not come easily. Flying comprises far more than just climbing into a plane, taking off, and discharging the guns when a target is sighted. Before ever leaving the airstrip Boyington donned winter clothing, including mittens, to ward off China's cold. Once inside the cockpit, he adjusted the earphones, goggles, and oxygen mask for comfort and checked the instruments before lifting into the air, where a new set of concerns occupied him—maneuvering the stick and rudder; adjusting the throttle and controls; checking the rearview mirror; making sure his wingman remained in position; watching the various gauges to ensure that he had sufficient fuel, oil, and altitude. Boyington performed these tasks while keeping an alert eye in every direction for the enemy, taking special care to guard against Japanese approaching to his rear, while his right hand grasped the pistol grip atop the control stick, ready to fire his six machine guns. If his guns jammed in the midst of combat, he had to manually clear them by yanking on a charging handle in the cockpit that ran to the guns.

Boyington, who lived for speed and flying and action, relished the challenges that flying entailed. Unfortunately for him, his squadron experienced little combat near Kunming in the war's opening weeks. Most of the action centered on Rangoon, eight hundred miles to the southwest, where the 3rd Squadron resisted repeated Japanese bombing attacks against that vital port city. Boyington did not calmly accept the inactivity. "In the meantime our Adam and Evers [sic] might just as well have been back in the United States blowing bubbles in the bathtub," he later lamented, "for nothing came over Kunming or even near it. Damn it to hell. Stuck here."[18]

George Burgard complained to his diary that even when a Japanese plane came into view, "we never get near enough to get a shot at them" because they always turned away. On December 21 he and Boyington rose to encounter a Japanese observation plane, "but the bird was smart and turned back short of Kunming. We accomplished the mission of keeping him out of here, but it was no consolation just to scare him away."[19]

Boyington's frustration mounted on Christmas Day when the 3rd Squadron, after listening to radio propagandist Tokyo Rose boast that the Japanese would spring a Christmas present on the AVG in Rangoon, intercepted a large formation of Japanese bombers and fighters. In the furious combat that ensued, the energized pilots turned back the attack and shot down at least ten enemy aircraft. Acclaim for the AVG grew in the United States, but Boyington knew the admirers referred to the actions above Rangoon, not to desolate Kunming where he languished.

Matters further deteriorated on December 30 when Chennault replaced the combat-experienced 3rd Squadron. Boyington hoped the 1st Squadron would be sent to Rangoon, but Chennault selected the 2nd Squadron instead. Once more Boyington was stuck in Kunming flying routine patrols. "How I envied the Panda Bears as they too left to join the battle at Rangoon, or take on where the Hell's Angels had left off," Boyington wrote of the dismal moment.[20] He had come to Burma to fly in combat, not to patrol desolate border regions.

Boyington did not stand alone in his discontent. Other pilots in the 1st Squadron, likewise irritated at missing out on the fighting, grew restless. Charlie Bond remarked in his diary that the bickering worsened as the end of December neared. Some men charged that Chennault favored the other two squadrons at their expense and wondered why they had not been given a crack at the Japanese where the hottest action was—specifically, at Rangoon.

The men focused their hostility on their squadron commander, Sandy Sandell, who had endeared himself to no one with his cold, irascible manner and his demands that the pilots and maintenance crew avoid associating with each other. The other pilots, younger and less experienced than Boyington and Charlie Bond, brought their complaints to the senior aviators. "The guys talk to me or Pappy because of our greater experience in the military," Bond wrote in his diary.[21]

On December 20 Boyington walked over to Bond's bunk to discuss the burgeoning crisis. "An undercurrent of dissatisfaction seems to be growing in our squadron," he told Bond. "Neither the pilots nor airmen seem to like Sandell. . . . It's Sandy's personality."[22] The two chatted for a while, then talked to other members of the squadron. Men listed their grievances, which seemed to center on a lack of organization and leadership, and offered suggestions to improve the situation.

Boyington and Bond decided they could not let the matter fester any longer. That same day they attempted to talk to Sandell about his problems. At first the commander "flew off the handle; he did not like our reaction."[23] Sandell finally calmed down and agreed to discuss the matter. The chat apparently did little to resolve the dilemma, as two days later George Burgard labeled the situation a mutiny and claimed that the squadron needed a more capable commander than the volatile Sandell. On December 30, with the 2nd Squadron departing for Rangoon, he added, "I like Sandell fine, as far as I am personally concerned, but he is a terribly inefficient Squadron head. Boyington would be the man for the job. Bond would also be a dandy if he only had the pursuit experience."[24]

Though the controversy still simmered as the New Year loomed, Boyington could look ahead with optimism. The year 1942 would be only the first in what was likely to be a long war that was certain to provide Boyington with plentiful opportunities for combat. His bunkmate, George Burgard, agreed that 1942 would be a memorable year. "The Japs broadcasting from Tokyo called us 'Savages' and cold blooded murderers," he wrote on December 29. "They h'aint seen nothing yet. Those rats shot at Joe Greene after he bailed out of his plane in the last fight at Rangoon. The American radio is giving us a big play, much greater, probably, than we deserve." Burgard added on New Year's Eve, "1942 is going to be a mighty interesting and unusual year."[25]

Boyington hoped that Burgard was as good a prophet as he was an aviator.

"All I do is sit around and wait"

The first half of January offered no evidence of change as the men at Kunming continued to grapple with lack of combat action and boredom. The Adam & Eves patrolled the China-Indochina border, but the routine flights offered little out of the ordinary. The intense action—the fighting and shooting and killing and dying—was still hundreds of miles away in Burma. To pass the interminably long hours, Boyington drank and played poker in the AVG bar, slept, and hunted wild animals. Men listened to radio station KGEI in San Francisco, so everyone knew that the home front closely followed the exploits of the Flying Tigers. But that only increased their desire to experience combat like their more fortunate mates in the other two squadrons. The people on the home front might consider them heroes, but the 1st Squadron would not accept the title until they had performed capably against the enemy.

Chennault sensed the growing discontent but had little sympathy for the pilots. On January 13 he offered all the men the chance to resign, although he added that anyone who accepted the offer would have to arrange his own way home; further, Chennault would make sure the man's resignation was processed as a dishonorable discharge. "He feels that anyone leaving now while we are at war and in actual contact with the enemy waxes of dishonor!"[26] scribbled Bond in his diary. Boyington may have laughed at Chennault's description that his squadron was "in actual contact with the enemy," but he declined the offer. He had not come this far only to leave before seeing action.

Good news finally arrived in mid-January when eight men, including Boyington, received orders for Mingaladon Aerodrome at Rangoon. He returned to a Burmese airfield much altered by recent action. Bomb craters potted the land, and machine-gun bullet holes aerated the barracks in which he was to stay. An unexploded bomb that had crashed through the barracks' roof and smacked harmlessly into the dirt beneath the wooden floor served as a cautionary reminder of war's perils. A sign, "Beware Unexploded Bomb," offered a grotesque welcome and let Boyington know that for the first time in his life he faced the real thing.[27]

Boyington's jubilation was short-lived. A few days after the eight men arrived, and before Boyington had the chance to experience combat, Chennault decided he had sent too many reinforcements and recalled two men to Kunming. The eight drew straws and, much to his chagrin, Boyington came out on the losing end along with pilot John Croft.

Boredom and inactivity once again filled Boyington's days. George Burgard peppered his diary with comments such as "No action of any importance," and "Spent the usual quiet day at the field except for good gunnery mission this afternoon." "Action is something that we had practically nothing of today," he remarked on January 21. "The nearest thing to any excitement was news from Rangoon that they got three Jap fighters while escorting British bombers on a raid into Thailand."[28]

Other AVG pilots reaped kills and honors while Boyington sat and fumed. As usual, he sought solace from Olga Greenlaw. He confided his feelings to the empathetic woman, who could only offer companionship to ease his tribulations. "I came out here to fight, and all I do is sit around and wait," he moaned to Greenlaw, who saw in Boyington's misery the seeds of future misfortune for the frustrated flier.[29]

Desperate battle conditions ended his discontent a few days later. Disastrous losses by the British army in Thailand forced a retreat back to Burma.

On January 23, when the Japanese, sensing the kill, commenced five days of air attacks on Rangoon, Chennault ordered Boyington back to Mingaladon to help check the advance. Boyington flew to Rangoon on January 25, ready to pursue Japanese aircraft. That first night he and a group of AVG pilots headed to the Royal Air Force club where British pilots congregated after hours. Like western gunslingers at opposite ends of the street, the two units glared at one another across the bar. "We stood there and frankly eyed one another," stated a British pilot, "and in our association felt the pride of manhood—like members of friendly bandit gangs meeting."[30] The American and British pilots overcame the initial discomfort and settled into a productive relationship.

It was a different matter in the sky, where Japanese aviators fresh from a series of triumphs as they spread Japan's rule throughout the Far East swept confidently into Burma. Boyington's first opportunity to encounter the enemy arrived on January 26, when he joined other AVG pilots to meet an incoming flight of twenty-three Nakajima Ki-27 "Nate" fighter planes from the 50th Sentai.

Boyington followed the lead aircraft, a P-40 piloted, he assumed, by a veteran from one of the other squadrons. As they rose to gain altitude Boyington wondered about the leader's tactics, because he seemed to be breaking one of Chennault's cardinal rules by keeping the P-40s at a lower altitude than the enemy. Not only was he ceding the altitude advantage, he was giving the Japanese the opportunity to dive out of the sun at the Americans. "When I went up on this first alert," said Boyington, "I did not know who was leading these eight planes . . . but I was very concerned because whoever was leading them, who I could not seem to contact on the radio, was taking us up directly under a huge umbrella of Japanese fighters."[31] Subsequent information clarified the confusion. Rather than following a veteran squadron commander, Boyington had charged into battle behind Albert "Red" Probst, another inexperienced combat pilot in his first day at Mingaladon.

The Japanese swarmed all over Boyington and the other outnumbered AVG pilots. "We were severely outnumbered by the enemy, who were flying I-97-type fighters," he recalled in a 2001 interview. "They were about 2,000 feet above us and diving down." Two set their sights on Boyington, and within moments a Nate pounced on Boyington's tail. Boyington dove to extricate himself as tracers zipped by his P-40, but he could not shake the stubborn Japanese pilot. No matter how hard he tried to reverse the situation and get behind the Japanese aircraft, nothing worked.

Soon another Japanese plane joined in the pursuit. Boyington fired wide of one, but the second Japanese looped over Boyington and forced him to break off. Boyington speedily dropped altitude to lose the pursuers, then climbed. "I spotted another fighter and decided to drop the nose and close in, firing as I gained on him. Suddenly, as he was almost filling the windscreen, he performed a split-S that any instructor would have envied, and I then noticed that I was not alone—his friends had joined in."[32]

Boyington, finally involved in his first combat action, calmly considered his options. He recalled an old wrestling trick and tightened his neck muscles to constrict the blood flow to enable him to absorb harder turns, but the lighter Japanese aircraft kept pursuing. What the AVG recruiter had told him about the poor quality of Japanese aviators had certainly proven erroneous. "In any event, I tried to tangle all on my own with several of these highly maneuverable Japanese fighters," Boyington later recalled. "I got nowhere at all because my plane could not begin to turn with them and furthermore, it could not begin to climb with them. The result was that my aircraft got shot full of holes. I even got a slug in my arm."[33]

With the odds stacked against him and his aircraft looking like a used target sleeve, Boyington decided that he had better flee and wait for another day. He finally shook free from his pursuers and returned to the airfield. "I got smart real fast and again took a dive and ran for home. When I landed I found a Jap 7.7-millimeter bullet in my arm, an incendiary that gave me a nice scar. This first crack at the Japs was a disaster, and all of us were seriously upset with our dismal performance, especially since Cokey Hoffman had been killed."[34]

While Boyington battled the Japanese, most of the other AVG pilots on the mission had safely withdrawn and returned to Mingaladon. When Boyington failed to return with them, Bob Prescott, his wingman for the flight, worried that the Japanese might have shot him down and was jubilant when he eventually landed. Prescott warmly greeted Boyington, who looked at his wingman and remarked glumly, "We didn't do so hot. Did we, podner?"[35] Boyington told Prescott not to worry about a poor first showing and promised they would improve in the next encounter. Though he tried to reassure Prescott, Boyington was seething inside about his own performance and declined to even submit an action report. "I hated myself so badly I didn't even bother to write up my first combat report, for this could have happened to others—but not to me."[36] In his first opportunity against the Japanese, the aviator limped home without a victory.

Three days later, twenty Japanese fighters challenged the AVG pilots. Boyington and nine other men rose to meet them, and in a swirling dogfight shot down sixteen of them. In the excitement Boyington heard Charlie Bond shout to the Japanese over his radio, "This is for Cokey, you son of a bitch."[37] Though AVG records do not credit Boyington with any kills that day, Boyington said in his autobiography and in postwar interviews that he downed two aircraft on the mission. No one can state with certainty what Boyington did or did not do on January 29, but it is not implausible that Boyington, already embarrassed over his dismal January 26 performance, hedged the truth.

Other than the gallant two-week stand of the outnumbered American Marines and naval personnel who had managed temporarily to halt the Japanese at Wake Island back in December, Americans had heard nothing but bad news coming out of the Pacific. Allied bastion after bastion fell to the Japanese invaders, and nothing dispelled the gloom that pervaded the home front. Now the Wake battlers had company in Chennault's hardy fliers, who received heavy play in the country's press. They were "the Wonderful Knights of the Air," and headlines trumpeted their feats. "American Pilots Rout Forty Jap Planes in Burma" one *Chicago Daily Tribune* headline blared, and the *New York Times* ran a banner stating, "Allied Fliers Rout Column in Burma."[38] *Time* magazine lionized Chennault as a gifted leader who proved that the United States possessed the qualities necessary for victory: "More than any flying man in World War II, 49-year-old Claire Chennault, leathery student of the split-second formation attack, has proved that fighting quality can triumph over numerical odds and superior equipment in the hands of the enemy. The proof is provided by the hottest, most destructive, most deadly accurate air-fighting outfit in the world: China's American Volunteer Group."[39] Overseas, the British Bulldog, Winston Churchill, praised the AVG in remarks to Parliament. "The victories of these Americans on the rice paddies of Burma are comparable in character if not in scope with those won by the RAF over the hop fields of Kent in the Battle of Britain."[40]

In the war's opening weeks and months, the spotlight thus shone on the Flying Tigers and its collection of crack aviators. Boyington longed to be included in that select group, but so far he had nothing to which he could point as justification other than his own report of two planes downed. Despite the accolades that came the AVG's way, inside the recesses of his troubled soul he knew that he had done little to justify anyone's praise. Worse, his fellow pilots knew it too.

"Devils in the sky and gods on the ground"

The next month Chennault handed him his opportunity. On February 3 he sent the 2nd Squadron back to Kunming, leaving the defense of Rangoon solely to the 1st Squadron. As the Japanese had advanced to within two hundred miles of the city, Boyington figured that he and the squadron would see plenty of action in what was shaping up as Rangoon's final moments. He was right. On February 6 thirty-five Japanese aircraft approached the city. Boyington, who had fired his guns only twice since he had been in Burma, skillfully maneuvered his P-40 behind an enemy plane, fired a brief burst, then watched as his first confirmed kill spun toward the ground. Boyington looked around, dropped on the tail of a second plane, and sent it in flames to the ground. The 1st Squadron recorded seven confirmed kills and five probable ones for the encounter. Boyington returned to Mingaladon elated that he could finally celebrate with those other pilots who had brought down enemy aircraft.

Euphoric over the victory, the home-front press heaped more adulation on the Flying Tigers. Though Tokyo Rose continued to taunt them for what she described as their cowardly hit-and-run tactics, *Time* magazine declared that the "A.V.G.'s 100-odd U.S. pilots brightened last week's dark record of war in the Pacific with great valor and victories." The article started that though badly outnumbered, the AVG gave the Japanese all they could handle, and labeled the feats of the pilots in their P-40s one of history's epic moments. One spectator in Rangoon told the reporter that the smaller fighters attacking Japan's larger bombers "looked like a fleet of rowboats attacking the Spanish Armada."[41] The magazine added that a Hollywood film director, if handed a script based on the Flying Tigers, would reject the heroics of the AVG as stretching the bounds of credibility. United Press correspondent Karl Eskelund took the praise even further on February 21, 1942: "They're devils in the sky and gods on the ground.

The majority are six feet tall and blond. 'We love our work here and miss only one thing—American blondes,' they say. They are the American Volunteer Group, commanded by wiry, wind battered Col. Claire L. Chennault."[42]

Boyington's joy over his two kills came to a sudden end on February 7 when Sandell crashed and died while testing an aircraft. Boyington assumed he would receive the open command slot, but instead Chennault asked Bob Neale to take over the Adam & Eves, with Boyington as his second in command. Neale hesitated, believing that Boyington deserved consideration because of his Marine experience and his undeniable flying skill, but nevertheless accepted the assignment. When Neale then ignored Boyington and instead discussed squadron affairs with Charles Bond, the operations officer, Boyington's sense that he was being slighted swelled. Bond noted in his diary that while Boyington had as much or more experience in fighter aircraft than anyone in the AVG, he simply did not care about what happened on the ground.

Boyington always believed that he would have performed well from the moment he landed in Burma had the men readily accepted him and followed his lead, but the AVG never welcomed him into the inner circle. An outsider when he arrived, Boyington remained on the edge of the group; his antics and drinking only increased the antagonism. He conveniently ignored the fact that his own reckless behavior was responsible for most of that antipathy. But Boyington was never one to assess himself objectively. He found it easier to blame his difficulties on others, particularly Chennault, than to point the finger at himself. He could show them if he only had the chance, he thought, but what could he do when everyone seemed to be aligned against him?

One officer chastised Boyington when he failed to taxi his aircraft to one of the satellite fields for the night, the task of every pilot to prevent the Japanese from catching all the aircraft at one location. The officer, upset over Boyington's insolent attitude, muttered, "If Boyington were in my squadron I'd send him back to Chennault in Kunming."[43] The situation continued to deteriorate. Already upset that Neale did not consult him on squadron matters, Boyington made the situation worse on February 15 by arriving late for an alert. The two exchanged such harsh words that they almost came to blows.

"Pappy Boyington is turning out to be a different man from what I had earlier thought," wrote Charlie Bond on February 15. "He is an ex-Marine flyer and an exceptionally fine fighter pilot from what I've seen, but he does not seem to care to do anything on the ground."[44] Bond had astutely observed the tendency that became a trademark of Boyington's command style. Tops in the air, he ignored paperwork and the "details" of his job when out of an aircraft. "He loved combat," explained Bond of his tempestuous compatriot. "He was one of those typical people that you have to have in time of war, but in time of peace what do you do with him? I still think Pappy basically was a good man. He just got off on the wrong foot early in his career."[45] He loved combat, the thrill of racing through the air while he chased a foe or the foe pursued him, but so far Burma and the Flying Tigers had offered little but routine patrols, a surefire prescription for trouble for the impatient aviator.

The crowning incident would occur on February 28 when Chiang Kaishek and Madame Chiang came to Kunming to host an appreciation banquet for the AVG. Though Chennault had ordered the men to abstain from drinking until after the dinner, Boyington and another pilot, Percy Bartlet, unwound in the hotel's bar instead of joining the banquet. Afterward, when Chennault and the visiting couple entered the bar, the inebriated Boyington and Bartlet could barely stand. Chennault said nothing about the embarrassing scene at the time, but it was clear to everyone that Boyington's days with the AVG were numbered.

"The streets were filled with the dead"

Boyington yearned for action, but he had no idea how much he was about to get. The situation at Rangoon in February 1942 was about to deteriorate drastically. "If Singapore falls, this spot is sure to catch hell," George Burgard wrote in his diary on February 10. With the victorious Japanese racing through Thailand and into Burma, the 1st Squadron faced the prospect of either fighting to the death or executing a speedy retreat to Kunming. When Singapore fell five days later, thousands in Rangoon fled. The Flying Tigers gallantly held on against overwhelming odds while the Burmese city crumbled. "Rangoon is certainly much more of a soft touch than Singapore," Burgard recorded on February 16, "and here we sit, 22 A.V.G. pilots trying to defend it against a nation. What prize chumps we are, holding down the hot spots for the British."[46]

Boyington and the other AVG members present watched the city collapse. British civilians joined thousands of Burmese citizens clogging the roads out of the city. The British left homes and belongings behind in their mad rush, inviting the AVG pilots to help themselves to whatever they wanted. Authorities opened the city's jails and asylums, allowing criminals and lepers to roam the streets. Violence and looting inevitably ensued, and wild dogs feasted on the carcasses of the dead animals and humans that littered the streets. Mayhem and murder became the norm in a city that once had offered exotic thrills.

Another pilot in Boyington's squadron, Jim Cross, wrote of a panic-stricken Rangoon: "The streets were filled with the dead, mangled, and wounded, and nobody was paying the slightest attention to them. As we drove along in our jeep, we tried to avoid running over dead bodies. . . . Along the docks, the smoke rose a mile high. Flames rolled and billowed from storage tanks of gasoline incinerating the dead bodies that lay nearby. As I left this city of burning dead, I found the roads jammed with refugees."[47]

With the Japanese drawing closer, Boyington flew escort missions in support of Chinese ground troops. He preferred air combat to escort, as the latter task required flying at low altitudes that brought him within range of Japanese antiaircraft and other guns, but in the desperate times the men had to focus on the most urgent needs. The AVG faced this calamity even as the number of available aircraft plunged due to overuse and lack of spare parts. Though pilots complained that under normal circumstances the rest of the fighters would be grounded too, they did the best they could with the patched-up aircraft. "Planes at Rangoon are almost unflyable," one pilot noted. "Tires are chewed up and baked hard. They blow out continually. We are short of them, and battery plates are thin. When we recharge them, they wear out within a day." He added that dust in the field fouled the engines and so heavily clogged the carburetion systems that engines malfunctioned. "This tendency of engines to quit makes it dangerous to dogfight or strafe."[48]

In light of the rapidly deteriorating situation, on February 22 Bob Neale placed the squadron on one-hour notice for evacuation. The next day he sent Boyington and five other men to the airfield at Magwe, two hundred miles north in central Burma, to fly escort and scout missions in that part of the country. Boyington's foul luck continued. Just two days after he left, the Japanese launched a massive aerial strike against Rangoon. In thick combat over the city, the AVG claimed more than forty kills. Boyington's dismay at missing this action lasted so long that he lied about the incident in his postwar memoirs, claiming that he shot down three Japanese aircraft over Rangoon at a time when he was posted two hundred miles away.

On February 27 Bob Neale learned that the British, expecting a collapse at any moment, had decided to pull their valuable radar station out of Mingaladon to prevent the Japanese from seizing it. Realizing that his pilots could do little to impede the enemy without it, he ordered the evacuation of the remaining pilots at Rangoon. After joining Boyington at Magwe for a brief time, the entire group flew to Kunming to begin preparations for that area's defense.

"Our reception was very cool"

Now ensconced in Kunming, Boyington flew raids against Japanese airfields and missions to keep the stretch of the Burma Road in that area open as long as possible. While flying with the Tigers he developed a valuable habit to prevent being surprised by an aircraft approaching out of the sun. Whenever he searched for enemy aircraft, Boyington closed one eye and held the tip of his thumb in front of the open one to block the sun's glare, allowing him to look directly at the sun without damaging his eyes and spot an aircraft coming at him from that direction. More than once, both in China and later in the South Pacific, this tactic helped Boyington detect enemy aircraft before they drew too close to be avoided.

Somehow, amid the turmoil and danger, Boyington managed to find trouble with his superiors once again. On March 5 he led a group of five P-40s assigned to escort an airplane taking Chiang Kai-shek and Madame Chiang to Chanyi, eighty miles to the east. On the return trip Boyington flew off course when he misjudged the wind speed. As a result, all of the aircraft ran out of gas and crash-landed in fields near the Indochina border. Though all five pilots survived, three of the aircraft were badly damaged.

Chennault was furious at the loss of the priceless P-40s, which George Burgard categorized as "terrible news" when he recorded the debacle in his diary. "Yesterday Boyington took five ships to escort Generalissimo Chang Kai-shek to Chan-Yi—75 miles to the northeast. The whole damn shooting match got lost completely and landed wheels up near Win-Shan, which is over 200 miles S.E. of Kunming. Five ships lost."[49] Boyington blamed the mishap on a faulty radio and compass, but few in the squadron believed the accidents were due to anything but lack of concentration and interest on the part of Boyington, who was doubtless bored with escorting the Chinese dignitaries.

Mechanics from the AVG flew to the scene and patched up three aircraft so they could at least hold together long enough for the flight back. Frank Losonsky warned Boyington that the landing gear might collapse on landing and that the bent props and dubious hydraulics imperiled any pilot's safe return to Kunming, but Boyington was determined to atone for his lapse. Boyington replied that when Losonsky judged the planes safe enough to fly, he would pilot the first back to Kunming, then drive back and do the same with the second and third. Losonsky questioned Boyington's sanity but agreed. He later judged Boyington's safe navigation in those rickety aircraft as one of the most impressive feats he had ever seen. Chennault, on the other hand, was not mollified. "Our reception was very cool, rightly so," wrote Boyington of Chennault's reaction.[50] Bob Neale removed Boyington as vice squadron leader because of the mishap.

The incident and its aftermath added impetus to Boyington's mad rush to self-destruction. On March 20 he broke into Charlie Bond's stash of liquor, which he and three others proceeded to enjoy. When Bond returned later that night, he tried to convince the four pilots to get some sleep because they had to be on alert the next morning, but the inebriated Boyington "as usual was wanting to fight with someone." Bond broke up a slugging match between Boyington and one of the other drunken pilots and finally coaxed them back to their quarters. "Pappy wants to fight me more than any other guy in the Flying Tigers," Bond wrote in his diary. "I did a lot of talking and his belligerence finally subsided. I told him that one of these days we would decide who could 'knock the other man on his can.' Pappy is a powerful man. No telling what would happen." Bond added that, "He is shorter than I am but outweighs me by at least thirty pounds. He is built like a bull."[51]

The Japanese added to their troubles on March 21 when 266 aircraft pounded AVG installations at Magwe, where the group had moved as a last-ditch stop before leaving Burma for Kunming. The onslaught ended AVG involvement in that country. The next day AVG ground personnel left by truck, handing Burma to the Japanese.

"As fine a team as Notre Dame ever was"

Boyington finally participated in a large-scale raid against the Japanese when the AVG assaulted the enemy airfield at Chiang Mai on March 24. The action partially atoned for those long months in Burma and China, when he had first been bypassed for a squadron command and then missed almost every opportunity to display his wizardry in aerial combat. The raid at Chiang Mai lacked the drama and scale of his later Pacific missions, but it was at least an offensive strike rather than a mundane escort mission. The plan called for five planes from Boyington's squadron to strafe aircraft at Chiang Mai in northern Thailand while five others from Newkirk's 2nd Squadron targeted planes at Lampang 45 miles to the south. To achieve surprise, the raiders would arrive at daybreak, the time of morning when invaders from the sky, aided by the first glitters of daylight ahead to their east, can more readily spot targets on the ground while personnel at the airfield struggle to locate aircraft attacking out of the darkness.

Because Chiang Mai was 150 miles inside Japanese-held territory, beyond the range of the P-40s, the group would have to stop first at Loiwing, China, to refuel, then at a second airstrip at Nam Sung, Burma, within range of Chiang Mai. They would remain at Nam Sung for the night before taking off in the early morning hours to arrive over Chiang Mai at dawn.

Chennault selected the ten best pilots in the AVG for the mission, which he organized in retaliation for the Japanese assault against Magwe. Six men— including Newkirk, Neale, and Bond—had shot down five or more aircraft to become aces, while Boyington and the others chosen had earned spots for their obvious talent in fighters. They would need those skills during the obstacle-ridden mission. They would have to fly deep into enemy territory, attack a well-defended base, and elude the swarms of enemy aircraft certain to be riled by the surprise assault. If forced down from enemy fire or malfunction—not unlikely considering their P-40s' state of disrepair—pilots faced hazards presented by near-impenetrable jungles and sharp, steep ridges. In his diary George Burgard labeled the mission "one of the most dangerous assignments so far."[52]

On March 22 at 4:05 AM, a Burmese servant awakened the pilots for a 5:25 takeoff. To add illumination in the still dark morning, the maintenance crew had parked an old truck at the far end of the grass strip with its headlights on. Boyington and the nine others were to aim for those headlights as they moved down the airstrip.

Bob Neale took off first, followed by Charlie Bond, who wondered if the ten pilots could successfully form up in the dark. "I followed and wondered how in hell those other guys will make it to rendezvous over the field at ten thousand feet," he later confided to his diary.[53] Boyington and Bill Bartling followed Neale and Bond, with Eddie Rector and Black Mac McGarry taking off as the top cover. Bartling, assigned to Boyington's wing, in the dark confused Neale's aircraft for Boyington's, but realized his error after a few minutes and slipped into his proper spot. The group circled the airfield as dawn broke, then set course toward Loiwing. The group was scheduled to refuel at Loiwing and continue to Nam Sung the same day, but the plan had to be changed when Newkirk flew off course and arrived too late in the day for them to reach the second airfield. They had no choice but to postpone the next leg until the morning.

The ten flew to Nam Sung on March 23 and spent the rest of the day checking equipment and preparing for the attack, now pushed back a day. With the runway lit by truck headlights and Chinese lanterns, the group lifted into the darkness at 5:45 AM on March 24, rendezvoused over the field, then turned toward Chiang Mai. As they neared their target shortly after 7 AM, Bond, the only pilot who had previously flown in the area, alerted the others that they should aim for a large mountain to their left. The airfield was at the southeast edge of that mountain.

Boyington veered into a dive. The field and hangar came into view at six thousand feet, and Boyington turned so that he could attack the field lengthwise, giving him the maximum opportunity to destroy parked aircraft. To his delight, it seemed that the AVG pilots had achieved the surprise they hoped for; the Japanese showed no signs of activity. Boyington dropped lower and made his first run at a string of Japanese aircraft that looked for all the world like shiny targets at an arcade game. So many aircraft lined the field that Bond wondered if the Japanese had parked their whole air force at Chiang Mai.

Aircraft engine noise blended with the rattle of AVG machine guns to alert the Japanese that trouble had arrived. Japanese aviators and mechanics rushed about the field or dropped to a prone position as Boyington, Bond, and others skimmed over the tops of parked planes and strafed the immobile aircraft. Explosions trashed the planes and cut down the Japanese where they stood, but also lit the area to unveil the attacking P-40s. Enemy tracers sped by Boyington, who knew that he could no longer count on surprise and darkness as allies.

Boyington strafed a line of aircraft, swung around, and prepared for a second strafing attack. "The aircraft on the field were parked mainly in two long lines," Boyington wrote in his action report. "All enemy planes were turning up, and the pilots and crews were running about their planes."[54] Machine gun crews joined antiaircraft batteries, transforming Chiang Mai into a theater of darting projectiles and flames. To reduce the chances of being struck, some of the AVG pilots began zigzagging.

In only six minutes Boyington completed two runs against the Japanese. For the first, and most likely the only, time in his stretch with Chennault's force, he felt alive, felt that he had contributed to a victory. Certain that he had destroyed at least seven aircraft, Boyington mentally calculated a huge bonus when he returned to base. As he completed his second run, Boyington heard a voice shout over the radio, "Let's get to hell out of here."[55] With the Japanese fire steadily thickening, and having completed a decent day's work by sunup, Boyington left behind a field covered with burning aircraft and injured men. The pilots returned to Nam Sung, refueled, and continued on to Loiwing, where they announced their victory by buzzing the field in a victory formation.

Eight of the ten returned safely to Loiwing. McGarry had to parachute out of his burning P-40. Thai police eventually rescued him but held him as a prisoner until 1945. Other fliers had seen Newkirk's airplane crash in a fiery ball that certainly took the aviator's life. The men observed a few moments of silence in his honor, then swaggered to the bar to swap stories and lay claim to their bonuses.

"It's surprising how quickly one gets over the horrible loss of his buddies in wartime and revels in the successes of the day," Charlie Bond wrote. "Everyone was laughing and enjoying the moment. Yet Jack was gone and we weren't sure of Black Mac. It makes one wonder about the nature of human beings."[56]

At $500 per aircraft, Boyington counted on receiving a staggering $3,500, an amount that would go far in steadying his sinking financial ship. When Chennault decided that all six pilots who attacked Chiang Mai would share equally in the mission's outcome—an estimated fifteen aircraft destroyed on the ground—Boyington's bounty dwindled. The AVG officially credited Boyington with one and a half kills, a tally for which he eventually received only $750. Boyington raged against what he perceived as another injustice, not only in the number of destroyed aircraft, but in the amount of money he received. To his dying day he maintained that no matter what the official record stated, he had destroyed more than two and half enemy planes on that raid.

Already considered heroes for their aggressive exploits against the Japanese at a time when much of America's armed forces seemed invisible or impotent, the AVG earned additional praise back in the United States for the raid against Chiang Mai. On March 25 the *Chicago Daily Tribune* reported that Chennault's aviators "smashed 40 Japanese planes at the Thailand airport of Chiengmai [*sic*] today in a dawn attack which caught the Japanese by surprise." The newspaper added that the pilots felled Japanese personnel as they ran to their planes "and pumped 3,500 rounds of ammunition into grounded planes and personnel." Five days later the *New York Times* quoted Chennault as saying of the mission, "For this raid I sent only ten pursuit planes—no bombers— who swooped down firing more than 10,000 rounds from machine guns and destroying thirty Japanese planes on the field." In its April 6 issue *Time* magazine stated that the Tigers "diced low, burned or shot up 40 planes on the ground, machine-gunned the Jap pilots as they ran for their cockpits."[57]

That the American press deified the men was hardly surprising. Other than Vice Adm. William F. Halsey's raids against a few Japanese-held islands, they represented at that time the only visible response that the United States had so far mustered to Japanese aggression. The *New York Times* editorial of March 30 typified the home-front reaction. "Equipped with P-40's, long outmoded by more modern planes, and with but a pitiful few of these, undergunned and so shy of replacement parts that many of their little complement of planes must continuously be grounded to provide spares for those in the air, they have performed the impossible by wonderful teamwork, by superb physical condition and by the application of tactics held unorthodox by many but part of the pursuit creed of their taciturn, indomitable leader." The editorial identified "romance of the first order" as well as "inspiration and a challenge" in what Chennault and his Tigers were trying to do, and urged the government to swiftly dispatch modern planes and other essential items to Chennault because "his men must be kept flying."[58]

Time magazine compared the AVG to one of the nation's most storied football programs:

> Chennault created the Flying Tigers as Knute Rockne created the great teams of Notre Dame. And in their sphere the Flying Tigers are as fine a team as Notre Dame ever was. Flying U.S.-made P-40s of outmoded

design, always short of equipment and ammunition, always hiding out from the Jap while they were on the ground, the A.V.G.s ran up a score never equaled. They knocked better than 300 Japanese planes out of the air, destroyed a hundred or so on the ground, saved many a ground force with its back to the wall. A.V.G.'s own losses: about 15 pilots.[59]

In the desperate times, with a demoralized home front seeking positive news from any source, the idolization extended almost to the unbelievable. The *New York Times* described an encounter in which one AVG pilot supposedly outmaneuvered twenty-seven Japanese opponents. The *Times* pictured the AVG men as wholesome, all-American types cut from the mold of film character Andy Hardy, played by Hollywood sensation Mickey Rooney. The newspaper quoted James Howard's reaction to being compared with hard-drinking World War I aviators, "Hard drinkers? Well, there seems to be always plenty of liquor around but, shucks, there isn't a man in our outfit who wouldn't trade you a quart of the best Scotch made for a real, honest to goodness, homemade milk shake or a coke."[60] Only a slice of apple pie and a picture of Mom were needed to complete the image.

Despite the successful raid against Chiang Mai, March had not been a benevolent month for the Allies in the region. Rangoon and other cities fell to the Japanese, causing British forces to beat a hasty retreat while the AVG had been forced to leave Burma for Kunming. Unfortunately, for both Boyington and the AVG, April would be worse.

Chapter Four
"Only Have to Fight the Japs Now"

Boyington was not the only flier with a morale problem. Many of his mates, in all three squadrons, were angry. Some were weary of the frequent combat over Rangoon; others, like Boyington, complained that there was not enough of it. Some groused about the food, the lack of spare aircraft parts, or the stiff odds against which they were expected to fly. A few simply had had enough and longed to return to the United States and all that was familiar. "Our twelve ships against the whole damn Jap Air Force," wrote one pilot in his diary. "It seems mighty futile to all of us and we're wondering what's taking the U.S. so damn long to get something over here."[1] Olga Greenlaw correctly concluded that the "pilots and ground crews had taken a terrific pounding and their nerves were starting to fray along the edges."[2]

Morale plummeted in April when Chennault informed the pilots that they would be expected to escort slow-moving British bombers and fly support missions for Chinese ground troops. They had volunteered to fight Japanese aircraft, not to accompany lumbering bombers or fly at low altitudes looking after the Chinese army, tasks that required the pilots to drop within easy range of Japanese ground fire. "My opinion of Chennault began to go downhill following his orders for a greater effort in ground attack missions," Boyington said in an interview published in 2001, "missions that were costing us in aircraft and pilots for no appreciable gain." Boyington added, "Many of the pilots refused to fly those missions, since there was no bonus in killing a tree."[3]

At the time the aviators did not realize that Chennault had little choice in the matter. Earlier that month the U.S. Army had inducted him into the Air Corps as a brigadier general, and orders from both his superiors and from Chiang Kai-shek directed him to conduct the ground support missions. On the other hand, Chennault did nothing to relieve the situation. Twenty-eight of thirty-four members of his 2nd and 3rd Squadrons had signed a petition demanding improved conditions in the AVG and threatened to resign if their requests were not met. Chennault flew to Loiwing and on April 19 conducted a meeting with the disgruntled men. He told them they had to follow orders, and unwisely hinted that those who refused to obey were cowards who could be charged with desertion in the face of the enemy. One pilot saw insult in Chennault's words and demanded an apology; sensibly, Chennault retracted them. When a second pilot, Tex Hill, stated that despite agreeing with his fellow pilots he would, in the name of patriotism, lead one of the escort missions, the revolt abated. The turmoil ended four days later when the Chinese informed Chennault that the AVG would no longer be asked to fly the distasteful missions.

The affair embittered many pilots, however, and handed Boyington another reason to detest the situation in China. Though he was not a direct part of the revolt—he was at Kunming at the time rather than Loiwing—Boyington concluded it was yet another example of the incompetence of colonels and generals. He later labeled the principals, including Chennault, Maj. Gen. Joseph W. Stilwell, and Chiang, "whores."[4]

The disconcerting news that the AVG would be disbanded in July worsened the morale problem. The pilots had agreed to fly in Burma before the United States was actively at war with Japan; what would become of them now that their country was involved in the hostilities? Boyington had assumed that he would return to the Marine Corps at his former rank, but it seemed that the U.S. Army might get him first; an induction date of July 1, 1942, had already been set. Boyington wanted nothing to do with the Army. He was a Marine, and a Marine he would remain. He wrote a letter to Chennault reminding his commander that he had signed a document stipulating his reinstatement in the Marines at his prior rank once his AVG service ended. Chennault ignored the note. Boyington, growing more incensed by the day, waited for a response, but Chennault refused to address the issue.

"I'm getting out of this comic-opera outfit"

Boyington felt as if he were standing in a giant vortex that whirled and spun around him while he watched events unfold. He had hoped that his tenure with the AVG would provide a respite from the marital and financial woes back home, but he instead faced more turmoil. He had sought combat but found little; he had assumed he would have his own squadron but commanded no one. "By April 1 I became so anxious to get out of Kunming, and all that it meant to me, that I damn nearly would have volunteered to walk back to the United States."[5] Boyington's already chaotic life tumbled further and further out of control.

The string of disastrous events never abated. While at a wedding on April 2, a ceremony that had to be halted because of an air raid alert, an inebriated Boyington stumbled down a hillside, badly injuring both knees and sustaining a large gash to his head. He spent two weeks in the AVG hospital recuperating from these self-inflicted wounds. He had barely returned to active duty when the next incident occurred.

On April 16 mechanic Leo Schramm inspected the P-40 under his charge, then left on an errand. While he was away, an alert sent pilots, including Boyington, rushing to their aircraft. By the time Schramm returned, he noticed that the plane he had worked on was taxiing in very unsteady fashion down the runway. Another mechanic told Schramm that Boyington was piloting the P-40. When Schramm asked why the plane was taking such an unsteady course, the other mechanic said of Boyington, "All I know is that I saw him drunker than a skunk about a half hour ago. He probably shouldn't be flying." Schramm watched helplessly as the plane lumbered erratically off the end of the runway, smacked into a ditch, and belly-flopped into a rice paddy. Before Schramm and the others could reach the damaged aircraft, Boyington had jumped out, hopped into a nearby truck, and sped away. Schramm pursued Boyington but failed to catch him, then returned to compile his report of the incident. Schramm's indignation at the abuse of his aircraft was nothing compared with what he felt when he learned that Boyington, in his own report of the incident, claimed that he could not lift off the runway because the plane lacked sufficient power for takeoff. "When I heard this I was beyond angry," wrote Schramm. "I wanted to confront him, in fact I had wanted to wrap my hands around his throat, but he had left the area."[6] Schramm knew the airplane had been fine and was furious that Boyington had tried to lay the blame at his feet.

As if that were not enough, Boyington added to his woes by reporting to night alert drunk. When Bob Neale confronted him, Boyington muttered, "Good-by [sic], fellows, I am going over to the Adjutant's office and turn in my resignation. . . . Guess that's what you all want."[7] Boyington's self-pitying attempt to blame the uproar in China for his drinking, and in the process perhaps gain sympathy, did not work with combat-hardened veterans like the AVG men. They expected results, not excuses, and Boyington had just about used up his allotment of the latter.

Even Tex Hill, one of the most understanding of the pilots, had trouble swallowing Boyington's antics. Hill claimed that they all drank too much, but whereas the other men set limits so that it would not interfere with their duties, Boyington never knew when to stop. "Time after time, he had disregarded his name on the nightly mission schedule, showing up the following morning too drunk to fly. On these occasions, someone always had to go up in Boyington's place, risking death. To Bob Neale and the other Adam and Eves taking that risk, it was unforgivable." Hill liked Boyington and wanted the best for him, but the man's actions antagonized everyone. "Boyington wasn't all bad. When he was in condition to fly, he flew with skill; and his comrades never questioned his courage. Many considered him the toughest man in the AVG. However, his penchant for drunkenness and fighting outweighed his contributions."[8]

The embittered Boyington, isolated in his world of self-pity and alcohol, normally turned to Olga Greenlaw for comfort, but that outlet disappeared when she left Kunming. As Greenlaw prepared to depart, Boyington walked up and told her he was going to resign. Greenlaw advised against the rash step, explaining that the move could gain a dishonorable discharge and end his career. "T'hell with it," Boyington told Greenlaw. "I'm getting out of this comic-opera outfit—and don't you worry about me, Olga. Someday you'll see me flying right up there on top."[9]

"I have resigned"

Boyington's usefulness to the AVG diminished after the pilots' revolt. He drank even more heavily and blustered to everyone that he intended to leave. Chennault groused to Tex Hill that if this were a regular military outfit, he could have Boyington shot. Chennault remained firm on the July 1 induction date into the Air Corps. When Boyington tried to explain to Chennault that he had a written agreement to return to the Marines, Chennault rebuffed him. "I have my orders," he stated brusquely. "Everybody is to be commissioned in the Air Corps not later than July 1, 1942."[10]

More than his military situation was weighing on Boyington's mind. He had received a letter from his mother informing him that the juvenile court, alarmed over neighborhood complaints that Helene was not taking proper care of their three children, had removed them from Helene and placed them in the custody of Boyington's mother. Already beset by troubles in China, and still in debt, Boyington now faced a domestic situation that urgently required his attention. On April 12, well aware that Chennault was likely to hand out a dishonorable discharge as a result, the frustrated Boyington telegraphed Marine Corps headquarters of his intent to resign from the AVG and asked for information regarding his status should he return to the Marines. Boyington submitted his resignation nine days later. He saw no sense in remaining in such an unproductive post. He had butted heads with Chennault at every turn, aerial combat always seemed to elude him, and most of the AVG considered him an outcast.

"Big news of the day was Boyington's resigning," wrote George Burgard on April 22. "This made most everybody happy, including Neale. Bond is the new Vice-Squadron Leader. Good for the old boy."[11] Word in the squadron was that Chennault, weary of Boyington's disruptions, had sent him packing. Though Boyington insisted that he had resigned, most AVG men believed otherwise. "Chennault finally got around to giving Boyington his discharge and sent him back to the States," concluded James Howard. "While he had antagonized nearly everyone in the AVG, Boyington claimed that he resigned."[12] Boyington did not help his cause when, later that night, he stumbled into the mess hall, obviously inebriated. Bob Neale told Charlie Bond that Boyington had been drunk for six straight days.

Whether Boyington resigned first and was discharged afterward is a moot question. His relationship with the AVG had been irreparably shattered, and that state of affairs lasted until Boyington's death. He had almost no contact with the Flying Tigers after the war, either individually or at unit reunions. With the rare exception, current Internet Flying Tiger chat boards contain harsh condemnations of Boyington, depicting him as a drunk with obvious flying skills who caused more trouble in the unit than he was worth.

The men of the AVG are for the most part justified in their antipathy toward Boyington. He contributed little to their success in his five months with the Flying Tigers. Boyington never felt comfortable with the unit, a group of men he erroneously concluded had no use for him, and their relations were rocky from day one. Often feeling sorry for himself, he turned to alcohol or the welcome friendship of Olga Greenlaw to escape their disapprobation. Like his marriage to Helene, it was a relationship best severed.

Boyington tried to explain his resignation to Olga Greenlaw in a subsequent letter, which contained the expected mixture of emotion and an attempt to gain sympathy. "I have resigned because I think it was the best thing to do," he confided to her, not inaccurately. "'For the good of the service' shall I say? I want you to know that I am not a coward, but I don't have to tell you that." Greenlaw was hardly surprised. "Another friend gone!" she wrote in her memoir. "I felt sad and sorry for this boy who had bobbled his chances."[13] At this stage of his career Boyington was indeed reacting to trying circumstances like a boy rather than a man. The AVG had given him a chance to steady his turbulent life, but he had tossed it away just as he had thrown away previous opportunities.

Boyington did succeed in one respect. Throughout the long ordeal that was his association with the AVG, Boyington observed. He may have grumbled, he may have drunk too much, and he may have hated Chennault, but he was too astute an aviator not to notice Chennault's innovative methods. He would take what he learned under Chennault, especially how to engage enemy aircraft, to the South Pacific and incorporate it into his own squadron. Boyington detested Chennault, but if imitation is indeed the sincerest form of flattery, in the South Pacific with the Black Sheep, Boyington flattered Chennault. Boyington exhibited many imperfections while he was with the AVG, but ignoring valuable advice was not one of them.

"This tyrant had to be taught a lesson"

As if Boyington had not created enough controversy, as soon as he reached the United States he further muddied the waters by claiming that he shot down six Japanese aircraft in the half year he spent with the Flying Tigers, a number he later reaffirmed in the South Pacific and again repeated in his autobiography. The murky details supporting his claims resulted in a debate that lingers to this day. Boyington's memory clashes with official AVG records and with research conducted by historians, particularly Bruce Gamble. All agree that he should be credited with no more than three and a half kills. No official record supports his statement that on at least two occasions—February 7 and February 25—he registered kills that were not later attributed to him.

James Howard, president of the AVG confirmation board, explained that the board required proof of a pilot's claim. "For years, Boyington promoted the fantasy he destroyed six Jap planes with the AVG," said Howard. But after examining the evidence, Howard and the board awarded him with only three and a half kills—two aircraft shot down over Rangoon on February 6, and credit for destroying one and a half planes on the ground at Chiang Mai on March 24, when all ten aviators shared equally in the outcome.[14]

Why did Boyington exaggerate his claims? It is not too much of a stretch to believe that he simply wanted to impress his Marine compatriots. He had long boasted of his prowess in the cockpit. How could he return from the vaunted Flying Tigers, the organization whose exploits newspapers had heralded in boldface type, in less than a starring role? He could not be so boastful as to claim he shot down more than any other Tiger; some men had recorded more than ten kills. However, he could slide comfortably along telling people that he shot down six—enough to be considered an ace but a figure sufficiently under the radar to be believable and that would avoid rigorous scrutiny at home while earning him accolades. Whether he shot down three and a half or six aircraft might seem irrelevant until one adds up his kills from later in the war, when he amassed one of the top records in the Pacific. If he is credited with six kills in Burma, Boyington stands as the leading Marine ace of all time. If not, another aviator takes his place.

"So, I ended up, in the Flying Tiger era, with six planes to my credit," he said in a 1977 interview, "and even though they were paying me three times my normal salary and giving me a bonus of $500, I never did get completely paid off. It only proved one thing. When I left there I was getting paid big money in those days and back in the Marine Corps where I got paid absolutely nothing extra for shooting down a plane, I shot down a lot more airplanes. . . . I seem to work better for nothing than I do for money."[15] The truth is that he worked better for those he felt appreciated him. Chennault and the Flying Tigers had little use for him. The Black Sheep did.

After resigning from the AVG Boyington embarked on a lengthy voyage to the United States. Because the Japanese navy blocked his return by the more direct trans-Pacific routes, Boyington had to travel west to return home. He first flew to Calcutta over the Hump, the portion of the Himalayas that aviators around the world feared for its turbulence and life-threatening conditions. Boyington concurred, later writing that the dangers of flying across the mountains "cannot be exaggerated in my opinion." Gale-force winds buffeted the transport "as though some gigantic animal had the plane in its mouth and was shaking it to pieces," and ice buildup on the aircraft placed everyone in peril. Boyington watched through a window as ice chunks broke off the right engine propeller and smacked against the cabin. "At times they sounded as if they would tear the plane apart. This was far worse than combat, as far as I was concerned, because there wasn't one damn thing I could do about anything."[16]

He spent a week in Calcutta waiting for another hop to Karachi, Pakistan, where he planned to board an Army Air Corps transport to Africa. When Boyington wired Chennault asking for his help in obtaining passage aboard a transport, Chennault sent a message to Army officials in Karachi stating that he could not assist Boyington and suggesting they draft him into the Tenth Air Force as a second lieutenant. "Who was this guy, God?" Boyington wrote in his autobiography of Chennault's calculated insult. "Why should he pick on me? . . . This tyrant had to be taught a lesson, even if it meant my swimming back to the Corps and shooting down a thousand Japs."[17]

Like many alcoholics, Boyington blamed someone else for his predicament. If people would just stop picking on him, he thought, his life would improve. On the positive side, Chennault's action prodded Boyington to succeed. Chennault and many of the Flying Tigers had written off Boyington. That abrupt dismissal motivated Boyington to prove them wrong, to show that he could capably perform in both an airplane and in command of a squadron.

Denied access to the speedier transport, Boyington purchased a ticket to New York on the SS *Brazil*. Amazingly, he met the same group of missionaries that had traveled to Burma aboard the *Boschfontein* with him in 1941. Though friendly with the men of God, Boyington spent most of his time pursuing a large group of females as the ship wended its way home from the war zone.

The *Brazil* pulled into New York Harbor on July 13, 1942, and Boyington hastened to Washington, D.C., to check on his military status, which his Marine superiors had been reviewing. Col. Ralph Mitchell, a promising officer Boyington would meet again in the South Pacific, thought the Marines would benefit from a combat-experienced aviator like Boyington and recommended that Boyington be accepted back into the Corps. Maj. Gen. Thomas Holcomb, the Marine commandant, agreed and forwarded Boyington's letter to the secretary of the navy for final approval. His superiors suggested that Boyington rejoin his family and straighten out his debts while he awaited orders for a new assignment.

Boyington followed their advice and returned to Seattle. As weeks turned into months, he impatiently waited for word from the Marines. He delivered speeches to civic groups in Washington and California in which he talked about his adventures in Burma and China. When he filed for custody of his children, the judge agreed that he should be the primary custodian but ordered the children to remain with his mother until Boyington could offer a more stable situation. To help pay his bills Boyington worked in the same parking garage where he had earned extra money to pay for college expenses. The owner was at first incredulous that Boyington, a Flying Tiger, needed to park cars for him, but happily assented once Boyington explained his dire straits and his hope that the job would be temporary. "For two long dreary months, right in the heart of the war, I parked cars—and with only high-school boys left on the job along with me. And still no word from Washington."[18]

Meanwhile, developments in Washington threatened to end his career before it resumed. Chennault wrote a damning letter recommending that the Marines reject Boyington, whom Chennault described as a "capable flyer [who] would have been of valuable service were it not for his excessive drinking."[19] Colonel Mitchell wondered about the wisdom of accepting damaged goods, but Holcomb dismissed the notion. On September 3 Boyington learned that his reinstatement had been approved and that he should await further instructions. Frustrated at the slow pace, Boyington sent a letter directly to the assistant secretary of the navy in early November. "I went on about how the United States was in a war and they needed pilots, because outside of the Flying Tigers, every American aviation unit had taken quite a drumming and so had the British out in that area. Fortunately, this man read it."[20]

His appeal apparently worked, as three days later he received orders for active duty as a major in the Marine Corps. He was to report to Air Regulating Squadron 2 San Diego for assignment overseas. "I'm all fixed up and only have to fight the Japs now, instead of everybody concerned," Boyington wrote to Olga Greenlaw. "It's a great feeling for a change."[21]

The Pacific, and fame, beckoned.

"I could not beg my way into an active squadron"

Fame would come, but not until Boyington passed through one more long round of boredom, drinking, and fighting. Boyington soon found himself in familiar territory—the hot seat. In early January 1943 he received orders to the South Pacific, and on January 7 he boarded the liner *Lurline*. This voyage across the Pacific was very different from his opulent journey to Burma. Escorted by two destroyers that kept a wary eye out for enemy submarines, the *Lurline* steamed straight ahead toward the war zone. Two weeks later Boyington debarked in Noumea, New Caledonia, where he was attached to Marine Air Group 11 (MAG-11) based in Espiritu Santo.

At last he had arrived in the right place for combat. Now that the Japanese had been checked at Guadalcanal in the lower Solomons, Adm. Ernest J. King, chief of naval operations and commander in chief of the U.S. Fleet, had decreed the offensive-defensive phase of the war. American planes and ships could begin taking the fight to the enemy and wrest away land that the Japanese had seized since the war's start. Tokyo lay in the distant future; for now, the center of aerial activity in the Pacific lay in the Solomons.

First on the agenda for King and Adm. Chester W. Nimitz, commander in chief of the Pacific Fleet at Pearl Harbor, was shutting down Japan's key island bastion: Rabaul, which lay 560 miles northwest of Guadalcanal. Almost everything pouring from Japan to the South Pacific—men, ships, aircraft, and supplies—flowed through Rabaul, a fortress protected by numerous antiaircraft batteries and 100,000 Japanese troops. From its immense harbor, supply lines reached westward to New Guinea and southeastward toward the Solomons, threatening Allied forces in both crucial locations. If King and Nimitz hoped to progress in either location, they first had to neutralize Rabaul.

Brutal naval battles off Guadalcanal had shorn Nimitz of all but two aircraft carriers, *Enterprise* and *Saratoga*, thus forcing him to look elsewhere for airplanes with which to hit Rabaul. To take the place of naval air groups operating off those remaining carriers, which he had to use sparingly until America's factories rebuilt his carrier arm, Nimitz turned to Marine aviators of the fourteen Marine air squadrons then stationed in the area. For the immediate future, the Marine Corps would serve as the South Pacific's air arm.

Since Nimitz could not operate bombers beyond the range of land-based fighter aircraft, which provided vital protection for the larger, slower planes, he had to climb a Solomons ladder toward Rabaul. The process repeated itself as American might spread from Guadalcanal: take the next island northward in the Solomons, construct air bases on the island from which Marine fighters could escort Allied bombers in bombing raids against targets still farther north, neutralize that next objective as preparation for an American assault, then seize that island. Each advance up the ladder would draw the Allies one step closer to Rabaul and the ultimate battle for supremacy in the region.[22]

Some of the most comprehensive and far-ranging aerial battles of the Pacific war now commenced in the skies above the Solomons as Marine aviators escorted Army bombers, attacked Japanese-held islands, and strafed enemy ships and troop transports. A happy set of circumstances thus awaited Boyington in the South Pacific: the Marines needed squadron commanders and expert aviators to challenge Japanese supremacy. For the first time in his military career, Boyington seemed to be in the right place at the right time.

That was certainly not apparent at first. When on February 1 he arrived at what aviators called the Fighter Strip, an airfield Seabees had fashioned out of the coral rock on Espiritu Santo, few signs pointed to imminent combat. The base facilities of Quonset huts and tents sat amid swaying palms on a former French coconut plantation. The base's task—to supply the fighter squadrons at Guadalcanal and serve as a reforming location for squadrons either leaving combat or preparing to enter the war zone—matched the serene environment.

Instead of combat, Boyington served as assistant operations officer, a tedious office job that carried little excitement or challenge. The entire Solomons region to his north offered all the aerial action a fighter pilot could want, but he remained in the rear, shuffling paperwork in a post he categorized as "about as next to nothing as I had ever hoped to be in charge of in my life. I had the say of nothing. All I did was count the planes when they went out for training flights, and count them again when they returned. What a life!" He realized that someone had to do the tedious chores, "but I knew I could never be happy doing it."[23] He occasionally flew a fighter to Guadalcanal and remained overnight, but he came no closer than that to combat. His ultimate destination lay tantalizingly close but seemed to be out of his reach.

The knowledge that other Marine aviators had already compiled impressive records fueled Boyington's impatience. His old friend Bob Galer had shot down eleven Japanese aircraft; Ken Walsh had taken down twenty; and Joe Foss, now weak and gaunt from malaria, had notched twenty-six to tie famed World War I pilot Eddie Rickenbacker as the top American ace. Always one who loved the "show," Boyington itched to get a crack at the Japanese and see how quickly he could move up the ranks of top pilots.

Boyington languished for six weeks before landing a new post on March 11 as executive officer of VMF-122. The prospect of joining a fighter squadron based at Guadalcanal had to thrill the pilot, but combat was no closer because the squadron was then going through its training phase. News correspondents, eager for a good story, reported the arrival of the former Flying Tiger and reprinted Boyington's claim that he had shot down six aircraft during his months with Chennault. In his memoirs, Capt. J. Hunter Reinburg, VMF-122's operations officer, wrote that every pilot had heard of Boyington and that prewar Marines knew of Boyington's reputation for carousing. The 1943 version, at first, did little to change those preconceptions.[24]

Instead of combat, VMF-122 flew defensive patrols over Guadalcanal and other relatively secure islands where the Japanese posed little threat. Boyington chafed at the inactivity, which did not improve when he was named commander of the squadron on April 19. He was in command, but of what? The squadron's war diary offers a steady diet of monotonous descriptions. April 21: "One flight on routine knucklehead patrol, and two flights on routine local patrol." "Routine plane service. Red alert at 1930, but no Japs showed up."[25]

Routine patrols were not what Boyington wanted. The thought of leading men into aerial combat had enticed him into the Marine Corps, but instead he was living in a pup tent near the Lunga River on Guadalcanal. His memoirs say of those mind-numbing weeks: "never saw so much as the vapor trail of a single Japanese plane."[26] As usual when he was bored, he turned to his long-standing remedy—the bottle. Boyington drank so heavily that Reinburg "was continuously flabbergasted how he could fly so well. . . . Greg never missed a mission assigned to him thanks mostly to the fact that his plane captain literally 'poured' him in the Wildcat's cockpit."[27] Boyington had enough sense to delegate the paperwork to his operations officer. He let Reinburg handle the assignments and fill out official forms—jobs that Boyington detested—so he could be free to fly. Fortunately recognizing his limitations, Boyington continued this practice of delegating his paperwork in his subsequent assignments.

Boyington's hopes for combat rose in the final weeks of May. The expected June landings against the Japanese in New Georgia, Nimitz's next step up the Solomons ladder, would keep every fighter pilot busy, not merely against barges and transports, but against what Boyington most sought—Japanese aviators. Again, though, Boyington's luck soured when he clashed with his old nemesis, Lt. Col. Joseph Smoak, the current operations officer for MAG-11. The bitter feelings generated when the two had butted heads during Boyington's time in flight school at Pensacola persisted. Smoak had already warned Boyington that continued drinking would lead to disciplinary action. Boyington ignored the threat. When Smoak confined Boyington to his quarters and relieved him of his command of VMF-122, the aggrieved major went over Smoak's head and contacted Brig. Gen. James Moore, chief of staff of the 1st Martine Aircraft Wing. Moore investigated the chain of events and, not wanting to waste the talents of a fine fighter pilot, ordered Boyington reinstated.

Boyington figured he could count on Moore, who was cut from similar cloth and "was a real stand-up guy. He took care of us and kept [Smoak] off our backs." Smoak on the other hand, "was a real by-the-book Marine, but unlike most of the characteristic backstabbers, he had pulled his time when it counted. He had served in China, and I respected him for that. I was simply the kind of officer he could not understand."[28]

Happy to be out of hot water for the time being, Boyington flew off to a scheduled rest and recreation week in Sydney, Australia. Like most servicemen enjoying civilization after weeks in forward areas, Boyington and Reinburg first stripped off their soiled uniforms so that a laundry service could remove the mildew and smudges. After consuming fresh milk and eggs, they rushed out for a drink and a warm reception from the pretty Australian girls. Predictably, trouble came along with them. Boyington and Reinburg made the rounds of Sydney's bars, downing shots and issuing wrestling challenges with frightening rapidity. Reinburg tagged along partly to keep his friend out of trouble but never guessed he would be kept so busy. On two separate occasions Reinburg had to convince Sydney police officers to let Boyington go after wrestling bouts spilled out into the streets.

Boyington continued the revelry even after he and Reinburg started on their way back to the Solomons. During a layover in New Caledonia, Reinburg witnessed in an officer's club the "most memorable wrestling match" involving his friend. "Greg succeeded in having his wrestling challenge accepted by a local police officer. We all went outside to watch." The affair turned comedic as Boyington grappled and rolled on the hard coral ground with the native constable. "It was almost like an 'Our Gang' comedy as the two tumbled over and over down the hill," recalled Reinburg. "At the bottom, the two declared the match a draw and returned to the bar for more drinking."[29] Bleeding from body lacerations caused by the coral rock and with their uniforms in tatters, Boyington and foe sat together at the bar, quaffing drinks like two school buddies.

Boyington's exuberance delayed his entry into the active combat zone when he broke an ankle in yet another fight. Boyington labeled it a free-for-all and explained that "somebody tackled me from the side in the darkness with a shoestring tackle. My anklebone . . . snapped audibly like a twig." Doctors put him in a cast up to his knee and ordered his evacuation. Once again his own actions had cost Boyington a golden opportunity. "If fate didn't get in my way . . . then I got in hers," he moaned. Boyington worried that he had ruined his final chance for combat. Because of his age and rank, his best prospect lay in landing his own squadron, but had his antics shattered that fragile hope? He chastised himself and muttered, "Man, oh man, you have loused up the detail now!"[30]

The injury required him to be evacuated to a New Zealand hospital, a sojourn Boyington regretted. Not only did Smoak suspend Boyington's flight status, thereby denying him flight pay until he returned, Boyington missed a chance to engage the enemy when VMF-122's pilots downed forty-eight Japanese aircraft in the fighting about New Georgia. "I guess they were waiting for me to leave," Boyington later lamented of his squadronmates' good fortune.[31]

After he recovered from his injury and flew back to the Solomons in early August, instead of rejoining VMF-122 Boyington received command of a different unit, VMF-112. A squadron in name only, its roster had yet to be filled with aviators. While Reinburg and his VMF-122 buddies registered more kills in the skies above New Georgia, Boyington chafed in the rear, waiting for his opportunity. "Try as I would, I could not beg or steal my way into an active squadron or get flying of any kind," he wrote in his memoirs. "Sometimes I believed I was so hard up I would have even jumped at a chance to fly dive bombers."[32]

"Bent-wing widow maker"

Flying a dive-bomber might have been suicidal, for Boyington would have been trying to match a slower plane against one of the war's most remarkable flying machines—the Mitsubishi A6M2 fighter, commonly called the Zero. The plane debuted in 1940, which corresponded to the year 2600 in the Japanese calendar. The Japanese thus dubbed it the Type "00" fighter, which the American press shortened first to "0" before settling on its illustrious nickname. The revolutionary aircraft featured an enclosed cockpit and retractable landing gear. Its outstanding performance was based on the lightweight metals from which it was fashioned. The lighter aircraft enjoyed enhanced maneuverability, greater range, and higher speed than anything the United States could field against it in the war's first fifteen months. Those American military experts who discounted Japanese capabilities before the war stood mute as aircraft after aircraft tumbled into the seas at the hands of the dashing Zero.

Everything has its weaknesses, however. The Zero sacrificed armor plating and pilot protection to ensure the lighter weight, and that made it more vulnerable to American bullets should a plane draw close enough. A burst fired into the Zero shredded the fuselage and ripped into the unprotected fuel tank, causing a violent explosion. As Chennault had taught Boyington and the other members of the AVG in Burma and China, the Zero also failed to match American aircraft in diving ability. A rapid attack followed by a snap-and-roll dive would take the American aviator out of harm's way. Unfortunately, American pilots had to learn the hard way how to exploit these weaknesses. In their initial encounters, Zeros all too often triumphantly left the scene of combat while smoking American aircraft fell helplessly to the water.

The war's first year sapped Japan's fighter corps. Lacking a sufficient pool of expert aviators and, even more critical, an adequate system of training and sending to the front lines a continuous stream of replacement pilots to take the place of the pilots killed or wounded in battle, Japanese effectiveness in the air had diminished. Despite the deficiency, however, the enemy still posed a significant threat when Boyington reached the South Pacific.

American aviators in the South Pacific faced other Japanese aircraft besides the Zero. Mitsubishi's factories also turned out two land-based bombers—the Mitsubishi G4M bomber, called the Betty, and the Mitsubishi Ki-21 heavy bomber, nicknamed the Sally. Escorted by the Zeros, these bombers made life miserable for American land forces on Guadalcanal. Carrier aircraft added their firepower to the fray, especially the Aichi D3A dive-bomber, called Val, and the Nakajima B5N torpedo bomber, nicknamed Kate.

Boyington would encounter each of these aircraft during his months in the South Pacific, but he most wanted to take on the Zero. Flying one on one against another pilot, he could test his skills in a deadlier version of his infamous barroom wrestling challenges. He would receive more than his share of chances, especially now that American factories had produced a fighter worthy of engaging the Zero—the Corsair.

When a foe labels an instrument of war "whistling death," a pilot knows he commands something special. The bent-wing Chance-Vought F4U Corsair, powered by a 2,000-horsepower Pratt and Whitney radial engine, recorded one of the Pacific War's most enviable records in blunting Japanese aerial power in the Solomons and helping transform what had been a last-ditch stand centering on Guadalcanal's Henderson Field to the first steps of the U.S. offensive leading to Tokyo.

The Corsair presented a deadly combination: it offered the benefits of the sleek Japanese Zero while sacrificing little in the way of protection for the pilot. It was faster—speeds in excess of 400 miles per hour at sea level made it the fastest fighter in the Pacific at the time—could climb 3,000 feet per minute, · and had twice the range of previous fighters. But unlike the Zero, it carried self-sealing gasoline tanks and armor plating to prevent quick explosions from well-placed bullets and to better shield the pilot from harm. Six 50-mm guns in the plane's wings meant that the Corsair, which Corsair pilots loved to call the "bent-wing widow maker," more than matched their Japanese opponents in armament.

Marine squadrons came by the Corsair by accident. The plane was initially earmarked for the Navy's carriers, but tests indicated that its massive nose too severely restricted forward visibility for the awkward takeoffs and landings required at sea. Unable to fully utilize the aircraft, the Navy handed the Corsair to the Marines. Once Marine aviators learned how to pilot the agile craft, they realized what a gift they had received. In their hands the Corsair became the first single-engine American fighter to rival the Japanese Zero, and for the remainder of 1943 and into 1944 the two fighters jousted in the skies over the Solomons for aerial supremacy.

The first Corsairs arrived in the Solomons in February 1943 while Boyington was waiting at Espiritu Santo for a combat post. The plane made its combat debut the next month, and shortly after that the Marine Corps began equipping all eight Marine fighter squadrons in the region with the new aircraft. It was love at first sight. The Marine aviators could now take off from forward airfields confident that they entered combat on equal terms. After only a few encounters, Japanese aviators realized that their aerial dominance had been broken. Dr. Jiro Horikoshi, the engineer who designed the Mitsubishi A6M Zero, agreed that "the first single-engine American fighter seriously to challenge the Zero was the Chance-Vought F4U Corsair." He also admitted that "the Corsairs soon proved to be a great nuisance to our fighters," and that the Corsair "clearly surpassed the Zero in performance."[33]

Marine aviators certainly agreed with Dr. Horikoshi's assessment. "The introduction of the 'Corsair,' with a capability that overwhelmed the 'Zero,' which had only about half its horsepower, was a great experience," remarked 1st Lt. John F. Bolt, who would soon be an integral part of Boyington's squadron. "We were just learning how to use the 'Corsair,' which I believe, was the real hero in the Pacific fighting."[34]

When Boyington returned to Espiritu Santo and inspected the new fighter, he agreed that this was the machine that could best the Zero in the South Pacific. "The Corsair was a sweet-flying baby if I ever flew one. No longer would we have to fight the Nip's fight, for we could make our own rules. Here was a ship that could climb with a Zero, only with a more shallow angle of climb, and one that had considerably more speed."[35] A future leader and ace many times over had found his aircraft. All he needed now was a squadron to take into battle.

The Marine command was quick to use the Corsair's assets. Pilots bombed and strafed enemy airfields and ships, conducted photo reconnaissance, escorted Allied bombers, and engaged in deadly duels with Japanese aviators, reinforced with a confidence that comes from operating a finely crafted airplane.

The plane's longer range brought Bougainville in the northern Solomons into the Allied sphere of attack for the first time, because the Corsair could provide the protection the vulnerable bombers needed as they penetrated deeper into Japanese-held territory. As the American military swept northward up the Solomons, other enemy airfields, even those at Rabaul, became targets.

Allied planners revised flight strategy, using fighters to make a "cocoon" for the bombers in an aerial version of the fast carriers and their escorting cruisers and destroyers that ruled the seas. During missions against the Japanese, bombers flew at 20,000 feet, surrounded by layers of fighters. Army P-38s flew high cover between 30,000 and 40,000 feet, while P-40s—Boyington's old aircraft from China—swept the skies below the bombers. Layers of Corsairs flew between the bombers and the high cover, with four to eight aircraft per layer weaving in and out of an area two to four miles wide. The sight of such a formidable formation, one capable of coughing thousands of bullets at intruders, gave enemy aviators pause. Hesitant to attack the airborne armadas because they would come under fire no matter how they approached the American bombers, Japanese pilots instead preferred to lie back and jump on stragglers or aircraft sputtering out of formation with a malfunction.

Now that Marine aviators had their weapon, the South Pacific lacked only a single dynamic leader who could mold a squadron into an effective machine and lead the way in the Solomons. Fate had been cruel to Boyington in China, but she now smiled on him by providing the Corsair, a word that appropriately means "pirate." In the hands of someone like Gregory Boyington, a twentieth-century buccaneer, the Corsair's full potential became obvious. The pairing could not come soon enough for Boyington, who lamented that shuffling papers for empty squadrons "kept me physically active until August 1943, but I was going mentally crazier by the day."[36]

Chapter Five

"I Am Going to Save You Guys"

After his turbulent years with Chennault and the Flying Tigers, a period of misery compounded by an array of personal problems, three factors converged in rapid succession to place Boyington in a situation ideal for his talents and temperament. First, the commander of the South Pacific, Adm. William Halsey, every inch the scraper and battler that Boyington was, sought more aircraft and squadrons for his crucial Allied push up the Solomons toward Rabaul. The forceful admiral especially wanted a squadron commander possessing the same grit and aggression Halsey had earlier exhibited in a series of daring carrier raids against Japanese-held islands and against Tokyo itself. Second, an incredible aircraft, the Corsair, became available for use in the South Pacific against the heralded Zero. And third, Boyington and a group of unattached aviators were waiting in the backwaters of the South Pacific for a combat assignment. Boyington needed men and planes, the Corsair required pilots, and Halsey was looking for all three. The gods finally smiled on Boyington during the summer of 1943.

"We need an aggressive combat leader"

Brig. Gen. James "Nuts" Moore, assistant commanding general of the 1st Marine Aircraft Wing at Espiritu Santo, six hundred miles southeast of Guadalcanal, saw a partial solution to Halsey's dilemma. The admiral pulled every string he could to bring another trained squadron to the South Pacific from the States, but none was available. He instead went with VMF-214, a squadron in name only. Its commander had recently been killed in combat, and the men, then in Australia for rest and recreation, would soon be dispersed to other squadrons. Moore recommended to his superior, Maj. Gen. Ralph J. Mitchell, wing commander of the 1st Marine Aircraft Wing, that the squadron be restaffed with a new commander, who could then select his pilots from a replacement pool of aviators awaiting assignment in Espiritu Santo.

Moore already had his commander in mind before receiving Mitchell's assent—his old friend Boyington. Despite his penchant for trouble, Boyington had attained the proper rank and acquired the valuable experience Moore needed in a commander. More important, he was available. Mitchell and Moore, in desperate need of forceful squadron commanders, concluded that Boyington's capabilities offset the shortcomings. "We need an aggressive combat leader," said Moore. "We'll go with Boyington."[1]

The former AVG flier wasted little time gathering the twenty-nine pilots for his squadron. Most were idling away their time at Espiritu Santo awaiting assignment to a forward unit. Like their leader in many regards, the eclectic collection of aviators presented an array of personalities and interests; but contrary to some accounts, Boyington did not simply free a bunch of malcontents and misfits from the island's brigs. He valued his own life too much to lead a collection of unbridled pilots into combat, so he looked for the best men available, not troublemakers who would constantly test his authority and make his job harder. None of the men he finally selected faced disciplinary action at the time, and for the duration of his command not one member committed a serious infraction.

Most of the new members of VMF-214 had either graduated from college or had some college experience. First Lt. James J. Hill had attended Northwestern University near his Chicago, Illinois, home; Lt. Paul A. "Moon" Mullen had gone to the University of Notre Dame; and 1st Lt. Robert M. Bragdon had been a psychology major while also a member of Princeton's boxing, rugby, track, and baseball teams. The squadron included an equestrian, Maj. Stanley R. Bailey; the studious economics major Capt. George M. Ashmun; and flight surgeon Dr. James M. Reames, who had already served eight months in the South Pacific. Boyington could no longer even claim to be the squadron's most flamboyant personality. That honor went to 1st Lt. Christopher L. Magee, an adventurer cut from the mold of the swashbucklers of old. Magee, who read books on philosophy and witchcraft in his spare hours, flew into combat wearing blue bathing trunks, tennis or bowling shoes, and a bandanna around his head. Because of his muscular build and penchant for lifting weights, no one, including Boyington, tested Magee's boxing prowess. First Lt. Frank Walton, a former Los Angeles police officer who served as the squadron's air combat intelligence officer, claimed that while Magee was quiet and reserved on the ground, "in the air he was a junior edition of Boyington, a wild man, man-handling his plane like a cowboy bulldogging a steer."[2]

Besides handling his duties as air combat intelligence officer and liaison with the press, Lieutenant Walton carried another responsibility, one specifically assigned by his superiors at headquarters—keeping Boyington out of trouble. At age thirty-four the oldest man in the squadron, Walton towered over the shorter Boyington and could utilize his policing skills to keep his superior officer in line. Wing Intelligence Officer Capt. David Decker told Walton that Boyington had "a reputation for getting drunk, and when he gets drunk, he gets belligerent and wants to wrestle. We need someone with him who won't get drunk and who is big enough to handle him if he gets too mean. Your background and your size make you a logical candidate."[3]

Walton accepted his new duties but wisely refrained from interjecting himself too often. His presence alone seemed sufficient to temper Boyington, and the two gradually fashioned a workable relationship. The new squadron commander displayed his respect for Walton on the unit's first night together. As the men sat around drinking beer and chatting about a variety of topics, Boyington, doubtless fortified by a fair share of alcohol, suddenly leapt to his feet. He glared at each man of his newly assembled unit, including Walton, and issued a challenge to wrestle anyone there—except the former Los Angeles police officer.

While the squadron was a diverse group, its members lacked combat experience—eighteen men had never flown in combat—and had yet to learn how to operate as a unit. With an average age of twenty-three, most of the pilots considered the thirty-year-old Boyington, whom they respectfully nicknamed "Pappy," ancient. All, however, had heard of his exploits with the Flying Tigers and looked forward to flying under his tutelage.

"I was there to coach them"

Pappy's informal introduction quickly established a casual mood in the squadron, but his men still had little idea what to expect from their leader or what kind of commander he would be. He looked more like a mechanic than a squadron leader. Rather than the spit-and-polish officer barking orders in nonstop fashion they were used to, Boyington rarely donned a regulation uniform, instead opting for dungarees and a shirt with the sleeves rolled up. The laid-back approach worked for Boyington, who preferred his own methods to those most officers adopted. He could no more follow a prescribed course for handling his squadron than a shark could survive in a desert. Boyington would do things his way, much like a college coach leads his charges onto a football field. "I looked at this group of young men as a coach would of a bunch of skilled young athletes," he explained in 1977. "I was there to coach them, tell them what the game was all about, to protect their lives with my knowledge, to control them, take care of them because of their lack of knowledge of the military, keep them out of trouble the best I could, keep the morale high."[4]

Boyington addressed six issues during the squadron's first instructional meeting. He covered his main points in meticulous fashion without resorting to notes, showing that he possessed both a thorough grasp of the subject and an astonishing ability to explain complex matters in simple terms. "Now listen," the new commander told his assembled fliers, "I am going to save you guys because you are the ones that have not seen as much action out here."[5] He told them that if they listened to his advice, their odds for returning safely would rise accordingly, and to consult him if they had any questions about the Japanese, their aircraft, or the Corsair, because he was the one best qualified to answer their queries.

Because he wanted his men to thoroughly understand not only their own aircraft but also that of the enemy, he immediately dove into a comparison of the Corsair and the Zero. He explained the strengths and weaknesses of each aircraft and how the men could utilize the Corsair's characteristics to their advantage. Never admitting that he was drawing on the lessons he had absorbed from Chennault, he emphasized that the men had to know the Corsair's limits if they were to survive.

"Don't try to loop with a Zero because the Zero is a lighter, more maneuverable plane and will loop inside you and he'll end up on your tail," explained

Boyington, growing more animated with each phrase. "The same goes for turning—don't try to turn with him. But your ship is faster; it will climb away from him in a shallow climb, and you can outdive anything they've got. So what does all this add up to? Just this: get above him; come in on him in a high stern pass; hold your fire till you're within good, close range; let him have it and watch him burn." If they missed their target, Boyington admonished them to avoid engaging in a dogfight and to instead dive away, regain altitude and speed, and attack when they could reengage from above. Above all, Boyington urged his men to trust the sturdy Corsair against the glorified Zero, because the American plane's armament and firepower had been designed to bring them back safely.

After thoroughly analyzing the differences between the two aircraft, Boyington cautioned his pilots that while he understood their eagerness to engage Zeros in aerial combat, they had a primary responsibility at all times—to successfully complete the day's mission. "There's one thing you must always keep in mind. Carry out your mission. If you're covering bombers, cover them to the target and back. Don't take off some place to attack a couple of Zeros off to one side. I know you all want to shoot down planes. But our first job is the completion of the mission, whatever it is."[6]

He spent more time emphasizing his third point—that everything that took place in battle depended on preparation. Was a pilot ready to encounter the enemy? Had he thought out his method of attack beforehand? When aerial combat began, reflexes would take over; there would be no time for thinking. All other things being equal entering a battle, the better-prepared pilot emerged triumphant. "The time you have to be really concerned is not when this enemy plane is about 250 yards directly behind you, but in the period before [combat]." Back at the airfield, before the mission, was the time to plan moves, not after the fighting started. "If you start figuring out—if you meet certain types of planes, what are you going to do next; if he does something, how are you going to counteract that? You do this when you are sitting around doing nothing [in your tent] and instead of feeling lonesome from being away from home and mother." He told them to think of the different situations they might face and plan a tactic to meet each. Thus prepared, they would not waste time trying to think during combat, but would instead instinctively react. "Do all your formal thinking before you ever go into action," he told them, and "the rest will come automatically. . . . [I]f anybody stops and thinks, he is not going to get a chance to shoot down an enemy plane and there is every likelihood that he himself is going to get shot down."[7]

For his fourth point he tackled a specter that no one wanted to talk about but that could not be ignored—fear, especially the trepidation that comes with a man's first encounter with the enemy. Boyington told them to expect that their first reaction in combat would be fear, but not to let it govern their actions. "Actually, this isn't the time to be frightened. It is a time to look at as an opportunity. In the first place, this man is off a thousand yards and is too far away from you to shoot at you. Another thing, too, he couldn't harm you in the first place unless he had his guns pointed directly at you."[8]

Safety existed in numbers, he told them, and they should remain together in the air whenever possible. When in combat, they should pick out one Japanese target and focus on it until they had destroyed it. He ended his lecture by emphasizing that aggression should rule their actions. Since they had arrived in the South Pacific to defeat the enemy, they should seek any opportunity to meet their foe. "Remember that fighter planes are built to fight. That's our primary general mission. Any time there are enemy planes in the air and we have fighters up, we should tangle with them if we can do so without leaving our own bombers or photo planes unprotected."[9]

Finally, Boyington told his men that while he had few rules they would have to follow, the one thing he would not tolerate was any man executing a victory roll after a mission. Then he explained why. Pilots during the Battle of Britain, after shooting down two or three German aircraft, flew low to the ground and executed a slow roll as they passed over their home airfield. In the process, some crashed and died because they did not realize that their plane had sustained damage during the fighting. He was not about to lose a valuable pilot or Corsair in such a foolhardy manner, and if any man perished doing a victory roll, Boyington would not gloss over the details. "I am the guy that has to write your parents a letter if you go down," Boyington said. "I'll be doggone if I am going to write anyone's parents telling them they died in action when they died being a damn fool. Any guy that does a victory roll, I am going to have him transferred out of the squadron that day."[10] Boyington could overlook a lot, but when it came to flying—the one thing in life he took seriously—he exhibited little tolerance. The men were not to treat it lightly.

Boyington used this initial meeting to set the tone for his squadron. If they were to emerge victorious, they had to first believe they were at least equal, if not superior, to their foe. His talk created confidence: in their leader, in their aircraft, and in themselves. Much like any football coach approaching a crucial weekend contest, Boyington wanted his charges to sweep into the skies convinced of victory.

The same Boyington who had repeatedly butted heads with superiors in Burma and China and earned the disdain of so many AVG aviators now displayed a talent for molding men. That version of Boyington had existed all along, but he had not been given the opportunity to command men in China, where most of his colleagues had viewed him as a divisive force and dismissed his opinions. In the South Pacific, Boyington found himself at the head of a group of men who listened eagerly to what he had to say. Scorned in Burma, Boyington felt needed and accepted in the South Pacific. The assembled aviators took Boyington's advice to heart. His words carried more validity because he had already flown against the Japanese, and besides, each man wanted a crack at the enemy. Under the leadership of Boyington, famed as a Flying Tiger, their opportunities seemed unlimited.

"Can I do what he is doing?"

After explaining his aerial philosophy, Boyington arranged as many practice flights as schedules and available aircraft allowed. While squadrons normally trained together in the States for as much as a year before being sent overseas, Boyington had only a few weeks to whip his unit into shape. Many pilots had never seen a Corsair, let alone flown one, so Boyington put his men into the air twice a day. He grabbed any aircraft he could locate, including beat-up Corsairs recently back from combat areas and planes patched together with spare parts. Boyington allotted more airtime to his less experienced aviators so they could learn the intricacies of flying and so that he could more fairly judge their abilities. Each night Boyington gathered his men around him to discuss the day's flights and chat about errors made and lessons learned.

Most of the squadron readily adapted to the Corsair, but one man tested Boyington's instructional talents. The first time 2nd Lt. Robert McClurg landed his Corsair, he swooped so low during his approach that palm branches from the trees lining the airfield wedged in the landing gear. Boyington examined the aircraft, then muttered, "Kid, you fly like a big bag of piss. You're never going to make it home unless I teach you something."[11] Instead of sending him packing, though, Boyington gave him extra attention. Boyington's faith in the neophyte pilot bolstered McClurg's confidence, and he responded by becoming one of the squadron's aces (five or more confirmed planes shot down).

The pilots willingly learned from Boyington not simply because of his reputation, but also for what they observed when he took the controls. He and the Corsair seemed a perfect match; like a sleek racehorse reacting to a jockey's prodding, Boyington's Corsair veered and dove and looped like few others could. "When we first got together with Boyington," recalled Lieutenant Hill, "he told us he would not ask them to do anything he couldn't do. But, boy, when we got in the air, he would do anything. We all thought, 'Gee, can I do what he is doing?'"[12]

First Lt. Don Fisher naively boasted that he could match Boyington's prowess and challenged his commander to a gunnery contest. Fisher approached first and pumped a stream of blue-painted bullets toward the target. Boyington followed, directing well-aimed bursts of red-painted bullets that all but obliterated the sleeve. An examination of the target afterward showed a few blue splats resting in a sea of red. "But, hell, that sleeve was red," said a chastened Fisher. "I never saw so many holes in a sleeve in my whole life. He sold me right then and there."[13] Any doubts about Boyington the pilots may have harbored quickly disappeared in the skies over Espiritu Santo.

The Corsair offered unique challenges. Its unusually large engine placed the cockpit farther back in the fuselage than in most aircraft. As the plane angled steeply upward during takeoff, the abnormally long nose blocked the pilot's frontal vision. Until the pilot gained sufficient airspeed—fifty miles per hour—for the aircraft to level out and clear his sight line, he had to veer to the right or left to determine if another aircraft was in his path. The pilot again lost vision when he dipped beneath fifty miles per hour on landing, requiring him to veer left or right to properly align the Corsair with the runway's center.

The plane's torque—the force that produces rotation and twisting—created problems as well. The engine turned the propeller clockwise, which in turn caused the aircraft to roll counterclockwise. In the air, especially at higher speeds, the pilot thus had to guard constantly against counterclockwise rotation. "It was a matter of knowing and respecting the airplane's characteristics,

Black Sheep pilots rushing to their aircraft at Espiritu Santo, September 1943. (National Archives and Records Administration, no. 54301)

Boyington instructing his Black Sheep pilots on the finer aspects of flying, Espiritu Santo, September 1943. (National Archives and Records Administration, no. 54303)

The Chance-Vought F4U Corsair. Photograph signed by legendary Japanese ace Saburo Sakai. (Courtesy Hap Halloran)

A Black Sheep F4U-1 on the roll from the Munda air strip. The coral island contributed a lot of dust during any activity, which kept the maintenance troops on their toes. Note the "extra" gun ports on the wing leading edges. (Peter B. Mersky collection)

Boyington, with ever-present cigarette, strikes a confident pose at Vella Lavella. (Personal Files Section, Marine Corps Research Center)

John Bolt—here a 1st lieutenant— holds a unique place in Marine Corps history. He is the Corps' only two-war ace and its only jet ace, with six kills over Zeros during World War II and six MiG-15s in Korea while flying Air Force F-86s. (Peter B. Mersky collection)

Boyington in the cockpit of a Corsair, December 1943, South Pacific. (National Archives and Records Administration, no. 043897)

Boyington instructing a group of pilots before a mission over Rabaul, December 1943. (National Archives and Records Administration, no. 403227)

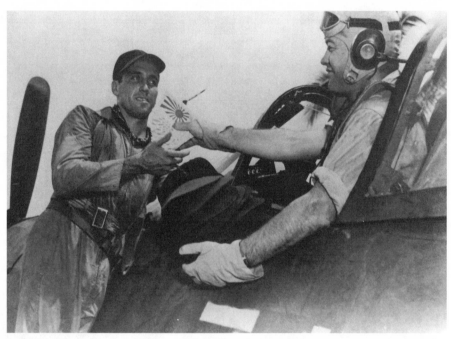

Boyington trades promotional cards with Capt. Chris Magee. Magee was the second leading Black Sheep ace with 9 kills. Like his commanding officer, he was a colorful character and later made his way to Israel to fight with the new nation's air force, flying bastardized Czech-built Messereschmitt 109s. (Peter B. Mersky collection)

Boyington (front row, third from right) posing with some of his Black Sheep at Vella Lavella wearing the baseball caps sent to them by the World Series champion St. Louis Cardinals, December 1943. (National Archives and Records Administration, no. 68323)

Boyington (center) posing with his entire Black Sheep Squadron on Vella Lavella, November 1943. (Courtesy Hap Halloran)

Poster on James Hill's wall showing ten Black Sheep aviators who flew with Boyington. (Author's collection)

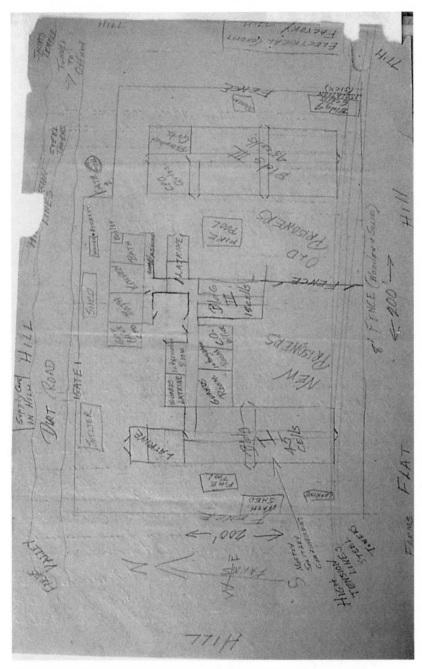

Sketch of the prison camp at Ofuna drawn by Navy Lt. (jg) Edwin Walasek. ("Prisoner of War Deposition of Navy Lt. [jg] Edwin Walasek," National Archives and Records Administration)

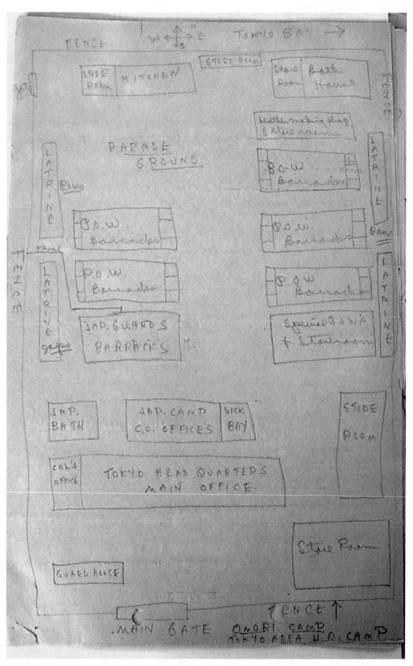

Drawing of Omori prison camp by Capt. Arthur L. Maher, USN, completed shortly after his liberation in 1945. The barracks where Boyington lived, labeled "Special POW's & Stateroom," is at middle right. ("Prisoner of War Deposition of Capt. Arthur L. Maher, USN," National Archives and Records Administration)

Photograph taken from a Navy aircraft showing the Omori camp shortly after the war ended. Signs posted on rooftops by the prisoners of war alert aircraft to what is below; Boyington's barracks is marked with a large sign. (Courtesy Joseph Goicoechea and Linda McCormick)

Hap Halloran (circled) celebrates Omori's liberation by the U.S. Navy. Obvious signs of malnourishment show the harsh conditions under which the inmates existed. (Courtesy Hap Halloran)

Boyington on the set of the 1977 television series Baa Baa Black Sheep. *Although he retired as a "bird" colonel, it is doubtful he got a chance to wear the uniform on active duty. The two men on the right were really enlisted Marines, not actors. (Peter B. Mersky collection)*

President Harry S. Truman presents the Medal of Honor to Lieutenant Colonel Boyington at a White House ceremony on October 5, 1945. (National Archives and Records Administration, no. 701141)

Boyington, uncomfortable with the national publicity, poses for a photograph after receiving the Medal of Honor, shown here around his neck. (Personal Files Section, Marine Corps Research Center)

Hap Halloran in 2007. (Author's collection)

Black Sheep member James Hill at his home in 2007. (Author's collection)

Boyington and his wife, Josephine, pose for a 1987 photograph at a Fresno, California, golf course. (Courtesy Hap Halloran)

A Marine honor guard at the airplane transporting Boyington's remains from California to Washington, D.C. (Courtesy Hap Halloran)

which were not unmanageable," Lieutenant McClurg later said, "but were horribly unforgiving in the case of an error."[14]

Despite the plane's quirks, pilots loved their Corsairs. The large nose provided a comforting security to the fliers, who felt that it served as a barrier between the pilot and enemy bullets, while the aircraft's powerful engine allowed the plane to carry a larger bomb load. Its improved maneuverability compared to earlier American fighters allowed it to engage the Zero on equal terms, while its reinforced armor plating enabled the Corsair to absorb a greater pounding than the less protected Zero. Finally, the fighter's speed allowed it to overtake enemy aircraft or, if in trouble, to turn for home and elude the slower foe.

Boyington also displayed a deft touch in gathering a capable staff that could tend to the more mundane tasks involved in running a squadron—which he detested—and free him to focus on combat missions. Boyington astutely selected the meticulous Capt. Stan Bailey as his executive officer. While Boyington whipped the squadron into shape on the airfield and in the air, Bailey and Intelligence Officer Walton handled the paperwork necessary for smooth operations. In addition, Boyington chose the most experienced aviators from his squadron to serve as his division leaders, then gave them free rein to run their divisions. A man who detested bureaucratic meddling from headquarters was not about to turn around and interfere with his division leaders.

On September 7 Boyington's squadron received its official designation, VMF-214. The unit trained for an additional four days before Boyington informed them that on September 12 they would fly first to Guadalcanal, then northwest to the Russell Islands to begin their first combat tour. "If nothing else," recalled Lieutenant McClurg, "we knew that we had a cohesive group and would be consistently flying missions."[15]

Over a few beers one night soon after being designated VMF-214, Boyington and his aviators discussed what nickname they should adopt for the squadron. Someone suggested "Boyington's Bastards" in reference to the hasty manner in which the squadron was assembled, but when they submitted the idea to headquarters a Marine Corps public relations officer quashed the notion as being too offensive for readers back home. Subsequent debate produced the more acceptable "Black Sheep," a label that carried the notion of outcasts but offended no one. Squadron members designed a squadron insignia, and Marine combat correspondent Penn Johnson drew it: a medieval shield bearing the

cowl and inverted gull wings of a Corsair with a bar sinister—a diagonal black
slash that is the heraldry symbol for a bastard. A sheep stood in the upper left
quadrant, the number 214 in the lower right, and a circle of stars in the center.

Having completed their hasty training and proudly possessing a nickname and an insignia, the Black Sheep Squadron was ready to enter the pages
of history.

"The scourge of the Japanese air force"

To gain control in the Solomons and begin rolling up Japan's southern flank,
the Allies had to neutralize the important port and fortress at Rabaul in New
Britain, 560 miles northwest of Guadalcanal. Men, supplies, ships, and aircraft
streamed from Japan's Home Islands through Truk, 2,000 miles to the southeast, and on to Rabaul, whence they poured into the Solomons. The key to seizing control in the Solomons thus lay in eliminating Rabaul as a supply source.

Planners developed a step-by-step approach up the string of islands.
Because the Navy dared not send its ships within range of Japanese land-based
aircraft, the Allies first had to gain air superiority in an area, construct airfields
from which fighter-escorted bombers could assault islands farther northward
up the Solomons chain, and repeat the process until they had drawn close
enough to take on Rabaul. In succession they had to advance northwest from
Guadalcanal to New Georgia, Vella Lavella, and finally Bougainville and its
array of airfields before drawing within air range of Rabaul. As the combined
chiefs of staff had decided at the Quebec Conference in August 1943 to iso-
late Rabaul rather than invade the island, the task of defusing Rabaul fell to
Army and Marine aviators. To that end Admiral Halsey rushed Marine fighter
squadrons to the southern Solomons. Without them, Japanese aircraft could
attack the Allied bombers with impunity. Boyington and his newly named
Black Sheep arrived at a crucial time for American forces and an opportune
time for themselves.

As Boyington formed and trained his squadron in August and September,
American forces had advanced northwest from Guadalcanal to the two major
islands next in succession—the Russell Islands and New Georgia, with its key
airfield at Munda. U.S. aircraft from those bases immediately started pounding Bougainville and its five potent airfields, the most important being Kahili
on the island's southern tip. Before cracking Rabaul, Halsey first had to knock

out Bougainville's air power, a tough task in its own right. Pilots already in the Solomons remarked that bold pilots took on Kahili, but few survived long enough to be considered old pilots. That was before Pappy Boyington, whom a Marine public relations officer called "the man who was to be the scourge of the Japanese Air Force in its latterly days in the South Pacific," and his Black Sheep appeared on September 13, 1943.[16] They first landed at Henderson Field on Guadalcanal, then flew to the Banika airstrip in the Russell Islands.

A strange dichotomy greeted the Black Sheep when they reached the Russell Islands. Crystal blue waters lapped at palm-fringed white beaches, but along the road to their airfield was posted a sign that no one could mistake for a tourism ad: "Marine Air Group 21, where the extermination of Japs is a business, not a pastime."[17] Boyington and his squadron might be surrounded by beauty, but the lush environment was the trappings of a deadly endeavor. The squadron would fly missions in the combat area for up to six weeks before receiving a week's breather in Australia. A few weeks of training and absorbing replacement pilots would follow before they returned to the combat zone for a second tour.

Life for a Marine pilot in the Solomons certainly offered more amenities than ground forces had available, but it was far from comfortable. Breakfast consisted of toast, powdered eggs, and coffee; lunch and dinner generally offered an endless repetition of Spam, rice, beans, and canned yams. Lieutenant McClurg sometimes supplemented their meals by wading into the waters offshore with the deep-sea fishing rod he brought from home and returning with red snapper, tuna, or even a barracuda dangling on his line. Grouped four to a hut, the men slept in plywood shelters with tentlike caps. Mosquito netting helped reduce the influx of mosquitoes and other insects, but nothing completely eliminated the nighttime hordes that infested the camps. Near unbearable heat and humidity smothered them around the clock and dampened their clothing. Hour-long daily torrential rains further heightened the misery, and each time the pilots took to the air they had to wonder whether they might have to land a damaged aircraft during one of the heavy downpours.

Combat operations invariably offered the same routine. The pilots walked to their fighters carrying their helmets, goggles, throat microphones, yellow Mae West life jackets, jungle survival backpacks, parachutes, and rubber boat packs, all of which had to be loaded onto their planes. At a "go" signal from the control tower, they lifted off the runway and veered out over shark-infested waters toward their target. When they returned, Lieutenant Walton concluded by their formation whether the men had engaged the enemy. A tight formation meant they had completed their mission without encountering enemy fighters, but if they arrived one at a time with engines coughing and sputtering, Walton knew the Japanese had been waiting.

"A born aviator"

With combat imminent, Boyington gathered the Black Sheep to remind them of the points they had discussed about aerial combat and what they might expect from the Japanese and their aircraft. "The first day in combat," Lieutenant Hill recalled, "Pappy told us, 'Now listen fellas, don't ever get into a dogfight with a Zero. It could get inside of you. If you try to pull away just on altitude initially, he can get a good shot. There is only one thing you can do. If you get a Jap under your tail, you do a back roll and straight down full throttle and he can never stay with you.'"[18] With their leader's remarks fresh in their minds, the next day the Black Sheep conducted their first mission by escorting twelve B-24 Liberator bombers in a strike against Kahili airfield on Bougainville. Walton briefed them on the objective, expected enemy resistance, and the time of takeoff.

Rather than each man flying his own assigned aircraft, the men took whatever Corsair was available. Because some aircraft performed perfectly while others had mechanical shortcomings from the wear and tear of battle, no one knew what to expect from the plane he received. Boyington, who asked for no preference just because he was the commanding officer, earned his men's respect by taking what was ready. "Some of them got shot up pretty bad," said Lieutenant Hill. "It got to the point sometimes we would get a plane and the mechanic that would say, 'You want the one with the oil leak, the hydraulic problem, or the one without a radio?' Pappy wanted to be one of the boys and did not want any preference in any way, so he said, 'I will take whatever plane is ready. That's fine.'"[19]

This first mission exemplified Boyington's later comment that "most of a combat pilot's missions are mundane and almost boring."[20] After rendezvousing with the B-24s over Guadalcanal, the squadron broke into three sections of eight planes each, with the sections flying at various altitudes. Eight Corsairs flew close cover 1,500 feet above the B-24s, another eight flew intermediate cover 1,500 feet higher, and the final eight were 4,500 feet above the bombers. As they droned northwest toward their target, the fighters weaved back and forth at their altitudes, the pilots constantly scanning the skies for unfriendly aircraft. One pilot turned back when the wing tanks failed to properly feed the fuel to the system, but the others continued on without mishap.

The squadron escorted the bombers up the Slot—the main channel running between the different Solomon islands—to Kahili. They were anxious yet excited at their prospects for action. The brief bombing ended in minutes and seemed to have caused little damage. Although a handful appeared to hit some of the installations, Boyington thought that most of the bombs exploded harmlessly into the water near the airfield. The Black Sheep, disappointed that no enemy fighters challenged them, shepherded the bombers back home.

The Black Sheep recorded a similar experience the following day, when twenty-four Corsairs escorted four B-24s conducting a photoreconnaissance mission over northern Choiseul, an island southeast of Bougainville. Malfunctions plagued the mission from start to end. One pilot turned back when his Corsair's fuel pressure dropped, one because of oxygen failure, one from a high blower malfunction, and another from loose intake manifold stacks. A fifth Corsair suffered a brake malfunction on landing.

Though they had sighted enemy Zeros on neither mission, Boyington's skill in the cockpit impressed those who flew with him. Lieutenant McClurg called Boyington "a born aviator—a natural at the controls of an airplane." McClurg added that few equaled their leader's talent at getting them to the target and back home. "Navigation was a forte of his, also; I don't think you'll find Boyington getting lost in any of the combat logs."[21]

The Black Sheep had witnessed Boyington's talents during training runs and in the first two escorting missions, but they had yet to observe him in action against an enemy fighter pilot. That changed dramatically on the September 16 mission.

"Zeros spilled out of the clouds"

The September 16 flight was no ordinary escort mission. More than one hundred bombers and fighters, including twenty-four Corsairs led by Boyington, took to the air to attack Ballale, an island off Bougainville's southeastern coast featuring an airfield that was layered with antiaircraft guns. Unlike the previous two missions, the attackers were likely to encounter opposition from enemy fighters determined to keep their airfield safe.

Though confident his experienced division leaders would perform capably, Boyington wondered how his Black Sheep would react to being in a battle. "My great concern was that the squadron might fall flat on its face or do something ridiculous," Boyington later remarked of the mission.[22] Before they climbed into their Corsairs he reminded his Black Sheep to conserve their fuel so they would have enough for a thirty-minute dogfight over Ballale as well as sufficient fuel to return to the Russell Islands.

At 1 PM twenty-four Corsairs coughed to life and lifted from the runway at Banika for a 1:50 rendezvous with the dive bombers, torpedo planes, and other fighter escorts over Munda airfield on New Georgia. The one hundred aircraft, one of the largest forces yet assembled in the South Pacific, veered northwest toward Ballale 130 miles away. The armada lumbered through the skies, the bombers nestled within a protective cocoon of fighters. The dive bombers and torpedo planes flew at 13,000 feet, 2,000 feet below a layer of New Zealand Warhawk fighters. Navy Hellcat fighters scouted the airspace at 19,000 feet while Boyington and the Black Sheep flew high cover at 21,000 feet.

Within an hour the bombers started their run in on the airfield while the three layers of fighters scrutinized the skies for approaching enemy aircraft. Boyington was scouting the right-hand sector when he heard someone shout, "Tally Ho!" indicating that the enemy had been sighted.

"Zeros spilled out of the clouds," Lt. J. F. Begert said of his initial glimpse of the thirty to forty Japanese Zeros led by Lieutenant (jg) Tetsuji Uenjo of the 204th Kokutai.[23] Tracer bullets zipped in all directions as the Japanese drew closer. The force broke into mad scrambles as fighters paired up in individual encounters like schoolboys in a playground brawl. Almost immediately the fray spread over two hundred square miles of sky, with opposing aircraft aligned in combat for brief moments before again losing sight of one another. "This was quite an initiation for me," Lieutenant McClurg recalled. "Complete pandemonium broke loose just when the bombers got on target. Japanese planes were waiting near our altitude and above, and they seemed to come from everywhere."[24] The aircraft darting and dashing in every direction reminded McClurg of a jar of bumblebees that had been shaken to anger and released. He marveled at how quickly a Zero would race into view and then disappear from sight within seconds. The pugnacious Boyington, practically reliving his schoolboy fights, veered to his left to avoid one Zero, then dropped down toward the bombers.

Like other Black Sheep, McClurg and his wingman were quickly separated in the chaos. "You might go in together and get a few shots together," explained Lieutenant Hill, "and then you break off and go after whatever you see."[25] Clouds provided both shelter from a pursuing Zero as well as the danger of colliding with another Zero lurking inside or on the other side. As Boyington had earlier warned, the pilots had little time to think in the heat of the moment. They could only spot, fire, and evade. Walton compared fighter pilots to racehorses: "They're an entirely different breed from bomber pilots. Accustomed to hurtling through the air at hundreds of miles an hour, they think fast, move fast; their minds and bodies are alert, quick."[26]

With mouths dry from the excitement and hearts pounding, the aviators fired in short bursts to avoid overheating their six 50-mm guns. The guns gave the Corsairs fearsome power but also slowed the aircraft and thereby made them more tempting targets. Lt. Warren Emrich recalled seeing "airplanes . . . all around. You look off to the left, there's airplanes going down in flames. There are airplanes crossing twenty feet in front of you. And I think, 'What am I doing here?' I'm scared to death. My mouth was so dry, if you'd have called me on the radio, I couldn't have answered you. That's how scared I was."[27]

Don Fisher, Boyington's wingman, followed Boyington down when a Zero suddenly charged in from the left toward the squadron leader. Fisher fired a short burst directly into the aircraft, which exploded and dropped to the water. Lt. Rolland Rinabarger spotted a daisy chain—a Corsair chased by a Zero, followed by a second Corsair pursued by a Zero—strung out in 200-yard line.

His squadron leader's words rushed to Lieutenant Hill's mind in the battle's opening moments. "I looked in my mirror and there is a Zero behind me," recalled Hill. "I see his guns blink and I thought, 'Man, Pappy, I remember what you said.' I did a snap roll and dove full throttle. I was not looking to see if I had lost him. I was just going full throttle down and I guess I did this from about 8,000 feet."[28]

While Hill followed his commander's advice, Boyington acted on instinct and ingrained habits. Mistaking Boyington's aircraft for one of his own, a Zero drew within 100 feet of Boyington, waggled his wings in a sign to join up, and then flew on, "showing the huge red roundel on his fuselage as he went by." Astonished at his good fortune, Boyington fired from fifty yards away. His Corsair's six guns, so aimed that the bullets came together with a force that could rip a plane in half, produced the desired effect. The Zero's "cockpit burst into flames, he rolled over to the left and went straight down, crashing into the water about 10 miles southeast of Ballale."[29] Though Boyington would never complain, this first Zero had been almost too easy. He had little time to celebrate as more Zeros quickly raced into view, hoping to deliver payback for their dead comrade. Boyington circled to his left and rose to 24,000 feet to evade the Japanese, then turned to the southwest toward Vella Lavella to rejoin the bombers on their way home.

Before he reached the bombers, Boyington spotted a group of Zeroes making passes on the American planes from 10,000 feet. Boyington selected a target, dropped behind the Zero, and opened fire from 300 yards. The action report recorded that "the Zero exploded completely as Boyington was about fifty feet from him."[30] The violent eruption tossed debris straight at Boyington, who instinctively threw his arms across his face as a defensive measure. Though he safely raced through the fragments, the plane sustained dents to the engine cowling and wing edges.

Boyington turned right and climbed to 18,000 feet to regain the crucial advantage of altitude. Searching around, he saw a Zero make a run at a Navy Hellcat fighter, waited until the Japanese pilot leveled out and began climbing, then attacked as the Zero rose slowly upward. Boyington opened fire at 300 yards and continued firing as the Japanese aircraft flipped on its back and exploded.

Now one-third of the way back to Vella Lavella, Boyington spotted what he thought was a solitary Japanese fighter at 6,000 feet. As he dove to approach the target, Boyington grew suspicious when the enemy pilot embarked on a gentle turn to the left, in effect presenting a perfect target. Recalling what he had learned from Chennault, he glanced behind to find a second Zero waiting to pounce on him as soon as he commenced his dive on the first. Ever aggressive, Boyington altered his tactics and charged directly at the second Zero, pumped bullets into it as he sped in from 300 yards, and watched it splash into the sea below for his fourth kill of the mission.

Not wanting to push his luck further, Boyington resumed his flight home. On the way back two Zeros attacked a fighter that, most likely due to damage, had sought shelter closer to the water. Though low on gas and ammunition, Boyington quickly dropped to aid the stricken American. The two Zeros took evasive measures, but Boyington followed one as it pulled straight upward and destroyed it with well-aimed bursts. The Zero spun out of control at 10,000 feet, rolled over, and, spewing flames, plunged to the water. In less than half an hour Boyington had shot down five enemy aircraft, qualifying him as an ace in just that single encounter.

Like most aviators, Boyington did not think of downing a plane as killing a man, but as removing a machine from the enemy's arsenal. After the war he said,

> I look back on the aviation part in combat not as a method to kill somebody. Our main purpose was to disable in any way you could an enemy aircraft because if it was disabled there is no way it could shoot down any of our forces or be of any threat to us. Actually, you didn't care about killing the pilot. It was more or less getting the airplane out of commission. That was the name of the game. You could have hit this aircraft in six, seven or eight places and downed it without ever injuring a pilot, but if you accidentally hit him, it was part of the game too.[31]

Now left without enough fuel to reach Banika, Boyington selected the closer, though less developed, airstrip at Munda. He landed with only ten gallons of fuel sloshing in his tanks and a meager thirty rounds of ammunition. After a ground crew topped his tanks, Boyington continued south to Banika to rejoin his squadron, where he learned that his mates had performed magnificently in their first encounter. In a fight that, according to the combat report, "spread out all over the sky for 150 to 200 square miles at all altitudes and continued for thirty minutes," the squadron accounted for eleven definite kills—planes someone actually witnessed either burn, explode, or crash—and nine probables.[32] Besides Boyington's five, Fisher and Begert notched two kills apiece, with McClurg and Alexander each adding one. Eight other pilots reported probable kills, but lacking an eyewitness to their action could not claim them as shot down.

The press heralded Boyington's feat. With that day's tally he became only the third Marine aviator to down five or more aircraft in a single encounter. Reporters praised him and trumpeted the fact that one of Chennault's Flying Tiger aces had gained similar status in the South Pacific in a mere thirty minutes.

The day was not entirely for celebration. The squadron suffered its first loss with the downing of Capt. Robert T. "Rootsnoot" Ewing. No one witnessed his end or knew if he had parachuted from his Corsair—as often occurs in the frantic pace of combat, he and his wingman, Lieutenant McClurg, had become separated to wage their own aerial jousts—so a slim hope still existed that he might yet safely return, but the odds appeared slim. "I had that awful feeling of knowing that a man I had gotten used to seeing around camp wouldn't be there any more," McClurg remembered.[33] Each Black Sheep had to push the thought out of his mind and focus on his tasks, for much more combat awaited them.

Boyington again gathered his men to discuss what they had learned from their first action. Every man praised the Corsair's performance, from the aircraft's speed to its potent battery of six machine guns. They joked that the plane's huge propeller and engine cowling must have made enemy aviators feel as if an enormous whirling windmill was racing through the skies to obliterate them.

The men had learned that the Japanese preferred to circle at high altitudes in groups of four or more aircraft while waiting for an American plane to appear; should a Corsair attack one Zero, the others in that circle would charge to their comrade's aid. They had also learned that the Japanese liked to use one plane as bait to draw Corsairs into unfavorable situations; that they deftly utilized cloud cover; and that they most often attacked with the sun at their back, making it more difficult for the Corsair pilot to spot them. As a countermeasure Boyington suggested that each pilot imitate the trick he used when looking toward the sun—hold up his thumb to block out the orb, then look to either side.

After Boyington left the gathering, the other Black Sheep chatted about their commander's prowess in the air. They had already been impressed with the knowledge he imparted during their brief training and in nightly discussions, but now their esteem for Boyington skyrocketed. He was not one who could only discuss what and how to perform an aerial maneuver during the heat of combat; he could show them as well. Over Ballale he had executed what he discussed. The men walked away with an enhanced respect for their leader and a desire to be better pilots themselves.

"He was the best aviator out there," said Lieutenant Hill. "I mean a fighter pilot, you have got to know aerodynamics to loop, shift, how to get out of a spin, invert a spin. But, Pappy went beyond that. He had a lot of guts. He was the bravest SOB. He was a leader and some of those commanding officers out there were not that kind of leader. They knew what they were doing, but Pappy just picked up on that and went further. You'd do anything Pappy would do and you did it because it's for him, but he made you feel like you wanted to do it for yourself."[34]

"Becoming a living legend"

For the remainder of September 1943 the Black Sheep Squadron operated out of the airstrip at Munda, a miserable place that made the Russells look like paradise in comparison. Boyington lived in a sixteen-foot-square tent with three other men and tried not to notice the foul odors that wafted in from the jungle, where hordes of flies feasted on decaying Japanese bodies. Torrential rains turned the airfield environs into a quagmire, four-foot-long lizards skittered through the underbrush, and rats the size of cats vied for food scraps or burrowed into the men's belongings. Coral dust filtered into everything—clothes, belongings, and food—and men enjoyed few restful nights because of nightly bombing runs by the Japanese and near-constant takeoffs and landings.

On September 17, their first day at Munda, Boyington called his men together for another discussion. Although largely satisfied with the men's performance in their first few missions, he wanted to "wise them up to a few things that hadn't been carried out to my satisfaction." He reemphasized the need to plan their tactics ahead of time and to anticipate "just exactly what one is going to insist that his plane do when the infrequent opportunity presents itself." If a pilot knew how he was going to react under certain conditions, he would be able to put his plane in the proper position to execute the move. "There is just a split second where everything is right, for the target is going to remain anything but stationary." He added, "In other words months of preparation, one of those few opportunities, and the judgment of a split second are what makes some pilot an ace, while others think back on what they could have done."[35]

To allay their fears, he explained that the men were safer in the air than they were when driving on a busy street back home. An opposing pilot could not touch them at a distance beyond 1,000 yards, and even inside that range he had to position his plane directly on the tail of his target because he could only shoot straight ahead.

Buttressed by those reminders, the Black Sheep embarked on one of their busiest periods, flying every day from dawn to sunset. Most missions consisted of escorting bombers to their targets and back, boring assignments in which they flew up to five hours over open water doing nothing but waiting for the enemy to appear. They usually had some sort of warning. Boyington always disregarded the rule against smoking in an airplane, and the other Black Sheep knew action was afoot when they saw their commander crack open the cockpit hood and toss out the butt. When not escorting bombers or on patrol, the aviators strafed enemy barges and gun or troop positions.

The September 23 flight underscored the point that most missions provided few thrills. Boyington and three other pilots took off at 12:30 PM to scout Mono Island south of Bougainville. Their mission was to determine the feasibility of dispatching PT boats close to enemy-held territory to rescue a group of downed pilots hiding there. The four flew to the objective, looked around a bit, and then flew back without incident. Once on the ground they delivered their reports, then returned to their tents and waited for another similar task. Engaging the enemy in close combat, it appeared, was to be the exception rather than the norm.[36]

A problem with malfunctioning Corsairs turned serious at Munda. The Black Sheep continued to use whatever Corsairs were available at the time of their mission. If a plane, often a hand-me-down from another squadron, failed to operate, the pilot climbed into the next one in line. Once in the air they struggled with faulty gasoline lines, radios, or engines—a disturbing thought to men whose lives depended on a combination of skill, good fortune, and a smoothly functioning aircraft. "Getting into a dogfight was horror enough," explained Lieutenant McClurg, "but there aren't any words I can use to convey the feeling that goes through a pilot when the engine sputters just as he's adding power on the 'tally ho' to enter a battle." He added that results would have been more disastrous had the Corsair not been such a sturdy machine. "The plane could take a terrible beating and still get us home."[37]

Nights at Munda compounded their discomfort as Japanese bombers, generally one or two intent solely on disrupting the pilots' sleep, flew over as often as four times a night and dropped a few bombs. At the sound of a siren blasting three times, the signal for an air raid, the men had to get off their bunks and scurry to the nearest foxhole, wait out the attack, then return to a slumber they assumed would again be curtailed. In what one member called the Battle of the Fox Hole, men at the beginning of the tour vied to be the first to reach shelter. Eventually, many, weary of the dreary routine, gave up and stayed at their bunks. During one raid a naked Walton raced out of his tent but then hesitated at the edge of the water-filled foxhole when two rats leaped in before him. A string of bombs proved to be more than sufficient motivation for Walton to join the rodents, and for the next thirty minutes he fended off the rats as they tried to climb up his chest and back.

Disrupted sleep produced short-tempered, weary, and inefficient pilots, a situation Boyington could not long tolerate. One day Boyington asked permission to take a Corsair up that night to wait for the enemy bombers. He circled the field for four hours, serving notice to the Japanese with his presence that the bombers should be wary of trying anything that night. Each time a Japanese bomber arrived and observed the Corsair in the distance, it turned back without incident. Not one bomb bothered the Black Sheep, who enjoyed their first restful sleep in days. "A good many thousand men [including other Allied personnel] blessed Pappy for giving them the first uninterrupted night's sleep they'd had in a long time," recalled Lieutenant Walton.[38]

Boyington logged his next kill on September 27 during a mission that started inauspiciously. According to the combat report, headquarters did not notify the squadron that it was to escort twenty-seven bombers to Kahili until fifteen minutes before they were supposed to take off. Only two flights of four planes each lifted off on time, with a tardy Boyington and three other pilots chasing after them.[39]

They arrived at Kahili to join up with the other six Black Sheep (two Corsairs had to return to the home base with an instrument malfunction) only moments before fifty Japanese aircraft pounced on the squadron. As Boyington had instructed, each pilot selected one target on which to focus, then dove to the attack. With so many Zeros congesting the sky, the action report stated, "there were plenty for everyone."[40] Boyington plunged into the melee as planes darted in loops and turns, emitting vapor trails that combined with the red tracer bullets that dissected the sky to paint a webbed pattern across the horizon. Boyington dropped behind one Zero and splashed it to the sea below with a well-aimed burst from two hundred yards.

The men flew back to Munda with four more kills to add to their squadron total. Lt. William Case coaxed his bullet-riddled Corsair back to Munda despite severe damage, justifying each man's faith in the sturdiness of his aircraft, but Lt. Walter Harris failed to return. Case reported seeing three Zeroes pursuing Harris, then later observed a Corsair hit the water over Kahili. He presumed that it was Harris' aircraft.

The Black Sheep had been in combat for less than three weeks and had already lost Captain Ewing and Lieutenant Harris. During the next day's patrol, two men with rage rather than reason guiding their actions spotted and strafed a barge filled with Japanese soldiers, shouting as they directed their bullets that the attack was for their lost comrade. "The atmosphere at camp changed when someone was lost, almost like dark weather closing in," wrote Lieutenant McClurg. "Things got quiet, and tempers became short. Only passing days and more missions would dull the sense of loss. Unfortunately, passing days and more missions often renewed those same feelings."[41]

Reporters began gravitating to the Black Sheep, slowly at first but in growing numbers as word of their prowess in the skies spread. A Marine Corps public relations officer said that "their clowning on the deck and cunning in the air captured the imagination of the Air Arm from Espiritu up to Munda, and Boyington was on his way to becoming a living legend."[42]

On September 29 George Weller, a war correspondent for the *Chicago Daily News,* landed at Munda in search of stories about the Sheep. Walton, who recognized the value of positive publicity for the squadron, handed over the personnel files of three men from the Chicago area, including Lt. Christopher Magee, the pilot who charged into battle wearing a gypsy-style bandanna around his head and comfortable shoes on his feet. Weller used the information provided by Walton to highlight the Black Sheep in a series of articles.

When asked to pose for a photograph in a Corsair splattered with Rising Sun decals, the Black Sheep obliged, utilizing a bit of chicanery to please the press while protecting themselves. They walked to the nearest aircraft, temporarily applied a handful of decals to the fuselage, chalked on their nickname, and then posed while the photographer captured the image. After the photographer had left, the Black Sheep removed the decals. The ruse was not because they lacked pride over their achievements but because they knew the Japanese would concentrate their efforts on any plane so gaudily bedecked.

Weller proved to be an ill omen. The day after he arrived, the squadron lost a third pilot, this time to friendly fire. At 7:40 the dawn patrol of four Corsairs spotted four boats off Kolombangara Island not far northwest of Munda. When the patrol's leader, Maj. Stanley Bailey, dropped down for a closer look, he determined that the vessels were American PT boats. The craft had taken the standard recognition procedure of throttling to full speed ahead, veering full right rudder, and waving the American flag. Bailey radioed the information to his three companions and ordered them to withhold their fire at the American vessels. Two of the three Corsair pilots received the message and wagged their wings in recognition, but the third, Lt. Robert Alexander, continued racing toward the ships. Whether Alexander's radio failed or he did not understand the message is not clear, but he strafed the PT boats, killing three men. When the boats' crews returned fire, Alexander's Corsair went into a slow turn and smashed into Kolombangara, cutting a black swath in the jungle.[43]

Alexander's death affected the Black Sheep more than usual because, after Boyington, he had been one of the squadron's most talented pilots. The incident emphasized a glaring fact about combat—death often had little to do with talent. Anyone, even the most gifted among them, could become a casualty in moments.

As usual when the squadron lost a man, the officer in charge of cataloguing his belongings created three piles: personal property, which included valuables such as money or wristwatches; nonvaluable items such as the man's uniform and photographs; and military equipment. He sent the first two piles home to the next of kin and returned the third pile to the quartermaster for reissue, but only after the squadron members had retrieved items they felt they could use, such as an extra pair of goggles. As reimbursement for such items, the men placed additional money into the package being sent home. The officer burned any mail belonging to the deceased lest an embarrassing detail about an unknown girlfriend or other such item distress family and loved ones.

Alexander's death marked the end of a stellar beginning for Boyington's Black Sheep. In September the men had flown 75 combat missions, including

456 individual flights, and engaged the enemy 60 times. Boyington participated in 23 flights, including 5 involving task force cover, 2 scrambles, 5 strike
escorts, 2 strafing missions, and 6 miscellaneous flights. Along the way he
had shot down 6 aircraft and begun the process of molding a squadron out of
replacements.[44]

October would prove to be even better.

Chapter Six

"We Had Pride; We Had Class; and We Were Winners"

On October 1 the squadron returned to the Russell Islands for one week before again operating out of Munda. Whereas September had served as their initiation to combat, in October the Black Sheep flew with one major purpose: to help eliminate Japanese air power from Bougainville's powerful airfields in preparation for a November assault on the island by ground forces. "In the month of October we were to be flown to a frazzle," Boyington recalled. "There was no such thing as rest, or a day off, a situation I had never experienced before."[1] More frequent strafing missions against enemy antiaircraft emplacements, ships, and ground forces broke up the tedious escorting assignments.

One nagging problem remained constant in the squadron's Solomons operations—aircraft maintenance. A pilot could count on either mechanical difficulties or outright failure from the overused Corsairs on one out of every two missions. Even newer aircraft succumbed with alarming frequency as severe heat and humidity caused parts to fail and the fine coral dust clogged engine parts and blocked fuel systems. Pilots complained almost daily in their squadron reports. The October 4 action report mentioned that the pilots had sent eight Corsairs to Munda for a long-delayed overhaul. Two Black Sheep had to return their "wheezing planes" to the airfield "because of a multitude of mechanical difficulties."[2]

No improvement was in evidence eleven days later when Lieutenant Walton, who wrote most of the squadron's reports, complained that "maintenance of our planes continues to be bad, three of the four planes in Lt. Bourgeois' division having to return to base because of various mechanical difficulties. One had carburetor problems, the high blower on another did not work, and Bourgeois had half inch dirt on his gas filter."[3]

"3 Zeros in less than 60 seconds"

Despite the mechanical issues, the squadron amassed another enviable record in October. Boyington added eight kills to his burgeoning total. On October 4 he and six other pilots were flying medium cover for dive-bombers hitting one of Kahili's strongest antiaircraft batteries when a strange occurrence unfolded. When he arrived at the location Boyington heard an Asian voice ask over his radio in perfect English, "Major Boyington, what is your position, please?"[4] Boyington knew the question was a ruse—the Japanese often listened in on their radio frequencies, and no man in his squadron would speak so properly— so he played along with his adversary. He reported his position as 20,000 feet over Treasury Island, miles southwest of his actual position, then the squadron waited in ambush for enemy aircraft to rise from the airfield.

Sure enough, enemy fighters on the move began kicking up dust clouds from a Kahili airfield. Boyington and his group dropped down on the right flank of thirty Zeros and engaged in a brief but furious dogfight. Boyington selected one Zero and fired from three hundred yards, chopped back on his throttle, skidded sideways, dropped behind his target, and shredded the enemy aircraft's tail with his bullets. As that plane spun out of control to the water, Boyington turned his Corsair for a run at a second Zero, which he speedily dispatched with another volley of bullets that produced smoke and a parachuting pilot. A few seconds later Boyington aligned a third enemy fighter in his gun sights and raced after it, maintaining his fire until the Zero exploded in flames. In an astonishing display of wizardry, Boyington, the action report stated, "bagged 3 Zeros in less than 60 seconds."[5] His squadronmates were beginning to believe that there was nothing Boyington could not do in the sky.

A postmission discussion produced more suggestions for the squadron. Boyington praised their hit-and-run tactic, adding, "The Zero can't dive with the F4U. In a diving stern approach it is safe to continue on past the Zero as he can't get his nose down to dive with you." He warned, however, that "the Zero's superior maneuverability makes it suicide to attempt a dogfight with him, particularly at low altitude."[6]

He made sure the pilots understood that in aerial combat the machine, not the man, was the objective, that nothing personal should fuel their actions. They were shooting down an aircraft, not an individual. "Your odds of aiming at a pilot are so slim," Boyington explained after the war. "What you are actually trying to do is put an airplane out of commission and the pilot is purely incidental. It would not make any difference what he looked like, who he was, or anything else, as long as the markings on his plane were different than yours, then you were in a high adventurous contest. The man who could fly the best and think the best came out ahead unless there was something that went radically wrong like an engine."[7]

Eleven days later Boyington added another aircraft to his tally when twelve to fifteen Zeros tried to approach the B-24 bombers he and his squadron were escorting near Kahili. The Corsairs shot down six Zeros, with one confirmed kill by their leader and two probables.[8] Boyington was jubilant. His Burmese exile with Chennault and the AVG was forgotten. Like an actor performing on stage or an athlete maneuvering on the playing field, Boyington was in his element in the South Pacific. Other aviators looked to him for guidance; he faced more action in a week than he had experienced in one month in China; and his superiors gave him autonomy to run the squadron in his own style, free from interference from a commanding figure like Chennault. "I'm working with the best bunch of guys in the South Pacific," he gushed. "I'm flying. I'm fighting. I'm killing Japs. I'm the happiest man in the world."[9]

Boyington notched another trio of kills on October 17. While a division of four Corsairs from VMF-221 flew toward Kahili as bait, Boyington and thirteen Black Sheep waited in ambush. The Black Sheep were elated with the aggressive nature of this mission, which seemed better suited to their talents than the more passive role of defending bombers. Boyington had long sought such an assignment for his squadron, which he thought superiors underutilized by assigning frequent escort tasks.

When they spotted the enemy fighters taking off from Kahili, Boyington barked into his throat mike, "Here they come, boys. Don't get too eager. Pick your targets." In a thirty-minute free-for-all that spread out over twenty square miles of sky, the squadron engaged forty Zeros, shouting encouragement or warnings to each other as they dove and circled. "Look out!" shouted one Black

Sheep to another. "I got the bastard!" yelled a third. "Watch behind you!" and "Coming in at eleven o'clock!" blared over the radios as the battle raged.[10] The Black Sheep lost no aircraft while downing twelve Zeros, including three shot down by Boyington. His total of nineteen tallies placed his name among the top aviators of the Pacific conflict, a feat that again had reporters inundating the airfield.[11]

He followed that success the next day with a fighter sweep over Kahili. Freed from the shackles of escorting bombers, Boyington led nineteen Corsairs to the aerodrome at Kahili, where he once more heard that melodious Asian voice asking for his position.

"Right over your lousy airfield, you yellow bellies. Come on up and fight," replied Boyington.

"Why don't you come down, Major Boyington?"

Never one to shy away from a challenge, whether in a schoolyard or in South Pacific combat, Boyington ordered the other aviators to hold their altitude, then dove on Kahili and strafed the airfield as antiaircraft fire buffeted his Corsair. After the strafing run Boyington rejoined the circling Black Sheep and issued his own challenge to his Japanese counterpart. "Now, come up and fight, you dirty yellow bastards!"[12]

Forty Zeros scrambled off the runway as Boyington led his men down. The formations broke into individual battles boiling across the sky at six thousand feet. The squadron destroyed another eight Zeros, including one taken by their leader, who had shot down eight in the last two weeks to bring his official tally in the South Pacific to fourteen.

"This was aggression, Pappy style"

Boyington had been pestering his superiors since September to allow more fighter sweeps. Escorting bombers hardly suited a man who sought combat every waking moment. "This escorting can be paralleled to the lineman's duty on the football field," Boyington explained; "a lot of work and the backs make all the touchdowns."[13] He wanted at least some of the glory for himself and his Black Sheep. He also argued that escorting bombers was not the best use for a unit of Corsair fighters, whose main task, he believed, was to knock the enemy out of the skies. Escorting did little to achieve that end. "Trying to protect the bombers while tangling with enemy fighters was like trying to box with one hand tied," claimed Lieutenant Walton of the frustrating situation. The enemy had the whole sky in which to work and maneuver while the Corsairs were limited to the small area around the bombers, a condition that severely limited the Black Sheep's ability to destroy the opposition. "We were pecking at them and knocking them down, but not nearly fast enough."[14]

Boyington suggested sending fighters out as independent groups to wait for the enemy. By arriving before the bombers, they could clear the area and hand the slower aircraft an open path to their target. Unspoken was that this proposal would also give Boyington and his squadron additional opportunities for engaging in aerial combat. The October 4 mission in which Boyington bagged three enemy fighters had accidentally turned into just such a fighter sweep. When the bombers failed to arrive for the scheduled rendezvous, Boyington took his fighters to Kahili for some action on his own initiative. "This was aggression, Pappy style," boasted Lieutenant McClurg, "in which we had the opportunity to go calling on the Japanese ourselves, with no bombers to watch."[15]

The October 15 combat report supported Boyington's arguments by recommending that fighter sweeps be dispatched before the bombers to engage enemy fighters, with a second sweep guarding the bombers' rear as they returned to base.[16] Other reports backed Boyington's contention, but he still had to overcome residual opposition at headquarters. Complete freedom to hunt the Japanese would not come for another month.

At least some of Boyington's success in the South Pacific might be attributed to his lack of excessive drinking. Whereas many Flying Tigers have said that Boyington flew while drunk, not one Black Sheep has leveled a similar claim. They admit that he drank while on the ground, as did many of them, but not to the point that it impaired his abilities in the sky. The Black Sheep bristle at the suggestion that their commander would criminally risk his life and the lives of those flying with him by flying drunk.

"Pappy's drinking caused him an awful lot of problems" off duty, said Lieutenant McClurg. "I never knew of him flying drunk, but he sure did spend many of his ground hours 'pickled.'" He added bluntly, "For the record, we never flew while intoxicated." Doc Reames "wouldn't have allowed us to jeopardize ourselves or our mates (or our precious aircraft, no matter how war-torn) by flying drunk. There may have been hangovers on occasion, but not drunkenness."[17] Other Black Sheep, such as Lieutenant Hill, backed McClurg's contention. "Pappy was doing some pretty heavy drinking, but there was no way he flew drunk. He may have flown with a hangover, but never drunk."[18] Whether or not Boyington sometimes climbed into his Corsair with a hangover, none of the men doubted their leader's capacity to command or worried that he flew inebriated.

Why the difference between Boyington's behavior in the AVG and that in the Black Sheep? Boyington stepped into a maddening situation in Burma and China. He arrived too late to be named a squadron commander, and he was often stationed at bases far from the active flying while others got the chance to excel in combat. In the absence of meaningful action, and with a lot of empty time on his hands, Boyington turned to the bottle. That situation did not exist in the South Pacific, however, where he enjoyed an abundance of combat, a free hand in running his own squadron, and men who looked to him for help rather than avoiding him as a nuisance.

"The hunters had become the hunted"

By the middle of October the Black Sheep had flown the six weeks of combat that a tour required and were ready for a week's respite in Australia. The break could not have arrived at a better time. Some of the men were suffering from dysentery or other tropical illnesses, and the daily grind had exhausted all of them.

Lt. William Case, in particular, looked forward to the tour's end because he was due to be sent stateside on its completion. Boyington made certain he survived to see his family. On a mission shortly before they were to leave for Australia, Case lowered his cockpit seat to gain extra protection from the Corsair's armor behind him. During the fighting, a bullet passed through his cockpit, grazed the top of his leather helmet, and knocked his head forward. Had he not lowered the seat the few inches, the bullet would have smacked into Case's head and sent the man to a watery grave. When Case landed and Boyington heard of his close call, he pulled Case off any further flights, saying, "Son, you just used up all your luck."[19]

Excitement rose to a high pitch on October 18 with the arrival of their replacement squadron. The night before they were due to leave, however, Boyington received orders to send four Black Sheep out on an unscheduled strafing mission over Kahili and an airport at nearby Kara. Boyington, chagrined at the thought that he might have to ask four men to risk their lives on the eve of well-earned rest and recreation, argued that the replacement aviators could handle the task, but headquarters insisted that the Black Sheep had to take it because the new squadron was unfamiliar with the target. Boyington could have selected any four men in the squadron for the dangerous mission, but he was not about to send someone else into peril while he remained in the safe confines of the base. He handled the issue in typically nonchalant fashion. "Which of you clowns wants to go with me to Kara for a little going away present?" he asked as he strutted into one of the tents.[20] Though certainly reluctant, three men volunteered, not as much from duty as to acknowledge their commander's refusal to shirk battle. The four lifted off, strafed Kahili, Kara, and a few barges, and safely returned.

The October 19 raid ended the Black Sheep's first tour. The squadron compiled an enviable record in their six-week tour of duty and contributed significantly to clearing the skies over Kahili in preparation for the American assault on Bougainville. In 15 days alone the Black Sheep had engaged the enemy 48 times in 358 individual flights and added to an already impressive tally of destroyed enemy aircraft.[21]

Lieutenant McClurg noticed a discernible drop in the Japanese pilots' aggressiveness in the course of that first tour. Whereas enemy pilots had at first appeared eager to match skills with the American aviators, more often than not they now remained on the defensive, as if conserving their forces. That trend would continue as the war progressed. Constant air combat around the Solomons and in the major carrier battles at the Coral Sea and Midway had decimated not only the number of aircraft available to the Japanese, but also their core of experienced aviators. They had to adopt a more cautious approach as American forces marched northward up the Solomon Islands and save their remaining pilots and aircraft for the crucial encounters yet to play out in Bougainville and over the Japanese bastion at Rabaul. While the Japanese carefully nurtured their depleting resources, a steady torrent of American aviators, aircraft, and the other tools of war gushed across the Pacific from mainland training bases and factories. In some measure the Pacific conflict proved to be a numbers game, one that favored the United States with its mighty industrial base and enormous population.

The superior performance of the Corsair was another reason for the Japanese hesitation. "The difference in planes was showing, too: while the Zeros could outmaneuver us, it took only one decent shot to splash one into the water," noted Lieutenant McClurg. "The Corsair, on the other hand, was like every Japanese barfighter's worst nightmare: he could smash on an F4U seemingly forever and it would still fly." McClurg added that while the squadron certainly had to shelve some Corsairs, "WE [sic] junked them, not the Japanese."[22]

After the war, a former Japanese pilot confirmed McClurg's assessment. Commander Masataka Okumiya, one of Japan's leading pilots, concluded of the aerial combat in September and October that forced the Japanese to retreat northward from Guadalcanal, "These successive withdrawals from our airbases could be regarded as nothing less than major disasters." Each time the Japanese abandoned a position and fell back toward Rabaul, the United States was that much closer to ending the fighting in the Solomons and advancing the seaborne attack toward Tokyo. Okumiya concluded that in the Solomons, where the Japanese had one year earlier enjoyed the upper hand, "The hunters had become the hunted."[23]

Boyington's increasing total of kills attracted more and more press coverage. In two months he had destroyed fourteen planes; that number added to the six he reportedly shot down in Burma made him the leading ace among active aviators. Matching or surpassing Eddie Rickenbacker's World War I record of twenty-six downed enemy aircraft seemed attainable.

On October 25 the squadron landed at Henderson Field on Guadalcanal, changed aircraft, and flew to Espiritu Santo. They remained there in the rear for six days while physicians administered malaria smears, then, with everyone cleared, headed to Australia and fun.[24]

Boyington's race for the record would have to wait.

"Gambler's guts"

Lieutenant McClurg would later say that Boyington had taken a diverse collection of mostly inexperienced pilots and by the middle of October had molded them into a team. "We had made it. We weren't worried about being replacement pilots any more. Difficult as it was sometimes, we had settled in to life as a squadron. We were a group, and we were doing our group duty."[25]

A booklet promoted by Boyington's superiors at headquarters explains in part how a man scorned by the Flying Tigers achieved such quick success with the Black Sheep. In a remarkable nod to Boyington's command talents, Headquarters, Marine Aircraft, South Pacific, Fleet Marine Force Intelligence Section printed and distributed to aviators throughout the Marine Corps a compilation of sixty-four points Boyington impressed on his men to make them effective combat pilots. Perhaps most telling is the fact that the booklet's material came from the Black Sheep themselves. Rather than an officer boasting of his methods in fashioning a squadron and successfully engaging the enemy in combat, the booklet in effect let his men speak to Boyington's talents.

Titled *The Combat Strategy and Tactics of Major Gregory Boyington, USMCR,* the booklet came out on January 19, 1944. Sections dealing with bomber escorts, fighter sweeps, strafing, and patrol constituted a primer on Boyington's success. The introduction referred to a new form of warfare in the struggle against Japan that had yet to achieve the recognition it deserved because "air strategy is still a new subject." It described a "vast change in the strategy of Marine fighter operations in the South Pacific area" made possible by the arrival of the Corsair and "a man who was to be responsible, more than any other, for changing our strategy." Previous fighter tactics in the South Pacific had restricted the pilots to escorting bombers and protecting shipping and airfields, a limited role that had emerged from older forms of training that focused on the defensive uses of fighters. The new tactics, "based upon offensive rather than defensive action," featured an aggressive brand of combat in which fighter pilots plunged deep into enemy territory to destroy Japanese aircraft and airfields.

The introduction noted that Major Boyington had learned the new tactics during his time in China and Burma with Chennault's Flying Tigers. "There the idea had grown upon him that the fighter airplane was a much more versatile weapon than the rest of the world seemed to realize. He found that he could fly deep into enemy territory, striking swiftly and by surprise, spreading destruction by strafing and bombing. With the success of these sorties there grew in his mind the germs of an offensive strategy which had not been used before. These ideas were born of a reasoning mind and a fighting heart."

Shortly after Boyington, the Black Sheep, and the Corsair came together, "the 'Black Sheep' and their leader were defeating the enemy so badly over his own Bougainville airfields that he not only refused to engage the Corsair in combat but even to leave the ground. Our bombers flew unmolested."[26] The Black Sheep's efforts helped gain air superiority in the northern Solomons in which bombers could operate more freely and a land assault against Bougainville could be better organized.

The booklet credited Boyington's success to his aggressive spirit. "First, last and always [the strategy] is based upon aggression, upon taking the initiative and upon holding that initiative by sheer force of attack. It is based upon keeping before us our points of strength and particularly the superior features of the Corsair. At the same time it is based upon keeping before us the Japs' points of weakness."

One of the themes the Black Sheep wanted emphasized when they supplied the information for the booklet was their leader's insistence that he wanted his fliers taking the offensive unless doing so would jeopardize their mission. "Fighter aircraft are designed, and fighter pilots are trained, to fight," the booklet quoted Boyington as saying to his men. "If there are enemy aircraft in the air, and contact is not made, something is wrong. The only exception to this are those situations where we must stay close to something we are expected to protect; where to attack means that we have been lured away."[27]

An aviator once asked Boyington to describe his strategy in battling the enemy. Boyington delivered an answer that not only summarized his thinking but also accurately described the man himself. "There is no such thing as strategy in fighting up there. Gambler's guts would be better to describe what a fighter pilot needs. Good aerial fighting is a gamble. And you've got . . . to take the consequences if you lose. It's just like street fighting. If you hit the other guy first, and hit him hard, you'll probably strike the last blow. That he'll hit you back harder than you hit him is the chance you have to take."[28]

The combative Boyington never relented in taking the offensive. "He didn't put forth a proposal for what we were going to 'try' to do; rather, he laid out what was going to happen," Lieutenant McClurg said. "We didn't spend much time worrying about how to respond with contingency plans; we concentrated on living in the offensive mode, and letting our opponents react to our initiatives."[29]

The defensive posture promoted in early aviation training had no part in Boyington's message. "One of the mistakes I think was made by Marine leaders in aviation at that time was that there was very little general instruction given to pilots about getting into a fight and slugging it out, dominating the enemy by your own aggressiveness," claimed Maj. Henry Miller. "The attitude was more or less to do your own thing. Boyington's characteristic was the desire and willingness to get right in there, ride as close as he could, do a lot of shooting without regard for himself."[30]

The squadron posted records matched by few others in part because Boyington taught the pilots to focus on their target and push all distractions out of their mind. "You see this in animals, such as lions or other predators," said 1st Lt. John Bolt. "When they attack a grass-eater, the other animals scatter in all directions, but the predator never changes targets. He selects his meal, and that is all there is to it. The others run all over the place, but the predator is not distracted. Call it a singleness of purpose; a dedication; a commitment." Bolt explained that the commitment lasted longer than a few moments in battle, that a pilot had to be committed each moment, "a dedication to it that gets you up early in the morning, and puts you to bed late at night. It's a commitment like anything else, but there, of course, you're playing with your life."[31] Boyington insisted that his Black Sheep adopt this commitment and a killer's instincts.

"Boyington was far ahead"

That a man so disorganized when it came to administrative details and almost every other aspect of his life should so vehemently emphasize meticulous preparation and knowledge to his squadron might seem ironic, but those became trademarks of Boyington's command. He insisted that "all missions must be preceded by thorough planning and briefing . . . because all of our present operations are over enemy territory far from our bases. Success in the air is a lot of little things. Most of them can be taken care of before takeoff."[32]

During frequent bull sessions with his men, Boyington, true to form, described combat in terms of an athletic endeavor, specifically boxing. He explained that in the ring a boxer has little time to think and has to take advantage of his opponent "strictly by reflex." A pilot likewise would face unexpected situations in combat, "things that happen that are not planned on or counted on like an engine not coming up to capacity or actually conking out." Boyington told his men that "if you think of this happening before you ever go up there, . . . when it does happen you don't just sit there and slow down and give somebody a chance to shoot you."[33] The pilot who pauses to think about what is occurring as the enemy approaches is the pilot who is shot down. Reflexes should take over. A reflex based on prior thought—planning before the mission started— brought a pilot safely back to his base. Good preparation led to other benefits. It reduced the need to use the radio while flying, for example, thereby diminishing the opportunities for the enemy to obtain a fix on their location. "With proper planning and briefing, no use of the radio should (be) necessary except in emergencies."[34]

Thorough preparation especially meant knowing what your plane could and could not do, as well as understanding the capabilities and weaknesses of the enemy's aircraft. "Boyington was far ahead in mechanical knowledge," Lt. John Begert said. The booklet noted that aviators in the South Pacific "had been indoctrinated with a respect for the Zero" that bordered on reverence and awe. Boyington wanted to shatter that attitude and show that success depended more on the pilot and his knowledge of aircraft than on the aircraft itself. "All fighters must realize the critical importance of recognition," stated the booklet, "in order to identify the enemy's different types so that his particular points of weakness can be exploited and his particular points of strength respected, etc."[35]

Boyington made his pilots repeat the cockpit checkout in a Corsair until they knew the routine by heart. He wanted them to understand their aircraft so intimately that they could fly it on instinct. Under the duress of battle, instinct saved those precious few moments that determined who lived and who died. McClurg noted that Boyington had him sit in that cockpit on the ground "over and over. Learn where the different knobs and gauges are in this bird. Learn where they are to the point where we didn't have to think about it because it was second nature. The F4U, like all fighters, could be a handful to fly, and if a pilot had to first think of where to find a particular knob when he needed it, he was finished before he had begun."[36]

Boyington did not want the men to think that all they had to do was concentrate on shooting down enemy planes. He harped just as frequently on premission details such as careful inspection of equipment. The booklet reiterated the point: "All pilots must check their oxygen equipment (as well as everything else) thoroughly before takeoff. To return to base early for oxygen reasons can hardly indicate anything less than negligence in preparation for the flight."

Boyington so thoroughly familiarized his men with the capabilities of the Corsair that the men took steps to improve the plane on their own initiative. Lieutenant Bolt experimented with and altered the way the plane's machine guns were belted. Bolt took a machine gun to the lagoon and fired different types of rounds—incendiary, armor piercing, and tracer—into oil drums to determine which better ignited the target. At the time, Navy doctrine called for using one of each shell in succession, but Bolt's experiment produced a better method, and his contribution to the booklet explained it: "As a result of tests of the comparative destructive power of tracer, armor piercing and incendiary ammunition, our squadron changed its belting from 1–1–1 to 2 incendiary–1 armor piercing–2 incendiary–1 tracer. In actual combat we found this load much more satisfactory."[37] The Navy studied Bolt's results and eventually switched the belting in all its fighters.

His experiences had taught Boyington that the most successful runs against the enemy were those that targeted either the Zero's front or its tail. He passed that information on to his Black Sheep, who added it to the booklet: "It is apparent that our most successful runs against fighter opposition are from eleven to one o'clock ahead and from five to seven o'clock astern, from a level just above to a level just below." He also wanted his men to realize that strafing enemy targets, though not as exciting as pursuing an enemy fighter, often had unforeseen dividends. "We in the air sometimes fail to appreciate the effect of strafing upon enemy morale. We know the actual physical destruction which .50 caliber guns can cause, but we sometimes forget the amount of less tangible damage which those guns can inflict. Often such a target as a bivouac area in a coconut plantation cannot be seen but strafing of such targets has inestimable value."[38] Effective strafing missions required planning and surprise.

In so constantly emphasizing knowledge of their Corsairs and knowledge of the enemy aircraft, Boyington had a purpose beyond preparing his men for battle. In showing the capabilities of the Corsair, the limitations of the Zero, and the most effective methods of challenging those aircraft, Boyington demystified the Zero. Many pilots in the South Pacific had heard so much about the maneuverability of the Zero and of its so-called invincibility that they embarked on missions at a disadvantage even before they entered combat. Boyington wanted his men to know that they were more than a match for the skills and machines of their foe. That he could speak from experience in China and Burma lent a relevance to his message that other squadron commanders lacked. His demystification of the Zero proved to be one of Boyington's most valuable contributions to the war in the Pacific.

"The vigil must be unceasing"

Having shown his men that there was nothing magical about their opponents and that with a decent understanding of their own machines and of the enemy's they could handle anything the Japanese tossed their way, Boyington fine-tuned the tactics he felt would most help during combat. Any edge he could impart meant the difference between life and death once action began.

Constant vigilance was crucial. From the moment they lifted off the runway until the instant they touched down back at their home base, Boyington wanted his men on high alert, inspecting the skies to sight the opposition before being spotted. A few seconds gained here could make all the difference in the world once combat began. The booklet urged pilots to "make steady careful observation a habit. They must have a system and a routine for scanning the air both above and below, behind, on the flanks and ahead. The vigil must be unceasing."[39]

Once the action started, Boyington cautioned his men to maintain their formation as much as possible because the Japanese loved to wait for and pounce on stragglers. As long as they remained in formation, "all the Zeros in the world won't touch you."[40] If a pilot found himself alone during battle and unable to locate any other member of the squadron, he should immediately return to home base. Above all, Boyington emphasized that a pilot had to maintain an altitude advantage. A pilot approaching his target from a higher altitude could embark on a steep dive, fire, and then veer away to regain altitude.

Boyington told his Black Sheep to come out of the sun whenever possible and to fire only when they had a clear target in sight and from close range. A pilot who shot too soon had little chance to hit the Zero, and the Japanese pilot, now forewarned, would begin taking evasive measures. In such a case, the pilot would have wasted time and ammunition because "in normal combat, if he [the Japanese pilot] cannot be hit before he has started down, he is usually gone."[41] As early as the September 16 action report, a time when the Black Sheep were still taking baby steps toward learning to fly as a cohesive squadron, Boyington underlined the admonition *Hold your fire till at close range*."[42] Once a pilot committed, Boyington cautioned, he had to direct his focus to that one target. "I always pick my target and plan my attack before I start on the original attack. I choose one target and stick to it. You can't do much good by spraying lead over a wide area."[43] Boyington said that he typically held his fire until he was within one hundred feet of his opponent.

Boyington told the men that the best run on a Zero was a stern run, but that the Black Sheep should not abandon a head-on run because they lacked "the guts to press it home." He suggested opening fire immediately in a head-on charge because "we are closing faster and because the plane opening fire last usually turns away first and is a good target during that run." The best defense if a Zero latched onto their tail was to nose over and dive because "they never or rarely follow you."[44]

Boyington had a final word of caution: be wary of a shot that looks too easy. Most likely the enemy "is suckering you in for his partner." If a Japanese plane started diving on them, "it is generally best to pull up sharply. He's going so fast he can't follow you and then you can come down on him." The Corsair's "speed is our defense," he said, and added, "the enemy can be outdistanced, and then altitude and position recovered for further attacks."[45]

Boyington warned the pilots to maintain their altitude advantage even as they were heading home, both to be in position to attack should they spot an enemy aircraft and to reduce the chances of being attacked. Too many pilots, thinking they were safe after the battle had ended or the mission was completed, let down their guard and flew home at low altitude. That was an invitation to enemy aircraft that pursued the returning American fliers, "and you're easy meat when you're down low."[46]

"It's up to me to teach him"

Boyington's teaching skills would likely have surprised anyone who had known him at any previous stage of his life, including his mates in the AVG. During his tenure with the Black Sheep, Boyington displayed the talents of a top-quality educator. At some point during the squadron's first few days, someone warned Boyington that the inexperienced Lieutenant McClurg would either soon be dead or would accidentally kill another Black Sheep. Undeterred by the challenge, Boyington said what any top-notch educator would say: "If the boy can't fly well enough, it's up to me to teach him."[47]

Boyington's legendary impatience was less in evidence after he took the helm of the Black Sheep. Once in command of a squadron compiled of aviators who respected him, Boyington no longer had to fall back on outrageous remarks or actions to get attention. He already had that, as well as their esteem, which meant that he could focus on shaping the squadron according to his principles. Boyington flowered as a squadron commander when all else—his previous record in the military, his disheveled appearance, his fistfights, his disastrous time with the AVG—pointed to calamity. He responded to respect, and in the process fashioned one of the most heralded units of the Pacific war. For one of the few times in his life, Boyington felt needed and accepted. Others listened to his words and considered what he said important.

The natural teacher in Boyington flourished in 1943–44. He not only told the men how to do something but also, more crucial, showed them how to do it. "I guess it was said that I was a good leader. I don't know whether I was or not, but it seemed that you can get people to follow you quite easily if you get in there and not tell them how to do it but show them how to do it and find out ways to help the men get rid of unnecessary fear." Like a top-notch educator, Boyington believed that "you can get along fine with the American boy if you show him and lead him and do not try to order him or drive him."[48]

Just as a good teacher comprehends the motivations of his students, Boyington possessed a profound understanding of what motivated one man to action and what froze another to inaction. "Of course, I realized that somebody going into one of these things for the first time would have a terrific amount of fear. In fact, the greatest fear any of us would have is fear of the unknown. We are just like mankind since the beginning of time. However, I was able to cut this fear down to a bare minimum."[49]

The teaching continued long after the flights ended. A night owl all his life, Boyington used informal nighttime bull sessions to discuss the positives and negatives of training flights or missions. John Begert claimed the Black Sheep did so well "because of training—we did more training with that squadron than we did with both the others—and the bull sessions we had at night about tactics." Lt. Ned Corman said of the discussions, "Ours was a free-thinking, free-speaking outfit. If you had some views, you expressed them. Whether they were accepted or not was immaterial—they were heard. You never got that in other squadrons, and to me that was the greatest difference."[50]

Even the missions most pilots shunned as a waste of time—routine patrols—were teaching opportunities. Boyington used them as instructional exercises to prove certain points or practice what they had discussed earlier. "Too often, fighters consider patrols and dumbo and task force covers a waste of time," the booklet describing his tactics noted. "However, along with performing the mission properly, the time involved can be utilized to good effect." During these routine flights Boyington had his pilots practice their formation flying. He asked leaders to exchange positions with their wingmen to see how well the wingmen could lead and how well the leaders could fly wing. The men practiced tight turns, violent scissors, and other tricky maneuvers, and developed their own systems of searching for distant objects.

A Marine ace from VMF-221, Lt. Harold E. "Murderous Manny" Segal, felt himself fortunate to have attended one of Boyington's bull sessions. Although the two aviators rarely crossed paths afterward, Segal, who shot down twelve Japanese aircraft, made a point to thank the Black Sheep commander when they met again after the war. Segal explained that one time a Zero locked on his tail and was about to finish him off when he recalled what Boyington had said in the tent that night about eluding a Japanese flier. Segal executed the maneuver Boyington recommended, shook the pursuer, and survived the war—and gave Boyington the credit.

"We were the *Black Sheep* Squadron"

Each step Boyington took with the Black Sheep became another building block in fashioning a team that thought first of their squadron and second of themselves. As a squadron commander Boyington put his men first, a trait the AVG never witnessed. Whenever the squadron received a new Corsair, for example, Boyington refused to requisition it for himself as a replacement for the well-worn Corsairs they had all been using, but instead let someone else take it. If the officer of the day assigned a new aircraft to Boyington, he would walk over to the board, erase the aircraft number after his name, and give the newer plane to one of his pilots, telling the OD: "Give me one of those old klunkers."[51]

A South Pacific aviator familiar with Boyington related that the Black Sheep commander said to Chaplain M. Paetznick of his fliers, "I never taxi out to take off on any mission that I don't pray; not for myself, but for their return and safety. It may not be an elegant prayer, but it always stated what needed to be said."[52] "Pappy could organize a group and inspire its members, just with who he was," said Lieutenant McClurg. "That is leadership. He was big on teamwork, and would grow large fangs at the first hint of any cliques or division within the group." He added, "I am sure his influence stayed with us through our lives."[53]

Boyington refused to send anyone on a mission that he would not go on as squadron leader, and he made it a point to be the first to volunteer for especially dangerous missions. He wanted to be the first to run in on strafing missions, which the pilots especially despised because they had to fly at lower altitudes against enemy antiaircraft fire. He believed that his example coaxed the rest to follow after him. He employed other morale boosters as well. Squadron bull sessions, often including alcohol, became legendary. Besides their discussions, Boyington and his men gathered at his tent for impromptu songfests that lasted long into the night. Calling themselves the Choral Society, they warbled popular songs such as "I Want a Girl Just Like the Girl That Married Dear Old Dad" and "For Me and My Gal," as well as others written by squadron members, especially Moon Mullen from the University of Notre Dame.

One song adapted the words of the Yale University "Whiffenpoof Song" to reflect their lives as Black Sheep:

We are poor little lambs who have lost our way.
Baa, baa, baa.
We are little Black Sheep who have gone astray.
Baa, baa, baa.
Gentlemen Black Sheep off on a spree,
Damned from here to Kahili,
God have mercy on such as we.
Baa, baa, baa.[54]

"It was fun," Lt. Harry Johnson later said. "It was a feeling that we were the best and we'd take any job. I liked the singing; I just liked it. You don't see the same loyalty now that we had—I don't believe I knew a one who wouldn't risk his life to save another." He added, "When you have pride, you have class. When the crunch comes, you're in there in your formation; you want to be a winner. In the Black Sheep, we had pride; we had class; and we were winners."[55]

Many men credited the pig roasts, fish fries using fish caught in the lagoon, beer busts, and other festivities with creating a tight-knit group. "I can recall no group I served with that had such esprit," said 1st Lt. Edwin Olander. "Part of that may have been the good feeling generated by success and by combat; part was a confidence instilled by Boyington. It was a good-times squadron. Everyone knows Greg's affinity for drink, and we all seemed to have a little, and we had some parties."[56]

Boyington even turned to Major League baseball to boost morale. To gain publicity for his men, on October 7 Boyington announced that his squadron would shoot down one Japanese Zero for each cap the winning World Series team agreed to send to them. He knew the caps were very popular with his men, less for the value of having a Major League ball cap than because the cap's long bill helped block the sun. Boyington was also certain that the caps of the winning team, which turned out to be the St. Louis Cardinals, would bring them luck.

Because pointless rules had been the bane of Boyington's career, he made certain not to bury his men in an avalanche of regulations. In his opinion, rules stifled imagination and initiative and allowed men like Colonel Smoak to throw their weight around. The only rules that mattered to Boyington pertained to the air, and those were to be implicitly followed. Otherwise, he commanded with a loose rein. If a man had to be disciplined, Boyington preferred talking to the individual about his errors to going through regular channels. "Boyington was very strict on air discipline, but he didn't worry too much about what went on on the ground," said Lieutenant Walton. "I liked the fact that he had few rules, all of which had to do with flight safety, and tried to enforce them," claimed 1st Lt. Edwin Harper. "When I had a squadron of my own, I tried to emulate some of that: not too many rules, but enforce those you have." First Lt. Rollie Rinaberger did the same.[57]

Boyington's system worked because he shared the responsibility rather than trying to keep all the controls in his own hands. Despite his abhorrence for anything official, Boyington realized that paperwork had to be filed and the nuts and bolts of a squadron had to be tended, so he delegated those duties to men who could capably execute them. Walton and the squadron executive, Capt. Stanley Bailey, took care of the paperwork and administrative details Boyington so detested, while Doc Reames served as the unofficial counselor. While he focused on the air, Boyington let his trio on the ground deal with the items he considered inconsequential to flying an aircraft. Boyington thus astutely took steps to neutralize what he recognized as his limitations. By utilizing his strengths and allowing others to compensate for his weaknesses, the undisciplined Boyington achieved tremendous results as a commander. He molded a team of individuals who believed in each other and in their leader, which in turn led to spectacular feats in the air.

"It was a time of extreme stress and action compressed into a brief period," admitted 1st Lt. Fred Losch, "but in just those couple of months, I became closer to that group than anyone except perhaps my brother." Losch added that because of Boyington and the skill of his fellow aviators, "We had a team, and we all tried to live up to it. We were the *Black Sheep* Squadron. Other squadrons were individuals—we were a *team*. . . . I'll always treasure those few weeks with the Black Sheep."[58]

"Pappy made me feel secure"

The most valid testimony attesting to a leader's effectiveness comes neither from the man himself nor from his superior officers. It springs from the men he commanded, the pilots who lived according to his precepts and flew into combat buttressed with the knowledge he imparted. There, among the Black Sheep, you will find universal acclaim.

Boyington made a lifelong impression on the men he led. Lieutenant McClurg dedicated his book to the Black Sheep and to Boyington, whom he dubbed "the greatest leader a pilot would ever want or need," and added, "I have looked back at times and felt very grateful for the things that enabled me to make it home from the war. I thank God. I credit Pappy, without whom I surely think I would not be here."[59] "Pappy made me feel secure," said Lt. Ed

Harper. "He made me feel aggressive. He gave me confidence. He was a leader. Sure, he got in trouble on the ground from time to time, and liked to drink and fight. But he was terrific in the air. And he made us young fighter pilots brave. And that's leadership."[60]

Walton, the man who maintained the records and thus knew more about the inner workings of the squadron than any of the others, summed up Boyington's impressive accomplishments in the Pacific war as follows: "Boyington had welded a conglomeration of casuals and replacements into one of the deadliest aerial combat squadrons in history. He was not only a savage past master of individual aerial combat; he was also an inspiring leader."[61] Even *Time* magazine's astute Pacific war correspondent, Robert Sherrod, who mingled with the war's top Navy and Marine commanders, saw a remarkable individual in Boyington, whom he called a wonderful commander. "He was not only a superb pilot, but also a natural leader, as he demonstrated among his Black Sheep pilots."[62]

When asked in 2007 about Boyington and the difference between his stint with the Flying Tigers and with the Black Sheep, Lieutenant Hill replied unhesitatingly that the AVG simply failed to understand Boyington. "The Black Sheep appreciated Boyington because he did not seek preferential treatment, because there were some officers who would ask for favored treatment." With the Flying Tigers, added Hill, "he was an ace and shot down six planes, but he was just one of the guys there. He was not the commanding officer. He didn't get along with anybody. I talked to a lot of Flying Tiger pilots and they all hated him." The Black Sheep responded when the AVG did not because they saw a different man in Boyington, a man they understood. "He was one of a kind that didn't give a damn about anything," Hill said. "Pappy was that kind of guy. He was the best damn commanding officer of a Marine fighter squadron during wartime. That was his thing. Other than wartime, he could get into a lot of trouble."[63]

Boyington excelled in the South Pacific because he was able to utilize the aviation skills that had been an integral part of him since he had first fallen in love with airplanes as a youth, when he wanted to unchain the F4B fighter and soar to the heavens. If other fliers had scorned the underutilized Boyington in Burma and China, in the South Pacific pilots frequently turned to him for advice, viewed him as a role model, and eagerly followed him into battle. Recognized and respected as a skilled aviator and looked up to as a leader, he responded in ways that would have astounded his family, the AVG, and most of his superior officers.

Chapter Seven

"They Can't Kill Me"

When the Black Sheep's first combat tour ended, Boyington led his squadron to Espiritu Santo before continuing on to Sydney. Weary after the long flight from the Solomons, Boyington and three other officers, including Lieutenant Walton, chose a hut, flopped onto their cots, and fell into deep slumber, not even noticing that the previous occupants had left behind a mess. They were awakened by a flashlight illuminating the inside. "A gruff voice came from behind the light, one that was only too familiar to me—and not pleasantly familiar, either," recalled Boyington: "Don't you know, Boyington, that there is an order against anyone sleeping without a mosquito net?"[1]

His old nemesis from Pensacola, Col. Joseph Smoak, now in command of the air group, shined the flashlight about the hut, berating Boyington for the mess in evidence. "You know the rules around here," he bellowed at Boyington. "Why haven't you and your men got your mosquito nets up? I've been around to the huts of all your squadron, and not one of them has his net up." Smoak, delighted at the chance to discipline a man he considered ill-fit for the Marine Corps, added, "Furthermore, your area is dirty. Why isn't it cleaned up? You know the rules. You're the commanding officer of your squadron. You will take immediate steps the first thing in the morning to remedy this situation, understand? And report to me as soon as you do. We don't live like a bunch of pigs down here." The next morning Boyington explained the situation to his men and told them to clean their areas, even though they had not been the guilty parties. "Do a thorough job; don't even leave a cigarette butt," he advised the

Black Sheep. "After everything is cleaned up, get your mosquito nets set up—and use them. I know it's silly, here where there are no mosquitoes and where our huts are screened in, but the regulations say that we must sleep under mosquito nets—so we'll sleep under mosquito nets."[2]

Boyington stormed over to Smoak's office to set the record straight but made no headway with the obstinate colonel. Smoak had detested Boyington since flight training in Florida, and he intended to make him suffer. Boyington argued that on merit alone, after his men had compiled such a glittering record in their first six weeks, he should be allowed to run the squadron in his own manner, but Smoak would not hear of it. Regulations were regulations, and they were to be followed. Boyington, unwilling to detain his men from the pleasures of Sydney, wisely stifled his anger and said no more. True to form, on the next fitness report Smoak criticized Boyington as a skilled pilot who could not competently run a squadron because of his excessive drinking.

All was not doom and gloom at Espiritu Santo, however. During his time there Boyington forged a rapport with a Catholic chaplain, and for the first time in his life he started to address his personal issues. The pair often chatted long into the night, sharing cigars and brandy as they discussed life, religion, and other topics that crossed their minds. Boyington could not explain why he, a man who had never had much use for religion, opened up to a man of God, but he felt the need to examine the course of his life in the lull between combat tours. "Apparently I must have been seeking something," Boyington explained, "although I wasn't quite certain what it might be. This man seemed to possess what I needed. I was seeking happiness and peace of mind, but the way to get these eluded me."[3]

Boyington took a few hesitant steps to face his demons. His blustery demeanor masked a host of insecurities, issues that required more time to resolve than the week at Espiritu Santo allowed. Unfortunately, the process stopped there. Boyington rarely opened up to anyone else in the years to come, guaranteeing a continued life of turmoil and unhappiness. His life might have been less fractious had he confided in more people like that Catholic chaplain.

"He's the best combat pilot we've got"

For six days beginning on November 6, Boyington and his Black Sheep left behind the perils of war for the enticements of Australia. Sydney, a metropolis of 1.5 million people, offered everything the Solomons lacked—decent quarters, exquisite food, free-flowing alcohol, and women. Forewarned by other aviators, the men had brought cigarettes and toilet paper, scarce items good for bartering in war-rationed Australia. The Black Sheep plunged into plates heaped with steak and eggs—both Boyington and Walton devoured a dozen eggs at their first breakfast—gulped beer and shots, and gathered each morning at the Snake Pit, a bar known for its vast assortment of enticing females.

As his memories of the respite indicate, Lieutenant Hill was determined to have a good time.

> After we spent six weeks in combat, we get a leave in Australia. Then we were trouble, because we were going back into combat the next week. We didn't know how long we were going to be around, so for that week we were really going to live life to the hilt. In Sydney, all the Australians were out fighting the war too. So, the Australian ladies were glad to see these GI's, these Marines. There would be all these girls all over you just waiting to get a date with one of the GI's, not just Marines or Air Corps. It got so that during a day's time, you could make dates with about three or four different girls.[4]

The brief sojourn ended all too quickly on November 12 when the squadron, laden with cases of beer to take back to the Solomons, assembled at the airport. Before they could board the airplane, though, two security officers told the group that the beer would have to stay behind because the extra weight would overburden the airplane. Considering the abandonment of the alcohol a near-traitorous act, the Black Sheep sat down at the airfield and consumed every bottle. "Most of us came back from the Sydney trip more tired than when we left," claimed Lieutenant McClurg, "but that was to be expected and was probably for the best."[5]

Two issues awaited the men when they reached Espiritu Santo on November 13: Colonel Smoak, and nineteen replacement pilots ordered in to fill out an enlarged squadron roster. Smoak, still seeking retribution, called Boyington to his office and informed him that he was being transferred to Vella Lavella as the operations officer. Stunned at this development, which meant the loss of his squadron and active combat in favor of a headquarters posting, Boyington went back and told his Black Sheep that Smoak had finally won. The men refused to accept it and urged Boyington to see Smoak's superior, Maj. Gen. James T. Moore, the assistant commanding general of the 1st Marine Aircraft Wing at Munda. Boyington and Moore had a long-standing friendly relationship, and the Black Sheep hoped Moore might step in and counter Smoak's order.

Rather than stomp directly to Moore's office and lodge a complaint, which he thought would look too much like seeking a favor, Boyington waited until he could "accidentally" bump into the general as he was walking to his office. The two struck up a routine conversation, and when Moore asked about the squadron's return to combat, Boyington replied that while the men looked forward to fighting the Japanese again, he had been ordered to remain behind for reassignment. Moore, irate that someone had removed his top squadron commander from combat, immediately strode to his office and called Smoak. "What's this about taking Boyington out of his squadron?" Moore shouted into the phone. Moore cut short Smoak's attempt to explain with a curt order to reinstate Boyington. "I don't care how senior he is; he's the best combat pilot we've got, and he's to be left in command of his squadron where he belongs, understand?"[6]

Smoak reluctantly followed the general's orders and tried another approach. He thought he could use his vast knowledge of the labyrinthine code of regulations to discipline Boyington. In order to see Moore, Boyington must have left the camp at Espiritu Santo and crossed the island—but he had forgotten to notify the group commander as regulations required. Confident that even Moore could not intervene against a clear violation of procedure, no matter how innocuous, on November 15 Smoak placed Boyington under arrest and ordered him to sign a letter acknowledging that he had violated the rule.

Smoak counted his victory too soon, though. Knowing Moore as well as he did, Boyington figured he could extricate himself from the mess fairly easily. In a letter addressed to Moore, he admitted breaking the rule, then quoted the regulation verbatim, sure that Moore, a fair-minded individual, would see the absurdity of cashiering a commander over such a minor regulation and would again intervene. The general did more than that. He not only informed Smoak that Boyington had proven his worth as a commander and as a combat pilot and was not to be disciplined, he also relieved Smoak of his duties and sent him to a different post—operations officer at Vella Lavella, the very spot to which Smoak had tried to banish Boyington.

Again secure in his position, Boyington greeted the replacement pilots, whose arrival brought the squadron to the newly designated number of forty aviators. As a way of welcoming the men, Boyington arranged a fish fry. He and some others "caught" their dinner by hurling hand grenades into the lagoon and gathering the fish that floated to the surface. Then he started training the replacements to make them as ready for combat as possible. For eleven days, beginning on November 15, Boyington, as he had done before the first tour, conducted frequent instructional sessions on the ground and practice flights in the air, much as a tutor prepares students for arduous exams.

Lt. Fred Losch, one of the new squadron members, remembered thinking, "God, those guys are professionals! A bunch of God-damned killers." He added, "I was the same age as several others, but they were six weeks ahead of me. We looked at them as if they were ten years older."[7]

"We intercepted whatever was coming at us"

On November 27 Boyington led his replenished Black Sheep Squadron from Espiritu Santo to Guadalcanal, where they refueled for the final hop to Vella Lavella. Their new home was a jungle-clad tropical island replete with coconut trees, exotic birds, and enticing fruit. While Vella Lavella teemed with insect life—the men put salamanders in their bedding to combat the hordes of mosquitoes and large black ants—the true danger lay to the north. Now that American forces had advanced up the Solomon chain, Kahili airfield was a mere seventy-five miles northwest, and Rabaul and its deadly ring of antiaircraft guns loomed three hundred miles beyond it. Before neutralizing Rabaul and knocking the enemy out of the Solomons, Boyington and the Black Sheep would have to fly into a hornet's nest.

Boyington faced another concern at the start of his second combat tour—mounting attention in the U.S. press as the number of aircraft he had downed neared twenty-six, a record first established by World War I aviator Eddie Rickenbacker and subsequently tied by Marine aviator Joe Foss, one of Guadalcanal's heroic fighter pilots. The tally from his first tour, when added to the aircraft Boyington claimed from his AVG days, had pulled him within six of the record. Each additional kill now attracted more newspaper and magazine reporters, all wanting to discuss his feelings about aerial combat and asking when he thought he might surpass Rickenbacker's and Foss' tally. Boyington loved the flattery accorded him and the squadron but detested the reporters' never-ceasing pursuit of headlines.

The attention stretched the boundaries of credibility at times. Boyington became a figure in a newspaper comic strip called *Fighting Marines,* and stories of his prowess reached ridiculous heights of exaggerations. One story circulated about an incident that supposedly happened during combat. According to the tale, in the heat of battle one of the Black Sheep asked if anyone had seen Pappy.

"I'm busy," Boyington supposedly blurted. "I've got five Zeros surrounded."

"Where are they?" asked the other pilot.

"Outside this cloud they've got me in!"[8]

Boyington's notoriety became so great that one colonel suggested that Boyington be awarded the Medal of Honor on the basis of the five kills he notched in the September 16 dogfight and for his aggressive leadership and sound tactics.

The tempestuous Boyington struggled to contain his impatience with the demands of the press. The reporters seemed to treat the entire episode as more of an athletic contest than a life-and-death struggle and seemed to forget what was at stake when he climbed into his Corsair. He told some of the other Black Sheep that the reporters "had very little idea what actual combat was like, and they didn't seem to care much."[9] Boyington's pilots also grew weary of the constant search for headlines and criticized the press for divulging information about Boyington that aided the enemy.

The reporters were not alone in their ignorance about war. Boyington believed that the people back home also had little idea of what the fighting men in the war sacrificed and endured. "How many months have you spent in the jungles with the heat and the insects?" he wanted to ask them. "How many times have you had malaria? How many of *your* best friends have you seen killed before *your* eyes? How many times have *you* had to stay in a foxhole all night? How often do *you* get up at 2:30 in the morning to go to work?"[10]

The initial portion of Boyington's second combat tour offered scant opportunity for aerial heroics. In the process of gathering their strength for the defense of Rabaul, the Japanese committed few aircraft to contest the American air attack over Bougainville, which ground forces had assaulted in early November. From November 27 until December 17, Boyington trained his squadron and participated in escort and strafing missions against Japanese land units on Bougainville. Supply dumps, machine-gun nests, trucks, and barges supplanted Japanese Zeros as prime targets during this stretch, as American forces battled to gain control of airfields around Cape Torokina along Bougainville's western coast and bring Rabaul within easy range of fighters and small bombers.

The Black Sheep were now providing close air support for ground forces, a tactic that had proved only marginally successful at Guadalcanal and New Georgia. Pilots had difficulty discerning the correct targets in the jungles below them and sometimes fired on friendly forces. Not surprisingly, infantry forces grew increasingly wary whenever an American fighter swooped low to the ground. Camouflaged as they were by the dense jungle, they were as likely as the Japanese to be the targets.

New tactics, including the use of colored smoke to denote American lines, resolved the issue. Boyington and his men flew as low as fifty feet above the ground, strafing enemy positions and bombing their supply routes and scaring up thousands of startled birds from their jungle sanctuaries. During one skirmish Marine units laid out a large white arrow pointing to Japanese mortar emplacements, which the Black Sheep demolished in eight separate runs. While initially regarding strafing with the same disdain they exhibited toward escorting bombers, the Black Sheep quickly realized the value of their services to the ground forces and took a more active interest. Soon anything moving at sea or outside American lines was fair game. "We intercepted whatever was coming at us in the Solomons and we strafed places where Japanese were seen," Capt. Fred Avey recalled years after the war. "We usually went up every day, sometimes twice. I flew so often that I got tired of sitting down. You can't stretch too well in those Corsairs, and even today people ask me why I stand so often."[11]

The constant daily repetition and grind of battle, added to the harsh conditions under which they fought, strained the Black Sheep to their limits. To relieve the stress they continued their nightly songfests and chat sessions, and drank whenever possible. The latter invariably raised concerns that Boyington, with his history of alcohol abuse, was sometimes flying into combat while intoxicated, but his Black Sheep denied the accusation. "Boyington loved to drink, but he never went into the air drunk, although he was hung over at times," admitted Captain Avey.[12] An inebriated Boyington might stumble into a shower and challenge a naked Avey to a wrestling match, as he once did, but the commander confined his faults to the ground. Never did he go on a mission with the Black Sheep while drunk. "Boyington couldn't have possibly been drunk when he was flying," agreed Lieutenant Hill. "How can you do what a pilot must do and be drunk?"[13]

"Just let me run this show my own way"

As soon as airfields had been secured on Bougainville, the focus of the American air effort turned toward Rabaul, three hundred miles to the northwest. Once the nexus of supplies and reinforcements for the Solomons, Rabaul now faced the prospect of an ever-strengthening American advance toward its five main and four secondary airfields. Shielded by five volcanoes rising more than two thousand feet and a potent ring of antiaircraft batteries, Rabaul posed a more rigorous test than Bougainville or any of the other Solomon islands. That the Japanese intended to hold the crucial base could not be denied—almost two hundred carrier aircraft had flown into Rabaul in early November. To retain the airfields Japan was willing to temporarily defuse its carrier arm, the instrument of war that garnered so many illustrious victories in the war's opening months, including the breathtaking raid against Pearl Harbor. For the next two months these aircraft joined the many antiaircraft batteries in attempting to repulse Boyington and the other American and Allied pilots who swept down in daily attacks.

To hit their targets Boyington and the Black Sheep had to fly long distances over water or thick jungles, elude any Japanese fighters that rose to meet them, plunge into thick antiaircraft fire, and return over the same water and jungles they passed on the way out. Should they sustain damage during the attack or encounter mechanical problems, they faced the unappetizing prospect of bailing out into a broad expanse of ocean or over a Japanese-held jungle island. "We always knew there'd be all kinds of antiaircraft," said Captain Avey. "That flak was scary—it burst all around you and was so thick you could hardly see the target. No matter which way you turned there was flak, so the best tactic was just to fly straight ahead, do your job, and get out. When you're in the air it was either kill or be killed. We were thought to be the bravest pilots, but honestly, I was frightened often."[14]

The Americans enjoyed a favorable edge in both available aircraft and experienced and rested pilots. Because the Japanese lacked sufficient spare parts to repair damaged aircraft, by the end of 1943 only 40 percent of their planes were airworthy. In contrast, American factories were churning out airplanes and the American training system was pouring a steady stream of knowledgeable pilots into the war zone. Aviators fresh from combat returned to the United States to explain to student fliers the nuances of air combat—what tricks to look for and how to handle each aircraft's idiosyncrasies. This efficient regimen ensured a constant flow of talented aviators at a time when the quality of Japanese replacement pilots steadily declined. Japan had lost many of its leading fliers in the great sea battles in the Coral Sea, at Midway, and in the wearying fights over Guadalcanal, leaving the admirals with less experienced aviators to fill the ranks. If an American flier was lost, a replacement quickly took his spot. In addition, American aviators knew that every six weeks or so they could look forward to a break in combat. Their Japanese counterparts enjoyed no such interlude. The Japanese system retained a man in combat until death or injury removed him from the contest.

Japanese aviators faced such trying conditions at Rabaul that they labeled the post "the graveyard of fighter pilots." The heady rush produced by the string of victories during the war's opening months had been replaced with a sense of resignation as the Japanese realized the futility of trying to defeat American power and numerical superiority. "Prior to the beginning of 1943, we still had hope and fought fiercely," Petty Officer Tetsuzo Iwamoto later said. "But now, we fought to uphold our honor. We didn't want to become cowards. . . . We believed that we were expendable, that we were all going to die. There was no hope of survival—no one cared anymore."[15]

Maj. Gen. Ralph J. Mitchell, the commander of air forces in the northern Solomons, wanted to supplement the bombing of Rabaul with Marine fighter sweeps. This was a strategy that Boyington, with the support of General Moore, had been promoting for some time. Sweeps appealed to Boyington for a simple reason—they left fighter pilots free to hit the enemy without escort duties to distract them. Mitchell, figuring that such a mission required an aggressive leader, selected Boyington to lead the first organized sweep against Rabaul, a massive eighty-four-aircraft strike set for December 17.

At 5:15 AM on December 17, Boyington and 7 other Black Sheep pilots lifted off the runway to rendezvous with 76 other Allied aircraft, including 31 F4U Corsairs, 23 New Zealand P-40 Kittyhawks, and 22 F6F Hellcat fighters.

The armada assembled in triple layers from 10,000 feet to 26,000 feet, then turned northwest along Bougainville's coastline toward Rabaul. With so many aircraft under his command, Boyington had trouble coordinating their movement, but the flotilla arrived over Rabaul at 10:05.

The pilots eagerly anticipated a wide-open fray. "Most fun of all were the fighter sweeps when we flew over their airfields to pick a fight—i.e., engage any enemy planes which chose to come up to meet us," Lieutenant Olander recalled. "Often, it was wild!" Olander's explanation of why he enjoyed fighter sweeps could readily be used to depict his commander, who made his reputation the hard way on schoolyard playgrounds. "My best description of a fighter sweep is: a bully goes into a school yard with a chip on his shoulder and says 'Let's fight.'"[16] No wonder Boyington loved the appeal of wide-open combat.

Boyington could see a conglomeration of enemy fighters aligned on the airfield below, but none appeared to be taking off. He fired a few rounds in an effort to prod them into action, and when that failed he broadcast taunts over his radio. One Japanese replied by challenging Boyington to "Come on down, sucker!" but only a handful of aircraft rose to meet them.[17] The lower-flying P-40s shot down eight enemy aircraft, but the large-scale aerial scuffle Boyington longed for was not to be. He had brought too many Allied fighters for the Japanese to risk their scant resources. The Black Sheep returned empty-handed.

The December 17 sweep "was balled up from the very beginning," complained Boyington. "The Allied fighters were of so many different types, we might just as well have been escorting bombers." He had discussed fighter sweeps with General Moore and had told Capt. John Foster of VMF-222 that "if they would just let me run this show my own way I would have Rabaul knocked out in two weeks."[18] He now took up the matter with General Mitchell.

Boyington contended that the sweep had employed too many aircraft to be effective. Rather than leading eighty or more fighters, a group he thought was too unwieldy to organize and command and so intimidating that the enemy simply remained on the ground, he suggested in the squadron's combat report that twenty-four would be sufficient, and by no means should more than forty-eight fighters participate. Boyington was certain that the Japanese would rise to meet a unit that size. He also took the opportunity to argue that the fighters should be the same type—preferably Corsairs—to eliminate the time-consuming task of checking the sky to identify aircraft, and that the fighting be confined to a limited area rather than a series of dogfights that occupied much of the sky.[19]

Boyington received his opportunity four days later when he guided forty-eight fighters to Rabaul. Boyington purposely held back his fighters so that they would arrive after a group of bombers had appeared, a time when Japanese Zeros would least suspect another attack. When the Zeros took the bait and swarmed around the bombers, Boyington and his fighters descended on one hundred targets spread out before them. Boyington spotted a Zero, dropped behind in a level run, held his fire until he had pulled within fifty feet, then splashed the enemy plane with a brief burst of gunfire. He quickly regained altitude to own the advantage in a second attack, which occurred minutes later when two Zeros materialized at ten thousand feet. Boyington chose the rear-most plane, which was sputtering with mechanical difficulties, opened fire from one hundred feet, and watched as the pilot leapt from his flame-engulfed aircraft. Boyington climbed back toward the sun, but when he observed the second Zero circling the area where his companion had gone down, he dropped behind the unsuspecting Zero and dispatched it in flames with a salvo from one hundred feet.

Energized by those three kills, Boyington circled Rabaul Harbor for twenty minutes in the hope of finding more targets. When a formation of nine Zeros emerged at ten thousand feet, Boyington again selected the rear plane as his target, ran in out of the sun, and fired from one hundred yards. He maintained his fire until he had plunged directly through the formation, passed underneath, and rolled out to the side. He observed pieces from his target's cowling and fuselage break away as the Zero spiraled into the channel below. The eight other Zeros turned toward Boyington, who relied on his Corsair's superior speed to put distance between him and the Japanese as he set a course home for Vella Lavella. When Boyington landed with the news that he had added four planes to his tally, the Black Sheep hoisted him to their shoulders and carried him around camp, shouting that he needed just three more kills for the record.

The next evening the squadron gathered for a Christmas Eve celebration. The men created a homemade eggnog concoction in a huge kettle by mixing together powdered eggs, powdered milk, sugar, nutmeg, and water—enhanced with five quarts of whiskey. Thus fortified, they sang, drank, and laughed to honor the holy occasion. The mood turned somber when Lt. Robert Bragdon said to Boyington, "Listen, Gramps, we all want to see you break the record, but we don't want you to go up there and get killed doing it." The Sheep had already observed how the ordeal of chasing the record added strain to their commander and wondered how much more he could endure.

Boyington had a ready reply. "Don't worry about me. They *can't* kill me. If you guys ever see me going down with 30 Zeros on my tail, don't give me up. Hell, I'll meet you in a San Diego bar six months after the war, and we'll all have a drink for old times' sake."[20]

"Why don't you guys leave me alone?"

Boyington admitted in his memoirs that on the day after Christmas, after ingesting too much alcoholic eggnog, he climbed into his Corsair with a mind-numbing hangover. "I had one hell of a tussle pulling myself out of the old rack," he said about being awakened that morning. "I was feeling really rough as I drove in silence down the hill to our ready shack by the strip with a load of duty pilots."[21] Heat, festering sores, and the pressure of breaking the record were also taking their toll on the commander.

The already arduous pace accelerated after Christmas. In monotonous fashion, the men took off before dawn each day, flew to the airstrip on Bougainville to refuel, then navigated to Rabaul and its antiaircraft batteries. Despite the exhaustion produced by the near-daily attacks, the Black Sheep never let up. "The Sheep were out there, seeking the enemy," said Lieutenant McClurg. "We didn't fight merely if our paths crossed; we made sure our paths crossed, and blasted away."[22] In another fighter sweep on December 27 Boyington drew within one of the record by downing his twenty-fifth aircraft. This was aerial combat at its finest, the aggressive sort Boyington had long sought and the type that most fit his personality. Unfortunately, he could hardly enjoy it because of the pressure from the press. After each mission the assembled reporters asked if he had tied or broken the record.

Boyington was determined to achieve the record, both for himself and for his squadron, but he was beginning to wonder if he could reach it before his second tour ended in early January. Once that tour was completed, Boyington would be sent back to the United States, and all hope of coming home as the leading Marine ace would evaporate. In an effort to increase his odds, Boyington flew morning and afternoon missions, in good and bad weather. "The Japs are getting pretty scarce out here," Boyington wrote in a letter during those trying days, "and I doubt if I will be able to beat Joe Foss' record before I am sent home."[23] The more missions he flew and returned without a tally, the more his frustration multiplied as he saw his chances dim.

The tension produced by the combination of combat and press demands exploded on December 30 when a reporter once again asked when he would tie Rickenbacker's and Foss' record. "Goddamn it, why don't you guys leave me alone?" he shouted. "I don't know if I'm going to break it or not. Just leave me alone till I do or go down trying."[24]

Doc Reames, alarmed over Boyington's deteriorating condition, attempted to persuade Boyington to take a break from flying, but the aviator adamantly refused. He had not drawn this close to the record only to let it slip away in the tour's dying moments. He was weary beyond words, though, and had to summon every ounce of strength to continue. He confessed to correspondent Fred Hampson that while he longed to own the record, he did not feel physically or mentally right. Heavy drinking obviously exacerbated the problem. He later explained that he was worried about what people thought of him and about gaining their acceptance, a lifelong trait often found in alcoholics. He admitted that the tendency "has only caused me to get into one predicament after another, all my life."[25]

Witnessing their leader's obvious discomfort at the circus unfolding around him, the Black Sheep ceased talking about the record. They could not control the press, but they could at least make Boyington comfortable when he was with them. Boyington's direction, guidance, and training had taken them safely through many tight encounters with the Japanese. They were now determined to shield their leader from as much of the pressure as possible. "He flew missions every day for correspondents," explained Captain Avey. "They wanted him to break the record for downing Japanese planes. There were always four or five guys who wanted to interview him. I resented them because they should have let Boyington and us rest. They didn't think about what it was like for us. Boyington was tired and at times shouldn't have gone up, but he did. I wonder if that didn't have something to do with his being shot down and captured."[26]

"The invincible lion had disappeared"

Though Boyington may at times have acted as if the record meant little to him, the desire to be recognized as the top ace motivated his activities as the new year opened. He admitted in a letter to his old China friend Olga Greenlaw that "getting killed has always been the least of my worries. I should have been killed a dozen times, considering all the things I have tried to do in my life. Strange as it may seem, I have done damn near everything I set out to do—and intend to do the rest."[27]

With monsoon season reducing the number of flights and the end of his second tour a few days away, Boyington worried more than ever that he might miss his chance to tie or surpass the record. Boyington wrote in his memoirs that an old flying buddy, Marion Carl, approached him and suggested that Boyington take his place in a fighter sweep Carl was to lead on January 3. Boyington agreed because it would give him an extra opportunity to break the record. Boyington repeated that assertion in a postwar interview, and some historians accept it. Carl, however, disputed that version, explaining that on January 2 Boyington came to him at Vella Lavella and asked if he could lead the sweep instead of Carl. Boyington, Carl stated, "was getting score-happy." Despite his reservations Carl agreed to the switch because Boyington had but a few days remaining in combat while Carl had plenty of time left.[28]

January 3 began inauspiciously for Boyington, who had to shuttle between various aircraft until he found an airworthy fighter. He lifted from the runway and steered his formation along Bougainville's west coast before turning northwest toward Rabaul. At 8 AM he led the sweep in a broad right turn and descended from 22,000 feet as seventy Japanese Zeros rose to challenge the intruders. Boyington selected a target, fired from four hundred yards, and watched as the pilot bailed out of his burning aircraft. Other aviators with Boyington confirmed the kill, which when counting all six claims with the AVG, put Boyington into a tie with Foss and Rickenbacker as the lead ace. An excited George Ashmun, who flew as Boyington's wing that day, congratulated his commander. "Gramps, you got a flamer!"[29]

As far as the other participants in the January 3 mission knew, that was the sole aircraft Boyington downed during that mission, and the action report filed at the time reflected the record-tying feat. After the war, however, Boyington, along with Frank Walton, wrote a supplemental action report in which he claimed that he shot down an additional two Zeros not witnessed by other fliers. The report claimed that when a flock of Zeros jumped him and Ashmun, the pair took evasive action, during which time Boyington supposedly splashed his twenty-seventh plane. Immediately afterward he noticed smoke billowing from Ashmun's Corsair but received no response when he attempted to contact his wingman. As other Zeros collected around Ashmun and pumped more bullets into the aircraft, Boyington, according to his supplemental report, dropped behind and sprayed the enemy formation in an effort to force them off Ashmun's tail. In the process he notched his twenty-eighth kill.

Despite his efforts, Boyington could not save Ashmun. He followed his wingman down and observed the Corsair crash into St. George Channel off Rabaul. Assuming that his friend was dead, Boyington veered toward home as the Zeros turned their attention to him, but he could not elude so many enemy pursuers. Bullets riddled his Corsair "like hail on a tin roof," puncturing the tail end, smacking against the armor plate behind his head, and shredding his wingtips. "I could hear and feel the shells striking the armor plate and fuselage," Boyington recalled after the war. "I remember my body being banged around, then suddenly I had a fire in the cockpit. The engine and fuel line had been shot up."[30]

Shrapnel from a 20-mm shell wounded Boyington in the left leg and ankle, spraying blood throughout the cockpit. Other pieces of metal sliced his forearm and head. Boyington dropped lower in an effort to shake the Zeros, but within a half mile his main gas tank exploded in flames, shrouding the cockpit in smoke and fire. Boyington described the situation as "much the same as opening the door of a furnace and sticking one's head into the thing."[31]

Unable to see clearly due to the flames, Boyington yanked at his ripcord and safety belt as the Corsair plunged to two hundred feet above the water's surface. His parachute opened only seconds before he splashed into the water five miles offshore from Cape St. George, New Ireland, hitting with such force that he felt like he had collided with a slab of concrete.

Aviators returning home heard someone shouting over the radio that he was about to hit the water, but no one could identify the voice. When they landed at Vella Lavella, absent their commander and Ashmun, the Black Sheep gathered quietly, anxiously awaiting the missing men. "The news spread like the chill wind from revetment to the 'ready room' to the tent camp on the hill," Associated Press correspondent Fred Hampson wrote in a January 4 article. "The war stood still for a hundred pilots and 500 ground crewmen. "For Maj. Gregory Boyington, leader of the marine's 'blacksheep squadron,' had failed to return from a mission during which he shot down his 26th enemy plane to tie the all-time American record."[32]

Stunned squadron members who had been convinced that Boyington would always be at their helm grappled with emotions as the day unfolded. "Thus, January 3, 1944 was the day that emptied Pappy's bunk," later wrote Lieutenant McClurg. "We were in a state of shock. The invincible lion had disappeared."[33]

Even aviators in other squadrons were crestfallen. Capt. John M. Foster of VMF-222, the Flying Deuces, termed the news "a severe mental blow. Gregory Boyington, the Indomitable, had been shot down!" Foster added, "If the Japs had been able to get Gregory Boyington—the man, above all men, who knew what to expect from a Jap in a fight, who had learned during four long, dangerous years how to hate and how to avenge that hate—then what was the chance for the rest of us, who were rank amateurs by comparison?"[34]

While the Black Sheep prayed for their leader's safe return, other officers realized that the war effort had suffered an irreplaceable loss. Maj. Gen. Ralph Mitchell, the commander of Allied air forces in the Solomons, said, "Not only was Boyington of immense value as a pilot but his instructional ability was almost immeasurable. We need men like him to 'read the Bible' to the kids back home who don't know it yet."[35]

In the United States, *Time* magazine announced in its January 17, 1944, issue that "tough, straight-shooting 'Pappy' Boyington, who had built his 'Black Sheep' into one of the best U.S. fighter squadrons, was missing in action." The *Chicago Daily Tribune*, which described Boyington as "stocky and square jawed, he looks not unlike a bulldog; in the air he fights like one," reported that on January 7 the Navy Department informed Boyington's mother of his loss. "I am confident he is all right and he will show up somehow, somewhere," she replied. In Seattle, Boyington's daughter Gloria included her father in her nighttime prayers. "Please God, bring Daddy back."[36]

"If it moved, it got shot"

The Black Sheep wasted no time taking to the air to look for their missing commander. They followed a January 3 search with another the next day, scouring the seas about New Ireland and Bougainville for almost three hours before returning empty-handed. Their futility and helplessness fueled a rage that each member vainly attempted to suppress, a fury that took form in exacting revenge on any enemy barge or ship they spotted. "The Black Sheep raged like wild men," stated Lieutenant Walton, "up and down the coasts of New Ireland and New Britain, shooting up barges, gun positions, buildings, bivouac areas; strafing airfields; killing Nip troops; cutting up supply dumps, trucks, small boats."[37]

"In the days immediately after January 3, the Black Sheep, who were previously known as aggressive, antagonistic fighters—became demons," explained Lieutenant McClurg. "If it moved, it got shot." He and the other Black Sheep took off with one goal in mind: make the Japanese pay. "Levels of destruction that previously left us satisfied that we had disabled something, now were not enough." He added, "We were out to make payment in full for the disappearance of Pappy."[38]

Boyington's memory and instructions lingered with his men. During a January 6 mission, for instance, Lt. H. C. Johnson spotted a solitary Zero over Rabaul. He started to dive on the lone plane when he recalled Boyington's admonition to look for a trap when there was an easy shot. Johnson looked behind and saw two other Zeros approaching on a high stern run. He embarked on a fast dive, veered sideways, took refuge in a cloudbank, and returned safely to Vella Lavella.

A flurry of rumors circulated about Boyington's fate. A few weeks after his disappearance, the unit received a report that a native chief on a Solomon island was harboring twenty aviators, including Boyington. Later in the war, Lieutenant Walton read a document obtained by Marines fighting on Saipan stating that Boyington had passed through the island on his way to Tokyo. Though delighted with the news, Walton fretted that once the Japanese found out who they had captured they would likely execute the famous pilot.

Though *Time* magazine proclaimed in its February 21, 1944, issue that Boyington had been killed, without solid evidence no one knew what had become of him. Walton expressed the feeling his squadronmates shared when he told a reporter, "He may show up and he may not. But if he doesn't, the American people ought to know that they lost the best and the bravest guy that ever came out here to fight for them. The Japs know it already."[39]

The Black Sheep flew their final mission as a squadron on January 6 before heading to Espiritu Santo and Australia. Unlike the first sojourn in Sydney, the somber mood prevented Boyington's men from enjoying their break from combat.

When the squadron members returned to the forward area, they faced the unpleasant prospect of being distributed to other squadrons. Some of the men had already completed their mandatory two tours and would go back to the United States, but the others were destined for squadrons badly in need of replacements. Maj. Henry Miller, who succeeded Boyington as commander of the Black Sheep, was determined not to let that happen. He wrote a letter to the commanding general of the 1st Marine Aircraft Wing urging that the Black Sheep be kept together: "The flight echelon referred to, known as the 'Black Sheep,' wishes to urge strongly that it be maintained as a unit in order not to destroy its high morale and its smooth operation as an aggressive squadron of the type which we believe of the most value to the Marine Corps."

To support his argument Miller included the booklet detailing Boyington's tactics and stated, "The record speaks for itself." The men know the tactics, he wrote, "believe in them, and feel that we as a unit are in the best position to carry them on." Miller contended that the surest way of continuing Boyington's effective tactics was to keep the squadron intact. The major ended his letter by referring to the camaraderie Boyington had built into the squadron. "Finally, under Major Boyington, the 'Black Sheep' developed an *esprit de corps* we believe unequalled in this area. This spirit will be lost if the unit is broken up."[40]

Though General Moore, Boyington's longtime advocate, added a ringing endorsement with a handwritten note attached to the recommendation to "keep this combat team intact. Do not split this group," war requirements took priority.[41] On March 1 the fifteen Black Sheep remaining in the theater received orders sending them to VMF-211. Boyington's squadron no longer existed.

Under Boyington's leadership the Black Sheep Squadron attained lofty triumphs. In only 84 days of combat the squadron's pilots shot down 97 enemy aircraft, destroyed 28 vessels of various sizes, strafed 125 Japanese land positions, and produced 8 aces. Their brief time together created one of the military's most distinguished units.

"You're not allowed to speak"

While his squadron splintered, Boyington was struggling to stay alive. After parachuting into the water he retrieved his Mae West, but the device would not inflate because it had been holed by Japanese bullets. For two hours he floated off New Ireland, ducking under the surface whenever a Zero dropped nearby. He was hesitant to inflate his rubber raft lest it draw the enemy's attention, but growing wearier every moment in the choppy waters, Boyington decided to risk capture and use it.

Once he had hauled himself on board, Boyington saw that his wounds were more serious than he had realized. Skin hung loosely from his scalp, his shattered left ankle sent shock waves of pain throughout his body, and shrapnel had ripped his left ear, arms, and shoulders. Alone at sea, Boyington assessed his situation. He wondered why he had survived the crash landing when other aviators died, and prayed that he had the courage to endure whatever lay ahead.

Eight hours after he hit the water, a sudden movement startled Boyington. In the distance a submarine surfaced, momentarily leading the downed pilot to think he had been rescued. As the boat neared his raft, however, Boyington detected a Japanese emblem. Rather than rescue and a return to Vella Lavella, he was headed to Rabaul and incarceration. Crew members from the submarine helped Boyington onto the boat, where an English-speaking pharmacist's mate questioned him. Their humane treatment happily surprised the Marine flier, "and I wondered if this was the type of treatment I could expect in the future. One of the crew spoke English and assured me that I was going to be all right."[42]

The submarine transported Boyington to Rabaul, the very place he and the other American pilots had been lambasting for the past months. Once he was ashore, sailors blindfolded him and led him to the Imperial Japanese Navy headquarters, where captors put him through the first of many harsh interrogations. Most questioners smacked him on the head and burned him with cigarettes, but one inquisitor treated him with kindness. Edward Chikaki Honda, a civilian interpreter who had been born in Hawaii and graduated from McKinley

High School in 1929 before being sent to Japan for university, advised Boying-ton that the officers who mistreated him would continue to ask the same questions and persist in beating him unless he thought of a single story and stuck to it. If he wavered from answer to answer, the abuse would intensify. "I took his advice. I couldn't argue with his logic. He understood my predicament."[43]

Boyington unwisely put personal feelings above duty when he may have placed his old enemy Colonel Smoak at risk. An interrogator threatened to order the execution of every other prisoner unless Boyington divulged the name of his base commander. Rather than give the name of the actual officer, Boyington not only substituted Smoak's name but pointed out on a map the location of Smoak's compound. As Boyington related in his autobiography, "I smiled to myself, thinking: 'I would love to see that no-good son of a bitch's face if it is at all possible for them to get through'" and bomb the spot. No harm came to Smoak as a result, but Boyington's rash—some would say traitorous—action potentially placed a fellow officer in danger.

In between interrogations Boyington shared a tiny cell with an American pilot who had been shot down over Ballale. Spoiled rice and thin soup provided meager sustenance, especially for someone suffering from wounds such as Boyington had. A man who was supposedly a physician examined his injuries but administered such minor, ineffective treatment that Boyington had to tolerate the pain and hope that nature and time would heal him.

Sparse food and poor health, including a bout with malaria, were bad enough for Boyington to endure; the thought that he might be killed by fellow countrymen proved almost unbearable. Allied bombing attacks kept him on alert day and night, and as an aviator who had played such a crucial part in those attacks, he clearly understood his danger.

In the end, those incessant bombing raids may have been partly responsible for Boyington's survival. Honda, far from being a Japanese patriot, wanted out of Rabaul. The Allies had been tightening the noose around the bastion for some time, and the daily bombings made him more anxious to leave. He figured that those who remained would either die or be captured, and neither option was appealing. Boyington was his ticket to safety. Honda first convinced his superiors that Boyington's fame as an aviator could be put to more beneficial propaganda use in Japan than at an outer defensive post, and then persuaded them that he should be Boyington's escort. On February 16 Honda herded Boyington and five other handcuffed and blindfolded prisoners—PBY pilot Cdr. John Arbuckle, fighter pilot Capt. Charles Taylor, Corsair pilot Maj. Don Boyle, and officers from Australia and New Zealand—aboard a Betty medium bomber for the trip from Rabaul to Truk in the Caroline Islands eight hundred miles to the northwest. Besides Honda and the plane's crew of three, only one armed guard accompanied the group.

Without a doubt Honda saved Boyington's life. Japanese naval policy stipulated that once interrogators had obtained whatever intelligence prisoners carried, they were to execute the captives rather than sending them to Japan. Had Boyington remained much longer at Rabaul, he most likely would have fallen subject to that provision and not survived the war.

Boyington claimed in his autobiography that as soon as he was in the air, he started thinking of ways to escape. He thought that the five prisoners could wriggle free from their bonds and subdue the solitary guard, who periodically dozed as the plane droned along. Armed with the soldier's weapon, they could commandeer the aircraft and fly it to an Allied-held airfield. He never enjoyed the chance. One of the other prisoners correctly guessed what was on Boyington's mind and said, "Greg, I pray you, don't try to make an escape and take over this plane." Boyington assented but bristled at what he considered excessive timidity. "None of my Black Sheep would have talked like that," he asserted in his book, "and everything would have been so damned easy if *only* I had had five of them there with me. All we would have had to do was knock over this guard. He was the only one with a gun handy."[44] That claim was typical Boyington braggadocio. Six weakened, shackled prisoners posed a poor match against an armed guard and four other Japanese soldiers. Had he made the attempt, Boyington and the other captives would most probably have been killed.

As luck would have it, he and the other men almost perished on landing at Truk. The Betty descended moments before American carrier aircraft swooped down for a thorough bombing of the airfield. Honda rushed the still-blindfolded prisoners from the aircraft into a slit trench, where they all huddled while American bombs exploded nearby. At times during the fracas, Boyington peeked from beneath his blindfold to witness Navy F6F Hellcat fighters strafe the airstrip and Japanese aircraft. Honda, who had already saved Boyington's life by extracting him from Rabaul, had again saved the aviator by hustling him to the trench.

Once the bombing ended, the Japanese crammed the six prisoners into a poorly ventilated cell big enough for one person. For sixteen days the men suffered from the equatorial heat and received little water. Their lips and tongues swelled and their mouths felt as if they were made of cotton, but they at least enjoyed sufficient quantities of rice and pickles. Honda shielded his charges from beatings by explaining to the Japanese guards that the six had long been captives and were already worn down by previous abuse.

Sixteen days after their arrival in Truk, Honda again escorted his prisoners to an aircraft for the flight to Japan. They stopped overnight at Saipan, where a kindly warrant officer arranged decent food for the prisoners, before going on to Iwo Jima. The final leg on March 7 took them to an airfield near Yokohama, a city fifty miles south of Tokyo. From there they traveled by truck and streetcar nine miles to the Yokohama suburb of Ofuna, where Honda removed the men's blindfolds.

The Japanese inhabitants stared at the captives as they trudged through the town on their way to the prison camp. When the prisoners asked Honda where they were being taken, he described their new locale in pleasant tones. "A navy camp, Ofuna, it's a suburb of Yokohama, the same as your Hollywood in Los Angeles, where they make motion pictures in Japan."[45]

Boyington's hopes for a comparatively pleasant experience rose as they paced through the countryside. The trees and gentle slopes reminded him of home, and what could be better than heading toward the Japanese Hollywood? His hopes plunged when he spotted the Ofuna camp, which would be his home for the next thirteen months. The wooden stockade seemed an open wound on the beautiful landscape that surrounded it. Once inside, Boyington surveyed the prisoners in the courtyard and spotted a man with whom he had been stationed aboard the USS *Yorktown* (CV-5) before the war. An elated Boyington shouted a greeting to the man, who failed to even turn his face in recognition.

"You're not allowed to speak until you have been in camp for a while," said Honda, "and then the [guards] will give you permission."[46]

Those were Boyington's first clues that Ofuna would be nothing like Hollywood.

Chapter Eight
"I'll Meet You Guys in a San Diego Bar"

At the Ofuna prison camp Boyington embarked on a different phase of his war career. After four exhausting months of near-daily combat in the South Pacific, where he pitted one of the Corps' most effective fighter squadrons against the best the Japanese could offer, he now commenced a nineteen-month stint as a prisoner of Japan, first at Ofuna and then at the Omori prison camp. His time as a prisoner of war could not have been more different from his handful of months with the Black Sheep, but in each case Boyington's intense desire to survive and pugnacious nature became allies in situations that demanded strength and resilience. As he had done with his Black Sheep, in prison camp Boyington helped to pull his mates through trying times.

"Intimidation camp"

Ofuna was not much to look at. One hour by bus from Yokohama, the camp offered three U-shaped unheated wooden barracks, grass sleeping mats, thin blankets, little food, a dearth of mail and medical treatment, and isolation from the outside world. Operated by the Japanese navy, it housed close to one hundred Allied officers and enlisted men whom the Japanese thought either had knowledge of Allied strategy or worked in crucial sectors such as communications or in submarines. They intended to extract all the information these captives had.

So masked in secrecy was Ofuna that not even the local civilian population knew of its existence. The Japanese never divulged the names of the camp's prisoners to the Red Cross or to the U.S. government, which meant that their families back home knew nothing of their fate. Japanese camp officials boasted to Boyington and the others that as far as the world was concerned, the men had ceased to exist and they could be killed at any moment. Because the men were considered special captives rather than prisoners of war, the Japanese claimed that they were not subject to the Geneva Convention. Other than a few Red Cross food packages received at Christmas 1944, the men had no contact with friendly organizations.

Pilot Louis Zamperini was a fellow prisoner. A former track star at the University of Southern California (USC) who ran in the 1936 Berlin Olympics, Zamperini had already learned the facts of life in Ofuna, which he described as "the despicable secret interrogation camp run by the Japanese navy, hidden even from prying Japanese eyes, certainly from any of the agencies from which I had expected help."[1] It was as if Boyington and the other incarcerated men had vanished for the duration of their stay there.

Interrogation by three Japanese inquisitors the men nicknamed the Quiz Kids occupied much of the captives' early weeks at Ofuna. The impeccably attired Kunichi Sasaki, called Handsome Harry by the inmates, conducted Boyington's first session. A graduate of USC who had attended the school at the same time as Zamperini, Sasaki spoke perfect English and at first seemed to befriend the Americans; he even gave Boyington cigarettes during their sessions. Like the rest of the guards, he turned out to be no friend.

The interrogations by the trio, which sometimes included beatings, con-tinued until the camp commander questioned Boyington a few weeks into his captivity. When Boyington saw what lay on the officer's desk—a transcript of an American radio broadcast announcing that Boyington had been awarded the Medal of Honor—he figured that he would be severely beaten or killed. To his surprise, his treatment improved over the next few days. The commander told Boyington that the Japanese honored heroes of any nation, and that a physician would treat the injuries he had sustained when he crashed off New Ireland.

Japanese indulgence only went so far, though, even for honored heroes. The frequent beatings earned Ofuna the labels "Intimidation Camp" and "hell-hole." Guards forced the men into the Ofuna crouch, in which the prisoner had to stand on the balls of his feet with his knees half bent and arms raised above his head. As soon as the man began to weaken and lower his arms, the guards administered a thrashing. Lt. (jg) William Ross said after the war that "at Ofuna when anybody broke the rules everybody was beaten. If the Japs, especially the young soldiers, wanted exercise they would take us and punch us around." In depositions given after the war, prisoners condemned the harsh conditions, which included, according to Ens. John Bertrang, being "imprisoned in cold weather in unheated prison, unclean, vermin infested. Stayed in cells during air raids. Incompetent sadistic prison doctor, six men died from malnutrition and improper medical care, mass beatings of groups for one man's offense."[2]

Guards beat prisoners whenever word arrived of an American victory, delivering both pain and hope to the captives. Gangs of guards often stalked the hallways at night, searching for prisoners on whom they could take out their wrath and aggression. Their violent overreactions confirmed that the war was progressing well for the United States and that liberation was a step closer.

Navy Lt. John M. Arbuckle, one of the men who had flown out of New Ireland with Boyington, witnessed men beaten with steel rods. He declared in his deposition that "the camp of Ofuna was just one big crime. [In] 13 months, I saw beatings with baseball bat [*sic*], sluggings, intimidations, humiliations, medical care refused, partial starvation and anything to make life miserable."[3] Hero or no hero, Boyington received the same deplorable treatment as the rest of the men. Once, after being caught smoking without permission, he had to stand inside a circle with his feet apart and endure successive beatings from two guards.

The meager food allotment barely kept the men alive. Most meals consisted of a cup of rice or barley and watery soup that might contain a few potato slices. Fruit, meat, and vegetables became luxuries the men dreamed of but rarely saw. Cdr. Richard H. O'Kane, commander of the submarine USS *Tang* and an inmate with Boyington, estimated that the rations provided only three hundred calories a day. Everyone lost weight under those conditions, including Boyington, who dropped from 180 pounds to 110.

While prisoners of war had a duty to try to escape, and those incarcerated in Germany had a chance of success, fleeing was not an option at Ofuna or any prison camp in Japan proper. Once out of camp the men would have no safe destination in which to seek shelter. They were on an island, and they looked nothing like the Asian inhabitants, making their recapture a matter of when, not if. Few of the men spoke more than a handful of Japanese phrases. "Easy to escape but nowhere to go," Navy Lt. (jg) Edwin Walasek declared in his deposition.[4]

With escape denied them, the prisoners defied their captors in less noticeable ways. Each morning the men reluctantly turned toward Tokyo and bowed to the emperor as required, but muttered expletives while doing so. Forbidden to speak with newer prisoners lest they learn how poorly the war was going for Japan, the men still discreetly relayed information to and from the recent arrivals as they shuffled about the compound, or picked up tidbits from amenable guards.

"We were kept updated on the war news," Boyington later explained, "usually by friendly guards who would tell us what was going on. Other news we learned by listening to the guards. I picked up the Japanese language pretty quickly, and I could understand many phrases and key words. New prisoners were also a great source of information. We knew the war was going badly for Japan, and in February 1945 we saw a massive raid on Yokosuka from our camp in Ofuna."[5]

"One of this war's sky legends"

While Boyington was lost in the enemy's prison camp system, news of his exploits continued to fascinate the American public. In fact, now that everyone assumed he had been killed, his deeds took on more of a legendary status. Newspapers and magazines ran articles detailing the aviator's career, especially his exploits in the South Pacific. His reputation reached a high point in March 1944 when President Franklin D. Roosevelt awarded Boyington the nation's highest accolade, the Medal of Honor, a tribute that another aggressive commander of the South Pacific, Adm. William Halsey, happily endorsed.

Despite fears of the downed aviator's demise, rumors that he survived continued to circulate. The *Chicago Daily Tribune* stated in May 1944 that although Boyington had been missing for five months, "there's an insistent rumor from Finschhafen to Sydney that the 26 plane marine ace is still alive." The article added that "wherever airmen gather they talk of Greg as if he were just temporarily missing, and they recall one of his last comments that 'I may disappear with 30 Zekes on my tail, but remember: I'll meet you guys in a San Diego bar six months after the war.'" The article also reported that a week after Boyington's disappearance, scout pilots thought they spotted him signaling from the beach of a Japanese-held island. Subsequent air searches located no traces of Boyington, but the reported sighting fueled hopes that never dimmed. Periodic reports of American airmen inhabiting isolated Pacific islets added to the mystique. "Boyington may grow into one of this war's sky legends," the article said, "like Georges Guynemer, the French ace of the last war who disappeared without a trace." The article added, "Few airmen have disappeared as quickly and as dramatically and with so few clues."[6]

Boyington's family knew little more than the American public. His mother, Grace, received a postcard from a man incarcerated in a different prison camp divulging that her son was alive, but without official confirmation from the government or the Red Cross, she could only have faith that the information was accurate and hope for the best.

"You just get through it"

Conditions for Boyington improved in September 1944 when the Japanese completed their interrogation and assigned him to the most prized duty in Ofuna—work in the camp's kitchen. Being in close proximity to the food supply enabled him to sneak extra rations, and the large cooking fires he started each morning at 4:30 kept him warm throughout the long winter. The Japanese also permitted him to bathe in the tubs used by the guards, an enormous privilege; the other prisoners were allowed to bathe only once a month. The daily sixteen-hour grind, during which Boyington carried barrels of water and sacks of rice, was exhausting, but the extra soup more than compensated. By the following spring he had regained most of the lost weight.

A kindly Japanese woman named Oba, whom Boyington called Auntie, helped during his tenure in the kitchen. She watched for guards while Boyington stole food, and she shared cigarettes with him while they rested from their work. "By the time I got there I was down sixty or seventy pounds and not looking so good," Boyington explained in an interview. "She took care of me, and I owe her as much as anyone."[7]

Boyington also credited another factor with helping improve his health— no alcohol. He had been sober since his capture, the longest stretch that he could remember. Only once, on New Year's Eve when celebrating guards handed Boyington some sake, did he taste alcohol. In a sense, Ofuna was Boyington's rehabilitation center, and free from the debilitating effects of alcohol, he gradually regained strength.

The New Year brought added reason to hope that the war would soon end. In February 1945 a devastating American carrier air strike blasted the area surrounding Ofuna. When air raid sirens sounded across the region, the prisoners assumed it was part of another drill, but "then all hell appeared to break loose over our peaceful country valley" as familiar-looking aircraft swooped down from the skies to attack the Yokosuka naval base twelve miles from camp. Boyington and the other inmates stared with a mixture of wonder, excitement, and fear. "Dive bomber after dive bomber started down," Boyington wrote, "the hills between the target area and our camp momentarily chopping each bomber from view, making it appear as though they were diving into the hills. But in a few seconds we saw them pull out about the same time we heard the ka-lumph of the exploding bomb." The men realized that this was far more than an isolated strike like the Doolittle bombing of Tokyo in 1942. They were witnessing an American carrier raid in full, "and we knew that this carrier raid was the beginning of the end for Japan."[8]

Carrier fighters lacked the range of larger bombers, which meant that the U.S. Navy controlled enough of the Pacific to bring the fighters within range of the Home Islands. The prisoners also concluded that the carriers would never approach so far to the north unless the Japanese navy had been neutralized and most of the rear areas, including the Philippines, had been seized. Japanese surrender had to be only a matter of months away. Despite their elation the captives could not yet celebrate, at least not overtly. Japanese guards beat anyone who watched the spectacle or cheered its progress, but in the excitement of the moment many captives ignored the risks to obtain a glimpse of the aerial clash. Boyington focused on a Navy F6F Hellcat as the aviator pursued a Zero low above the nearby hills and then shot him down with an accurate burst from his guns.

Boyington remained a prisoner until war's end, but he did not spend all of that time in Ofuna. On April 16 he and seventeen others learned that they were being transferred to the Japanese prisoner-of-war camp at Omori twenty-five miles away. The news raised hopes that they would now enjoy the advantages of regular prisoners of war, including the safeguards offered by the Geneva Convention. At long last Boyington's family might learn that he was still alive. Boyington's departure from Ofuna differed dramatically from his arrival. Then he had noticed the beautiful countryside and had hoped that the camp would be, if not luxurious, at least civilized. The dismal location offered nothing he now wanted to recall, and as he and the others boarded a streetcar for the trip, he hoped to leave all memories behind.

After completing the journey along the shores of Tokyo Bay, the group of prisoners walked another five miles to their new camp, the last six hundred feet across a wooden causeway connecting the prison camp—essentially an island in the bay—with the mainland. Boyington had heard that Omori served as the headquarters camp for the area, a visible installation to civilians and to neutral observers. If that were true, he could look forward to better treatment. Red Cross visits would see to that. His optimism sustained a quick blow. Japanese guards lined up the new prisoners in front of the administrative building, and they stood there all day in the cold, blustery winds waiting for an officer to address them. Finally, near evening, a colonel emerged and spoke. His words ended any expectations that their time in Omori would be different. "You are to remain in this camp as 'special prisoners,'" barked the officer. "If any of you try to escape you will be killed."[9]

At first glance, Omori appeared no different from Ofuna. A ten-foot wall enclosed the camp, which consisted of one barracks for the Japanese guards and six prisoner barracks. Because he, like most pilots, was considered a special prisoner, Boyington was taken to Barracks 1 and isolated from the rest of the inmates, a mixture of American, British, and other Allied nationalities that included men captured early in the war at Wake Island and in the Philippines. Army TSgt. Harry C. Liskowsky stated in his postwar deposition that the special prisoners "were segregated from us. Their ration was much less than what we got. They weren't allowed any privileges. They were confined to their barracks and to the grounds around the barracks."[10]

The spartan barracks featured little comfort. Twenty-three feet wide by one hundred feet long, the wooden structures sported two tiers of sleeping decks protruding from the walls, one eighteen inches above the dirt floor and the second five feet higher. The Japanese packed as many as five hundred men into Omori's six barracks. The men felt like cattle in a boxcar. "I had a blanket," explained Ray "Hap" Halloran, a B-29 airman incarcerated with Boyington, "and after a week or two we picked a partner you could sleep with to generate some body heat. We'd put his blanket on the bottom and mine on top, and the bugs were solid in both of them."[11]

A rigid schedule ruled the prisoners' lives. At 6 AM guards shouted the men awake. After a meager breakfast of thin soup and rice, by 7:30 the men gathered in their work details. Most labored outside the camp, either working for Japanese companies that had contracted for workers or removing debris from American bombing raids. At 5 PM the workers returned to camp, stopping to be searched before entering, swallowed their evening meal, then "enjoyed" time off until lights-out at 10 PM.

As the threat of an American invasion of the Home Islands grew closer, the Japanese forced Boyington and the other prisoners to excavate large caves as bomb shelters. Each day the men trudged six miles to the cave site, toiled all day long, then walked six miles back to camp and an inadequate supper. Men paired off during the walk to help each other—if one fell or stumbled, the other quickly came to his aid to prevent a beating.

Japanese civilians sometimes surreptitiously helped the prisoners by leaving cigarette butts on the ground or by sneaking food to them. Prisoners learned to look for handfuls of roasted soybeans but had to be careful lest a guard catch them eating or hiding the bounty. "There was an elderly lady who gave us seven beans each," said Halloran. "You had to eat quickly because if a guard saw it the lady was killed. There was a gal who walked by our work area, and once she stopped and gave us a sweet potato that another prisoner and I split. She felt sorry for us. There are good people everywhere."[12]

Since the men on the outside work details benefited from the extra food, they remained in relatively decent physical condition compared with men kept inside, but that hardly compensated for the deplorable state of affairs at Omori. Hunger never abated, and men talked about food as if discussing long-lost treasure. Standing near or at the top of everyone's list was that American standard, the cheeseburger. Despite the lack of food, the prisoners enjoyed a healthier diet than at Ofuna. Some actually started to gain weight. "We looked at the POWs there," said Joseph Goicoechea, a civilian construction worker captured in December 1941 at Wake Island and confined at various camps before arriving at Omori. "Boy they looked much better than we did. We found out they were eating better and taken better care of."[13]

Even though Omori offered benefits other camps might not possess, the squalid conditions still caused men to use words like "deplorable" and "atrocious" in describing it. Halloran explained that the men in his barracks, which included Boyington, lived by three rules: cry only when alone, everyone must finish their food at the same time so that one man could not hoard his allotment and enjoy it when the other men had nothing, and equally share any food smuggled in from outside the camp.

Because Omori had more prisoners than Ofuna, Boyington and the others found it simpler to blend in and avoid abuse from guards, but no one completely escaped the guards' attention. Some Japanese resented Boyington's elevated status and took pleasure in beating him; others treated him with deference. Halloran still marvels at the time when Boyington, angry over something a guard did or said, threw a squash at the guard. The Japanese soldier surprised Halloran by walking away rather than beating Boyington. "He had no fear," Halloran said of the Marine aviator.[14] All of the men suffered, however, and, according to Halloran, no captive resented Boyington or thought he received preferential treatment. As the war continued and the outlook worsened for the Japanese, abuse of the prisoners escalated. "Nothing you could do about it," said Halloran, who was stripped naked, tied to a bar, and beaten. "You just get through it."[15]

The men loathed the hordes of fleas, bedbugs, body lice, and other critters that cohabited their world. "More vermin than I thought existed," concluded Sgt. James E. Hinkle in his postwar deposition on conditions at Omori.[16] Swarms of flies so inundated the camp during the hot summer months that Japanese commanders offered extra food portions or other rewards for every one hundred flies the men killed.

Medical care was all but nonexistent at Omori. Captive American military doctors did what they could with the handful of drugs issued from Red Cross parcels, but lacking supplies and proper facilities, they could offer only stopgap measures. The two Japanese physicians who periodically visited the camp from outside were lackadaisical in tending their patients. "These two doctors were indifferent concerning medical care for the prisoners," explained TSgt. Harry C. Liskowsky. "They were more concerned with their own theories of experimenting to find different medical reactions under the circumstances of what the men were suffering from and the primary object was to get the men out to work rather than to keep them hospitalized, even though the American doctors were strongly against sending them out to work." Lt. John M. Arbuckle, who accompanied Boyington at every stage of the prisoner ordeal, stated that "as *special* prisoners we were refused medical attention, no baths, starvation, over work, and general mistreatment."[17]

Cpl. Arthur Gill of the Army Air Corps, who arrived at Omori along with Boyington, succumbed within three months from malnourishment and lack of proper medical attention. More would have died without the aid of a friendly guard named Kano, who smuggled food into the special barracks that housed Boyington. The courageous Kano also risked his life to sneak special prisoners from their barracks so that American physicians elsewhere in Omori could treat their maladies.

As occurred at every prison of war camp in both the European and Pacific theaters, ingenious men found ways to beat the system. They hid smuggled food and other items in cleverly concealed places behind walls or under the boards of their sleeping deck. The men quartered in the rest of the camp surreptitiously passed information to Boyington and others in the special barracks so they could keep pace with the war's progress, which helped raise their morale. Some men attached makeshift hotplates to a solitary electrical wire leading to the barracks, while those on outside work details took every opportunity to smuggle food back into camp in false pockets, oversized hats and shoes, or socks suspended underneath their arms by rope.

Prisoners took every opportunity to impede the Japanese war effort. Those laboring on railroad tracks altered the railcars' numbers to confuse Japanese controllers, and other men poured sugar or dirt into gasoline tanks or purposely dropped and broke items so the Japanese could not use them. Though insignificant to the total war picture, the sabotage and smuggling made the men feel that even in their distant hideaway they were aiding their nation in some small manner.

"If Pappy's here, we're all gonna make it"

Boyington did what he could to help the other prisoners. Just as he blossomed when given command of the Black Sheep, a group of pilots who needed and recognized his expertise, Boyington now came through for others in the prison camp. After being shot down and captured, a dejected Hap Halloran entered Barracks 1 demoralized that his service in the war had so abruptly ended. His spirits immediately rose when he learned that Boyington, whom he and everyone else on the outside had assumed had perished in January 1944, was actually alive and living in the same barracks. Halloran had followed Boyington's career like a boy keeps track of his sports hero, and he was thrilled that the aviator was still alive. "Someone said Pappy Boyington is up in the front section," recalled Halloran. "'Pappy Boyington!' I said. I thought it was a miracle. He was in the front section with eighteen other men, including Commander [Richard] O'Kane of the submarine *Tang.*"

Because Halloran and the rest of his B-29 crew were kept separate from Boyington and his smaller group, he had to wait for an opportunity to speak to his idol. The best chance arose when both had to use the *benjo,* the sanitary facilities. "You had to get a ticket from the guard. When Boyington went by I went up and got a ticket. We could speak, at some risk, in there. There'd be dividers, but you could speak. I was so proud. I introduced myself and told him I was glad to see him."[18] On a second visit to the *benjo* Halloran told Boyington that he had been awarded a Medal of Honor. Boyington replied that he would gladly trade the medal for a hamburger.

Halloran noticed that Boyington seemed thin, but "he maintained the sparkle in his eyes—the built in look and mannerisms of a natural leader. He instilled confidence in us in a quiet way." Halloran, who had been severely beaten by his captors and confined in squalid conditions before arriving in Omori, took comfort that a man like Boyington stood only yards from him. "One of my thoughts was, if Pappy's here, we're all gonna make it. He's not going to die. I felt safer. He was only ten to twelve feet from me on the other side of that dirty blanket separating us. He helped pull me through."[19]

Boyington aided his fellow inmates in other ways. As one of the senior officers present, he helped maintain order by intervening when two prisoners argued or fought. He listened to their arguments and helped adjudicate disputes. "He took things in stride and did not complain," explained Halloran. "He set the pace. He was extremely solicitous for fellow P.O.W.s in our special barrack at Omori—especially the very young fellows. He spent many evening hours tending to them—talking to them and exhorting them to hang in there and to perpetuate their desire to survive." Prisoners whom Joe Morang of the *Chicago Daily Tribune* interviewed after the war claimed that Boyington was "an inspiration to their morale, and that he once withstood 47 blows with a baseball bat without outcry."[20]

Boyington in particular focused on one young prisoner whom everyone could see was rapidly losing the desire to live. Boyington talked to him like a father chatting with his son, telling him the war would end soon and urging him to hold on a little longer. Boyington intensified his labors when the prisoner refused to eat, even scolding the young captive and forcing food down his throat. Despite his endeavors and entreaties, the boy died. "Please, Greg, don't scold me," he said feebly shortly before succumbing. The effort Boyington exhibited in trying to pull the young man through impressed everyone else in the barracks. "The boy Greg helped was next to us in the barracks," said Halloran. "Greg was sitting there, and the boy was eighteen or nineteen, off a sub. Boyington told me the kid couldn't eat anymore and was bloating up. Boyington kept telling him to hang in there. This is the side the press never covered— the loving, caring side of Boyington." Halloran later added, "Pappy never gave up. That love and concern exhibited by Pappy impressed us all."[21]

News of the war's progress and other important events filtered into Japanese camps even though they were isolated from the outside world. Some of the news was good; some of it wasn't. On April 13, three days before leaving Ofuna for Omori, Boyington was working in the prison garden when a guard approached with the information that President Roosevelt, the leader who had occupied the White House for twelve years and had guided an uneasy nation through the double perils of the Great Depression and entry into a world war, had died. Men later shared their thoughts on the fallen president and wondered how the new chief executive, Harry Truman, would perform.

The death of a second world figure the next month electrified the camp and made even the most pessimistic captive conclude that the war's end was very near. When they learned on May 3 that German leader Adolf Hitler had committed suicide, jubilant prisoners were certain that Japan's reign in the Pacific was about to end. Hitler's death and the fall of Germany would allow the Allies to end the fighting in Europe and free millions of soldiers for duty in the Pacific. Japan could not long hold out against the full might of the Allies.

"Dispose of them as the situation dictates"

Increased Allied bombing attacks against the Home Islands were additional positive indications that the war was coming to an end. As much as the prisoners welcomed the intensified bombing raids, the raids brought a new concern: would they perish at the hands of their own nation's military? Bombs dropped indiscriminately can just as easily ravage a barracks packed with prisoners of war as they can demolish a Japanese supply depot. Boyington and his comrades lived with the irony that they might have endured months of atrocious treatment only to die by friendly fire. As special prisoners, the men in Barracks 1 could not even seek shelter to evade the rain of bombs.

Two factors worked in their favor. First, because the men were living on a small island, they were separated and thus relatively safe from the fires that raged ashore. Second, Omori was outside the main zone of attack, which centered on Tokyo and the adjoining regions. Off-target bombs sometimes landed perilously close to the camp, however, which Allied aviators had no idea housed Allied prisoners. During the most destructive raids, Boyington could feel the heat emanating from massive conflagrations and the concussions caused by the bombs blasting Yokohama, and shrapnel peppered the barracks roofs like a stream of hail.

"Our fears of not surviving the rigors of Japanese imprisonment and treatment were now replaced by fears we could now be killed by American bombs," captive Robert Martindale, a bomber pilot shot down over the Bismarck Sea three years earlier, later wrote. After each attack he and the men gazed across the channel toward shore, a once-bustling conglomeration of buildings and roads that had been reduced to a "field of rubble extending as far as the eye could see."[22] Frightened rats seeking refuge swarmed onto the island from shore, and bloated bodies floated to Omori with each tide.

Boyington and the other occupants of Barracks 1 quietly cheered the near-daily assaults, masking their joy lest angry guards smack them with rifle butts or batter them to the ground. Despite the risk, Boyington, who longed to be with those aviators racing through the sky, gazed at the aircraft, especially the impressive B-29 bombers. "From that moment on," he later said, "I had no doubts whatsoever that the Nips were really in for something." He added, "We realized that we had to go through so much in order to get out of there. We knew that some of us would be killed, but that the majority of us would get out." Calling the massive bombers "The Music" after the sound the air raid sirens made, Boyington described the bombings as "something to behold, great hordes of silver B-29s coming over in the daylight. They looked beautiful."[23] During one raid Boyington was returning from the latrine when a dive-bomber hit the causeway between the camp and mainland, coughing up a huge slab of concrete that landed only twenty feet ahead of him. In the last week of May he huddled in his barracks as five hundred Allied aircraft blasted the Tokyo-Yokohama area with incendiaries.

After many of the bombings Boyington and the special prisoners faced the unpleasant task of going into Yokohama and the outlying regions of Tokyo to clear debris. Though the Americans suffered their own brand of agonies, their sympathy went out to the Japanese civilians searching for family members amid the rubble that had once been their homes.

As devastating as were these bombings, they paled compared with what occurred in early August. On August 6 the prisoners noticed that the guards seemed especially vexed. They gathered in small groups, mumbling in hushed tones, but all the captives could determine was that a great raid had taken place. Tales circulated that one bomber had destroyed a city with a single bomb, but Boyington dismissed those as fables. Other unfounded rumors had only raised hopes that reality later dashed. This time, however, rumor understated reality. News filtered in that Hiroshima had been laid to waste by something called an atom bomb, and a few days later a guard informed Boyington that a single bomb had totally demolished one of Japan's largest cities, Nagasaki. More than 100,000 perished at Hiroshima, while upward of 75,000 died at Nagasaki. Fear cut short any jubilation the prisoners felt, because the sprawling city of Tokyo— and with it, Omori—had to be next on the list. They realized that the war's end must be drawing near but now doubted they would live to witness it. If an American bomb did not kill them, their angry Japanese captors surely would.

Additional signs pointed to a speedy conclusion. As he unloaded railroad cars in July, prisoner Joseph Goicoechea spotted a group of foreigners loading boxes of office materials and documents onto the same train. Some of those individuals informed the prisoners that they worked at the German embassy in Tokyo, that the war in Europe had already ended, and that the fighting in the Pacific would soon terminate. Shortly afterward a guard asked Boyington how he was holding up. When Boyington replied that he could be doing better, the guard said, "Well, it will only be another month or so and the thing will be all over."[24]

The men received the news for which they had so long waited on the morning of August 15, when Emperor Hirohito informed the nation that the war had ended. Inside Omori silent Japanese guards gathered, heads bowed, as their leader's voice issued from the radio. They then returned to their duties, obviously distraught.

Ill with yellow jaundice, Boyington did not hear the emperor's announcement. He learned that joyous news from a disconsolate guard. Still in a state of disbelief, Boyington noticed that the prisoners on outside work detail returned early from their tasks, something unprecedented. They were followed by a group of British prisoners lustily singing as they marched back to camp. Boyington finally believed that at long last his prison ordeal was ending.

Or had it? That night a friendly guard awoke the prisoners to warn them that drunken guards had discussed breaking into the barracks and killing all the captives. The guard said that he would stand outside and do what he could to prevent any violence, but cautioned that the prisoners must be prepared to fight for their lives. He handed the men a hammer and nails to reinforce the door, then headed outside. A short time later Boyington and the others heard a group of guards approaching the barracks. As angry shouts filled the air, Boyington stood beside the front entrance, hammer in hand, ready to crack the first skull that appeared. Though the friendly guard persuaded his drunken comrades to leave, Boyington wondered if the event presaged more peril for the inmates.

The prisoners gathered together and discussed their options should a slaughter appear likely. Their fears were not unfounded. Some Japanese civilians had already told them that the prisoners were to be killed if it seemed the war was lost, and a document unearthed after the war divulged that orders had been issued for the speedy dispatch of Allied prisoners. The document stated, "Whether they [prisoners] are destroyed individually or in groups, or however it is done, with mass bombing, poisonous smoke, poisons, drowning, decapitation, or what, dispose of them as the situation dictates." The order ended with chilling words: "In any case it is the aim not to allow the escape of a single one, to annihilate them all, and not to leave any traces."[25]

The prisoners came to one conclusion. Some had heard that they would be told they were being escorted out of camp to the mountains to avoid bombing attacks, but instead of being safely removed they would be machine-gunned as they crossed the causeway. Senior officers decided that should that occur, the men would make a break for it, and every man would be on his own.

Even the prospect of death failed to dampen the men's joy. Dreams long cherished, in Boyington's case through twenty months of confinement, drew nearer. Freedom, home, family—all became distinct possibilities rather than remote images. In the book he wrote about his wartime experiences Robert Martindale said that "what had been the subjects of dreams and idle talk now began to have more meaning."[26]

"They're our boys—now go and get them out"

Changes occurred at a rapid pace. The Japanese handed out fresh clothes and vitamins to the prisoners and switched the men to different quarters. Boyington noticed that almost every officer and all the cruel guards had suddenly disappeared. U.S. Navy observation planes swooped low to take photographs of Omori, and within days Army Air Corps bombers parachuted fifty-five-gallon drums filled with food, medicine, and clothing to the captives. Unfortunately, some of the men were injured and a few were killed when a handful of the parachutes failed to open and the crates smashed into the camp. Robert Martindale was sitting in an office when a parachuted container bounced on the ground a few times, smashed into the building, and spewed its contents all about the office. Fortunately, Martindale and the others in the office escaped without injury. The senior officers placed observers in Omori's watchtowers to warn the men when aircraft approached. Men also painted signs on barrack roofs stating, "Please Drop Outside." One added for good measure, "Boyington Here."

Boyington would have welcomed the package that contained a crate of alcohol, but the senior camp commander confiscated it, fearing what the alcohol might do to the weakened men. Besides, Boyington was not about to be caught outside with massive crates falling from the sky. While other inmates scurried out in the open to retrieve the supplies, he sought cover. "Nuts to that," he explained to a prisoner near him who wondered why Boyington did not rush out to grab the food. "After living through all I have, I'm damned if I'm going to be killed by being hit on the head by a crate of peaches."[27]

The first indication of imminent release occurred on August 28 in a note dropped by a Navy aircraft from the USS *Yorktown*:

Hi Fellows.

You'll be free by tomorrow . . .
Our planes have landed
on field nearby. Give
the girls back home
a kiss for me. Loads
of luck—God Bless You.
[signed] Ens. L. Komisarek[28]

The electrifying news raced through the camp.

While the U.S. Army handled the prison camps in Japan's interior, the Navy liberated those located closer to the coastline, including Omori. The day after the men received Ensign Komisarek's note, an armada of American warships steamed into Tokyo Bay, causing wild outbursts among Omori's prison population. A short time later three landing barges separated from the battleships and cruisers and veered toward the camp. One of the occupants, Cdr. Harold Stassen, had received word from his boss to rescue the prisoners of war as speedily as possible. When Admiral Halsey learned of the deplorable conditions at Omori and other prison camps, he turned to Stassen, a member of his staff, and said, "They're our boys—now go and get them out."[29]

Stassen stood ready to do whatever he could to expedite the men's liberation. As the Higgins boats drew near to the island, sailors leapt from the craft and planted three flags in the dirt. A shirtless Boyington stood at attention and saluted the American flag, then gazed toward Stassen. "God sakes, Pappy," said Stassen, as the two shook hands, "we didn't know you were alive until we saw that picture the plane took this morning."[30] A reconnaissance photograph had revealed the painted sign pointing out Boyington's presence.

Stassen took Halsey's order to heart. When the camp's Japanese commander claimed he had no authority to release the prisoners to Stassen, the officer replied, "You have no authority, period!" He added, "We are under Admiral Halsey's orders, and those are the only orders that count in Japan now!"[31] Beginning with the sickest first, Stassen began evacuating men from Omori that same day. Within forty-eight hours Boyington and every other former prisoner had been freed from their wartime hell.

News that Boyington was alive and safe reached the United States on August 29. "Ace Boyington Safe in Tokyo, 3d Fleet Told," proclaimed a headline in the *Chicago Daily Tribune* that day. The accompanying story reported that "the fabulous Maj. Gregory (Pappy) Boyington, marine flying ace who disappeared in a dog fight with Jap planes over Rabaul Jan. 1, 1944, and presumably was killed, was reported alive in Tokyo today, in an Associated Press report transmitted from the U.S.S. *Ancon* in Tokyo bay [sic]." The article added that while the news "electrified the fleet," it did not surprise his Black Sheep, who had never given up hope that their leader was alive. Back home, Boyington's daughter Gloria, when informed of her father's rescue, said, "I know it. I just said my prayers for him."[32]

A Higgins boat took Boyington from Omori to the hospital ship *Benevolence,* where he received a shower, a delousing, and a medical examination. Then, like all the famished prisoners who had gone months or years without their favorite food, he dug into five helpings of ham and eggs.

On September 2 the former prisoners watched in awe as 500 B-29 bombers flew over Tokyo Bay as part of the official surrender ceremony. The sight of more than 250 Allied warships brought tears to the eyes of Hap Halloran and other men. They stared incredulously at the assembled might of the U.S. Navy, a force that had devastated Japan and freed them from their prison camp nightmare.

A collection of news reporters gathered on the *Benevolence,* each with questions for the liberated aviator. What was his captivity like? What were his thoughts on being awarded the Medal of Honor? What was his reaction to a September 6 promotion to lieutenant colonel? The publicity startled Boyington, who said little except to state that he was happy to be on his way home.

Boyington had no idea the Marine Corps had built him into such a hero during his confinement, and he later contended that had headquarters known he had survived the January 1944 dogfight, it would not have done so. "There was no question in their minds that my watery grave would hold me," he claimed in his book, "and that I would never return to disgrace them or haunt them, or, one thing for certain, they would never have let those releases out of their hands."[33]

After recovering sufficiently, Boyington left the *Benevolence* for an airfield near Tokyo, where he boarded a transport to begin his journey home. The plane took him to Guam, where Boyington remained two days, then to Kwajalein and on to Pearl Harbor, where General Moore, his longtime advocate, waited to welcome him. "Major General Moore met me at Pearl Harbor," Boyington said later, "and I can't explain the feeling I had on seeing my old friend and benefactor. He gave me the use of his quarters, car and driver, and that was great. I had decided to change my ways, accept my fate and clean myself up. I felt that if the nation was going to honor me as a hero, I should honor the nation by acting like one, or at least looking like one."[34]

Bill Millington, one of Boyington's longtime friends, bumped into him in Hawaii. The two caught up on events, then Boyington said, "But I want you guys to know something. During my confinement with those damn nuts, I saw life in an entirely different fashion. I'm a different man now, and, by God, I'm going to prove it too." Millington left thinking that his friend had possibly turned the corner, but Boyington's good intentions did not last long. That night a drunken Boyington totaled the Jeep he was driving. "He couldn't resist it," Millington told biographer Bruce Gamble. "One taste of alcohol in some damn bar, and he was off on a binge again."[35]

Boyington enjoyed a lovely week in Hawaii, where again he was fêted as a celebrity. He decided that if the Marine Corps intended to make him a war hero, he would go along with it, and perhaps escape the problems of his past, but Boyington was never comfortable with the adulation. In a revealing sentence that divulged the stimulus that lay behind his childhood troubles and his tumultuous relationship with the AVG, and yet propelled him to success with the Black Sheep, Boyington wrote in his memoirs, "For *all this* was not sufficient for a man who just wanted to be *wanted,* and for some reason or another had felt that he never had been since childhood."[36] The hardened ace, like thousands of troubled individuals, longed to be loved and accepted.

He extended that feeling of acceptance toward his former captor, Honda. When Allied officials arrested the interrogator after the war, he was wearing a wristwatch that belonged to Boyington. Disbelieving Honda's explanation that Boyington had given him the valuable timepiece, officials contacted Boyington, who confirmed the story. Boyington wrote that Honda had aided him and others and should be treated decently. "Yes, I gave him the watch," he stated in his letter. "It was broken, so I had no more use for it, and told him he could fix it up and keep it. He is a good gent, treat him right, and please wish him the Season's

Greetings, most sincerely, for me."[37] The same Boyington who felt such antipathy toward Chennault and others whom he believed had cast him aside was surprisingly generous to his former enemy. Rather than villains, he considered Honda and many other Japanese unfortunate victims of circumstance. "As far as holding a grudge, no," he said in a postwar interview. "That would be silly. There are good and bad people everywhere. The Japanese civilians who had been bombed out and were always around us showed us respect, not antipathy. Many of them went out of their way to help us at great risk to themselves, slipping us food. When I think about how the Japanese civilians treated us as POWs in their country, I can only feel very ashamed at how we treated our own Japanese Americans, taking their homes and businesses and placing them in camps."[38]

Another aircraft transported Boyington to the mainland, where a hero's welcome awaited him in San Francisco on September 12. He would be fêted with banquets and parades in the weeks to come, but none meant more than this initial reception. There, in the midst of the revelers, stood a group of his Black Sheep pilots that Walton had hurriedly assembled. The Black Sheep lifted him to their shoulders and carried him to a reception room, where he chatted with reporters. Then, recalling his promise to meet them after the war in a bar, Boyington and his Black Sheep adjourned to the St. Francis Hotel for a night of partying. To honor the occasion his men handed Boyington, whom one newspaper described as the "roughest, toughest, most aggressive air combat leader to come out of the Pacific war," a beautiful wristwatch engraved with the inscription "To Gramps from his Black Sheep."[39]

The heady welcome home handed momentary hope to the troubled aviator. People hailed him as a hero and his Black Sheep had assembled around him. Maybe he could gain a fresh start in life, one free from the disturbances and distractions that had marked his past. Unfortunately, those hopes soon dissipated in a downward spiral fueled by debilitating self-pity. Though he hoped "we could just return as some other person," Boyington instead discovered that "my drinking past was waiting back home, to pick up where I left off, whether I wanted to or not."[40]

Chapter Nine

"I Knew Greg Boyington at His Best—in Combat"

Once back in the United States, Boyington faced an exhausting schedule. Instead of taking time to decompress and relax in familiar surroundings, he immediately embarked on a two-month nationwide bond tour arranged by the Marine Corps. The ordeal fatigued the worn-down aviator, who needed time to rehabilitate as well as to restore a semblance of stability to his shaky finances and his even more tenuous family ties. Not surprisingly he turned once again to a familiar remedy in times of crisis—alcohol.

"You absolutely *must* control the booze"

Frank Walton, his friend from the Black Sheep Squadron, accompanied Boyington on the tour, partly to assist him in any way he could but mainly to ensure that the war hero did not embarrass himself or the Marine Corps with drunken antics. A worried Walton, who knew Boyington as well as any man, directly addressed his main concern before he and Boyington set out on the tour's first stop. "Greg, you can be or do anything you want. Your name is a household word. Your picture has been in every paper in the country. Your story has been told and retold. You can be a congressman; you can be governor of your home state; you have your choice of positions in a dozen corporations—everyone wants you. But you absolutely *must* control the booze. Liquor has been your major problem to date. If you don't solve it, this will all turn to ashes."[1]

Boyington agreed, then explained that his tenure in prison camp gave him time to ponder the direction of his life. He vowed to behave. "Don't worry, old boy, I am forced to take a few on this tour to be polite like you are. But after it is over, I'm going to quit."[2] Walton wanted to believe Boyington but knew that proof would come with his actions.

A series of parades and banquets ensued. New York staged a huge ticker-tape pageant, and Chicago, Seattle, and other large cities hosted fêtes. Boyington, never comfortable in large, formal settings, struggled from speech to speech and town to town. Every stop seemed to offer another friendly hand passing along a drink, which Boyington never declined. "This is killing me," he confided to a friend. "I just can't go anyplace without somebody giving me a double shot of whiskey."[3]

The bond tour terminated in a messy affair in Portland, Oregon. Boyington once again overimbibed before speaking to a group of Portland's prominent citizens, and as he later recorded it, alcohol "rear[ed] its ugly head." The inebriated aviator rambled on incoherently during the speech, slurring his words and uttering outlandish statements. "You came here to be entertained by some sideshow freak, I know," he said at one moment to a hushed, uncomfortable crowd.[4] When he finished his embarrassing ramblings, not one person applauded. Boyington returned to his seat in an unsettling stillness.

Equally disastrous was Boyington's relationship with his family. Grace and the children traveled to San Francisco right after he returned to the States, but after a few moments together the demands of other well-wishers took Boyington away. The rocky relationship that had characterized the prewar years remained unchanged for the remainder of his life, with Boyington unable or unwilling to bridge the chasm preventing him from being a good father, and his family never quite able to forgive the absent father/husband.

At least the bond tour ended on a positive note. During a White House ceremony on October 5, Boyington received the Medal of Honor that had been awarded to him while he was incarcerated in Japan. Though he had earlier joked to Hap Halloran that he would gladly trade the medal for a hamburger, his perspective as a free man altered his outlook. Boyington proudly accepted the honor from a grateful nation.

"I've been rankled by the 'top gun' title"

It was while he was in Washington, D.C., for the medal festivities that Boyington, accompanied by Walton, submitted the supplemental action report that anointed him as the Marine's top ace. He and Walton walked into Marine headquarters the day before Boyington's White House ceremony and added a supplement to the January 3, 1944, action report that summarized the details of two additional kills. The handwritten report increased Boyington's tally to twenty-eight, enthroning him as the undisputed Marine ace.

Boyington made clear that the supplemental report was not meant to be a complete summary of what the other Black Sheep members did that day, but only recorded the activities of his wingman and himself. On the standard Marine Aircraft Action Report form, Boyington wrote in pencil "Supplemental Report" across the top, bypassed most of the sections by scribbling "Covered in original report," and then added the new details pertaining to the two additional destroyed aircraft.

He repeated the particulars of shooting down his twenty-sixth enemy plane, then moved into the new material. After registering his first kill of the day, Boyington, accompanied by Ashmun, had dropped to 12,000 feet as enemy aircraft quickly surrounded them. The pair started to scissors, during which time both Boyington and Ashmun shot down another plane—in Boyington's case, his twenty-seventh. Immediately after the dual kills smoke billowed from Ashmun's plane and he plunged downward at a forty-five-degree angle. Boyington shouted to Ashmun through the radio to jump out but received no response. As more Zeros pumped fire into Ashmun's Corsair from propeller to tail, Boyington pulled in behind and skidded from side to side, spraying the Zeros in an effort to dislodge them from Ashmun's tail. While he executed that move to aid Ashmun, other Zeros pounced on Boyington from behind and shot holes in his wings and fuselage. In this melee, according to the supplemental report, Boyington shot down his third plane of the day, elevating his overall total to twenty-eight. Boyington followed Ashmun down and saw the plane burn and crash into St. George Channel. Assuming that his buddy was dead, Boyington leveled out and headed for home, but had traveled less than half a mile when his main gas tank erupted in flames, filling the cockpit with smoke and fire. The rest of the supplemental report covered the details of Boyington's crash and capture.[5]

The Marine Corps readily accepted the supplemental report, perhaps out of reluctance to wage a distasteful public battle with a war hero, but other individuals have disputed Boyington's claims. In 1987 James H. Howard, who had flown with Boyington in Burma, told historian Robert Sherrod that in 1942 he served as the head of AVG confirmation board, and that Boyington should have been credited with only three and a half kills in Burma. Four years later Howard repeated that contention in his autobiography and expanded his misgivings to the South Pacific total. "Knowing how Boyington exaggerated his AVG claims, I often wonder if the claims he made later with his squadron in the South Pacific could stand up to the scrutiny of a confirmation board such as we had in the Flying Tigers. His claim to have shot down two more Japanese near Rabaul just before he was shot down and captured makes many of us suspicious. Neither of those two claims had been witnessed by another pilot."[6]

Marion Carl, the aviator Boyington claimed had offered his Corsair so that Boyington could fly on his final mission, agreed with Sherrod and Howard that Boyington's claims were exaggerated. In his 1994 autobiography, written with historian Barrett Tillman, Carl asserted that "the medal [Medal of Honor] was deserved—Greg was a talented aviator and an aggressive combat leader—but I've been rankled by the 'top gun' title ever since." Carl cited Japanese records of that final day showing only two planes lost, and noted that witnesses saw only one of the three kills Boyington claimed. Carl added that even if Boyington received credit for the extra two Zeros reported downed on January 3, he would still trail Foss because of his disputed AVG claims. Carl admitted to frustration over the controversy and added, "For the Marine Corps officially to recognize Boyington as its top ace, despite documentation to the contrary, defies all logic. I suspect it's a bureaucratic inability to admit such a long-standing error."[7]

The controversy incensed Boyington, who stoutly maintained that he should be considered the top ace. In the spring of 1981 Robert Sherrod published an article about the matter in *Fortitudine* magazine that included excerpts from the forthcoming revised version of his book on Marine Corps aviation. On reading it, Boyington mailed a letter to the editor of *Fortitudine,* V. Keith Fleming Jr., on July 23, 1981, in which he said that he was "deeply concerned" that the magazine had "permitted Robert Sherrod to move virtually unshackled in his rather clumsy attempt to create seeds of doubt concerning myself and war record." Boyington claimed that Sherrod had taken material out of context from his memoirs and showed bias in his handling of the matter. He blamed Chennault for lowering his total from six to three and a half kills; asserted that his associates had persuaded Chennault to take such action; and claimed that while Sherrod correctly stated that no other aviator witnessed his final two kills, the reason was because only he and Ashmun had dropped below the cloud cover to tangle with the Japanese. "For if anyone had gone below the clouds near Rabaul that morning, they would have witnessed one of the goddamnest dog fights ever put on by two Marines versus close to thirty enemy fighters." Exhibiting his rage as well as his ability to twist facts, Boyington added, "My words to follow ought to add a few more human dimensions to the botched up conclusion Sherrod gave you. These are sex, revenge, and jealousy of anyone thought to be getting more recognition than themselves."[8]

In his biography of Boyington published in 2000, Bruce Gamble condemned the aviator for falsifying the records in his own behalf. Gamble explained that Boyington mentioned nothing of the two extra kills in interviews immediately after being liberated, a time when he most likely assumed that Joe Foss would have added handsomely to his total and placed the record beyond reach. When he learned that the two of them remained tied, Boyington "saw an opportunity to become the high-scoring marine fighter ace, and simply took it."[9]

Gamble's harsh assessment is probably not far from the truth. Other than his times in combat or in prison camp, Boyington was never known for clear thinking. Now, nearing the end of an exhausting bond tour that included heavy drinking at every stop, Boyington might have resorted to such chicanery to add to his record and establish his fame for all time. If so, Walton assisted in the action most likely because he believed his commander. Because we have only Boyington's own word as proof, the argument over those two additional planes will never be resolved.

"I was a nasty, quarrelsome drunk"

The Marine Corps decided to retire its most infamous pilot, who had gone from being a public relations asset to a liability because of his excessive drinking. The Corps placed Boyington on the retired list effective August 1, 1947, sending him back to civilian life at a time when he was neither prepared nor willing to go. Consequently, controversy, sadness, and instability marked the ensuing years. Fellow Black Sheep member Bob McClurg spoke of Boyington's "disappointment in his life after retiring"; the former squadron leader was a fish out of water away from the military.[10] The arena in which Boyington excelled—a place where people respected his talents and needed him—no longer existed.

"Shortly after the war the glamour was gone," wrote Boyington in 1958 of those hectic times, "and there was nothing in my life but turbulence for nearly ten years." Sadly for the war hero, the mayhem stretched far beyond those ten years. Work—or the lack thereof—was a problem. Boyington never could hold onto a job for long. People hired him mostly because of his lofty status, then let him go once his drinking became such a severe problem that it could no longer be overlooked. He underperformed at a series of sales jobs; he worked at—of all places—a brewery; and he even officiated wrestling matches throughout the nation. All ended in similar fashion, with the war hero and former employer parting in awkward embarrassment. Each time he failed, Boyington sank deeper into the morass that was his personal life, and as alcoholics do, used his crises as excuses to justify further bad behavior, to gain sympathy from loved ones, and to drink even more.

Conditions improved slightly in 1956, the year after he lost his job at the brewery, when Boyington reentered the world of aviation by piloting a five-engine aircraft ferrying air-freight executives around the country. The task certainly lacked the excitement and drama of combat with his Black Sheep, but it at least reunited him with the milieu in which he had been most comfortable. Aircraft seemed to lift him above his terrestrial struggles and give him the peace of mind he could so rarely find on the ground. When friends wondered why he chose to live in the San Fernando Valley in California only five minutes from the roar of a nearby airfield, Boyington replied, "They probably don't stop to think that this particular noise is music to me."[11]

The music never lasted, though. In 1964 he accepted a position with the Electronic Specialty Company, a high-paying job that offered security for Boyington's future, but the combination of ample pay and the need to embark on frequent out-of-town jaunts proved lethal. Boyington lapsed into drinking and embarked on a string of short-term love affairs that created even more havoc. For a time he resumed his affair with Lucy Malcolmson, whom he had met aboard a ship returning from Burma, and promised to marry her. Then, with startling swiftness, he met Frances Baker, agreed to marry her, and dumped Lucy. The chaotic string of events provided fodder for gossip columnists and newspaper headlines across the country. On January 6, 1946, for instance, the *Chicago Daily Tribune* featured an article stating that Boyington would marry Lucy; on January 8 the newspaper quoted Lucy as saying Boyington had abandoned her and "I wouldn't marry him now if he crawled here on his hands and knees"; on January 10 the publication announced that Boyington and Frances Baker had wed.[12] Boyington's friends shook their heads in dismay over the soap opera antics.

Another detail further complicated matters—to provide for his children during the war, Boyington had given Lucy control of his finances, such as they were. He now wanted $9,000 of the money returned, but Lucy claimed that not only had she used the money to pay his children's expenses, she had contributed some of her own as well. In August 1946, amid great publicity, the case went to court, where a judge found in Lucy's behalf.

The acrimony hurled back and forth along with his other personal problems depressed the aviator. "I can handle Japs okay, but I can't do much with women," a dispirited Boyington groaned to Walton. He added to Walton's wife, "You know, Carol, the happiest time of my life was when I was in that Japanese prison camp. I was told what to do. Everything was arranged. I had no decisions to make."[13] Boyington's life had careened so severely out of control that he preferred prison camp to life back home.

At this stage Boyington, who had never shied from charging at an enemy Zero, lacked the inner strength to tackle his personal demons. In 1959 he complicated matters by divorcing Frances Baker and marrying Dolores Shade, an aspiring actress. Marriage number two had proven to be no better than number one. Boyington's already rocky relationship with his children, whom he continued to ignore after the war, deteriorated as well. In his absence, two of his children had fallen victim to Ellsworth Hallenbeck's pedophilia, and by the time Boyington took a belated interest, it was too late. Boyington never enjoyed a normal father-child relationship with any of his children.

In its September 2, 1946, issue, *Time* magazine aptly summed up Boyington's postwar life: "To Pappy, peace had been something less than wonderful; to peace he had been something less than wonderful, too."[14]

As it had during his entire adult life, alcohol stood at the center of Boyington's problems. He may have thought that drinking helped him get through the day, but alcohol only weakened him when he most needed strength. A chain of automobile accidents landed the inebriated Boyington in police custody and compiled repair bills in excess of $11,000. The Los Angeles Police Department and county sheriff's office grew accustomed to picking him up during his bouts and transporting him home. He tried to shrug off his behavior by telling a reporter, "After all, I didn't grow up emotionally until after I was 40." But then he admitted, "I wouldn't accept responsibility. I was a nasty, quarrelsome drunk on my periodic binges."[15]

A vicious cycle trapped Boyington. The more he drank, the more his work and marital situations worsened; the worse his personal life became, the more he drank. A potential movie project about his World War II experiences fizzled. Boyington finished third in a race to determine the Democratic congressional candidate in a district near Los Angeles. Any letdown provided ample reason for another bourbon or Scotch. At one point Boyington sought the advice of a psychiatrist, attended Alcoholics Anonymous meetings, and even retreated to a sanitarium, but nothing worked for long. He sobered up briefly after his more serious accidents, only to plunge back into the bottle.

He thought he saw a path out of the morass with the July 1958 publication of his best-selling memoirs, *Baa Baa Black Sheep,* which momentarily brought him financial stability. He appeared on television, including the most-watched program at the time, *The Ed Sullivan Show,* and became the darling of air shows, where fans swarmed around him to obtain an autographed book or a photo with the hero.

If he expected money to enhance his happiness, Boyington forgot the words with which he had closed the book. "If this story were to have a moral, then I would say: 'Just name a hero and I'll prove he's a bum.'"[16] Boyington's negativism resonates through the words, but the sentence illustrates his basic insecurity. Underneath the fleeting success stood a man in pain, not due to war injuries or automobile accidents, but because of a frail psyche and a physical addiction. Nothing could improve until he corrected those maladies.

Boyington followed his memoirs with a second attempt at writing two years later. The lurid and poorly written novel *Tonya,* a piece of historical fiction based on his experiences in China, shattered any tenuous relationship he may still have had with the AVG. The novel scathingly depicted Chennault and the Flying Tigers and further enraged members of the AVG, who had never been in Boyington's corner to begin with.

Conditions improved when Boyington, going through another messy divorce, moved to Cathedral City, California, near Palm Springs and met Josephine Moseman. A recovering alcoholic herself, Moseman was able to cut through Boyington's bravado and help him understand the harm his drinking caused to himself and those around him. Though Boyington relapsed more than once, her encouragement nudged him toward Alcoholics Anonymous and a happier life. On August 4, 1975, the couple married, the fourth union for Boyington.

"As phony as a three-dollar bill"

Events in Boyington's tumultuous life even threatened to impair his relationship with the Black Sheep, the only group of individuals with whom he had maintained solid ties. In 1976 the National Broadcasting Company (NBC) aired the television series *Baa Baa Black Sheep,* starring actor Robert Conrad as Boyington. Just as *Tonya* had enraged the AVG, this television series angered Boyington's Black Sheep. Instead of focusing on their actual exploits and talents, the series portrayed Boyington's men as hard-drinking vagabonds whom Boyington rescued from brigs throughout the South Pacific. Rather than the skilled Japanese aviators the real Black Sheep had faced, their enemies were either Colonel Smoak, thinly disguised as a character named Colonel Lard, or anyone who attempted to stop them from drinking and fighting.

The Black Sheep wasted little time letting Boyington know how they felt during a 1976 reunion in Hawaii. "Television made it look like all we did was party," said Black Sheep pilot Fred Avey, "but that was in no way true. We never went up drunk. The only thing accurate about the show was that we flew Corsairs." Avey, who said he was happy the program used substitute names rather than their real names, said Boyington received the message in Hawaii. "Boyington realized how upset we were and apologized to us, and he was not one to apologize very often."[17]

Fellow Black Sheep member Robert McClurg agreed with Avey that the television show, newspapers, and magazines have perpetuated a mistaken view of the squadron "as a gang of misfit, violent, law breaking individuals who shot down a bunch of Japanese airplanes, almost as a secondary thing whilst satisfying our own lusts and fighting among ourselves." He added, "What came out on film was a bunch of cutups, always scheming. They sometimes made it look like we treated our combat with the Japanese almost as a distraction to our other unsavory conduct."[18]

Frank Walton took special offense at the NBC series. The friend who had accompanied Boyington on his postwar bond drive was so incensed that he wrote an article for *TV Guide* expressing his rage. "*Baa Baa Black Sheep,* the new NBC TV series starring Robert Conrad, is as phony as a three-dollar bill," Walton bluntly stated in the April 23, 1977, issue. "It is ironic that the Hollywood 'showbiz' technique, with its admitted penchant for distortion, should have twisted what is one of the great performances of the war into such an inept travesty. The dramatization of the real facts about the Black Sheep's performance could be a high adventure story of which we all could be proud."[19]

Walton had more to say about the show in his 1986 memoir, *Once They Were Eagles.* The television series had Boyington "recruit[ing] the squadron pilots by giving them the choice of standing trial for various unspecified misdeeds or joining him in the Black Sheep Squadron," Walton wrote. "Not only was nothing further from the facts (no Black Sheep pilot had ever been charged with a court-martial offense), but such false allegations had a detrimental effect on the professional careers of a number of the former Black Sheep. These lawyers, college professors, businessmen, government officials, artists, and engineers did not appreciate the label of bums and misfits. Nor, certainly, did the widows, mothers, fathers, and children of those Black Sheep who had given their lives in the service of their country."[20]

However inaccurate the depiction of the Black Sheep, the program at least brought attention to the men, who nevertheless made it a point to rectify the errors at every opportunity. Robert McClurg explained that the show gave added notoriety to the squadron, and Black Sheep member James Hill brushed it off as another example of Hollywood being Hollywood. "I thought there is something that the kids enjoy seeing. I thought the flying was terrific. It was just the stories were all made up. It was show-biz. You know. This is what the public wants to see."[21] Hill added that as a result of the show, he and other Black Sheep received numerous requests to appear at air shows around the country.

"An unusual sight"

Boyington took advantage of those same air shows to sell copies of his autobiography. Aviation devotees of all ages flocked to his table, where they purchased inscribed books or posed for photographs with the famous pilot. Though some of the younger females left disappointed that Boyington shared few physical similarities with good-looking Robert Conrad from the television series, the air shows did help to promote the achievements of the Black Sheep Squadron.

In 1977 Boyington followed his books with a recorded account of his life called *Pappy Boyington, World War II Ace.*

At some of the air shows Boyington shared space with Petty Officer 3rd Class Masajiro Kawato of the 253rd Kokutai (Air Group), a Japanese aviator who claimed that he had been the pilot who shot down Gregory Boyington. In his 1978 book, *Bye Bye Black Sheep,* Kawato wrote that on January 3, 1944, "I saw an unusual sight. An F4U Corsair was after a Zero and right behind the F4U another Zero was followed by another F4U." As Kawato observed the dogfight, the first Zero exploded, and soon afterward smoke billowed from the first Corsair, which would in this case have been Capt. George Ashmun's aircraft. Kawato dropped behind the second Corsair and pumped 20-mm gunfire into it. The Corsair "rolled over to the right and went in for a dive," Kawato wrote, "but I was able to stay with him because of my speed." One thousand feet above the water the canopy opened and the pilot leaped out. According to Kawato, "Imagine my surprise to find that the pilot happened to be a well known Marine, Major Gregory 'Pappy' Boyington, commanding the Black Sheep Squadron."[22]

Kawato tells a gripping story but, unfortunately, it lacks validity. World War II aviation expert Henry Sakaida scoured Japanese records for his book *Pacific Air Combat WWII: Voices from the Past,* and found that while thirty-seven Zeros of the 253rd and thirty-three Zeros of 204th Kokotai engaged an estimated thirty Corsairs that morning, fellow pilots dispute Kawato's claims. They assert that rather than being in the thick of the fighting, Kawato flew above as a protective cover for the Zeros that dropped down to attack. Those pilots state that Kawato stretched the truth in claiming credit for Boyington. Sakaida found other discrepancies in the story as well. Kawato claimed he spotted Boyington over Duke of York Island, but Boyington actually flew off Cape St. George, New Ireland. In the book Kawato used a painting depicting him shooting down Boyington's aircraft, a Corsair bearing the number 86. While Boyington often flew in that Corsair, on that day he flew Marion Carl's plane rather than the one Kawato claimed to have destroyed. In fact, no one can be certain which pilot sent Boyington down in flames in the frantic fighting that day.

A May 25, 1981, letter from the Zero Fighter Pilots Association found in Boyington's personal file at the Marine Corps Research Center in Quantico, Virginia, castigates Kawato, an astonishing condemnation considering that it originates from Kawato's fellow aviators. The letter contends that to ascertain the facts, the association interviewed men who served with Kawato at Rabaul, and that the pilot's claims are "100% lie and the upmost [*sic*] fabrication we have ever heard." The association declared its shame over the claims and its embarrassment for Kawato. As the Japanese pilot was then living in the United States, he posed no problem for the Zero Fighter Pilots Association, "But, we regret he is now a problem to you as he now lives in your country. Good for us, bad for you."[23]

A second controversy that occurred long after Boyington's death illustrates people's tendency to take sides when Boyington is involved. In 2006 the Student Senate at Boyington's alma mater, the University of Washington, voted down a proposal to erect a monument honoring its famous alumnus. The "Resolution Calling for a Tribute for Col. Gregory 'Pappy' Boyington, USMC" stated, "We consider Col. Gregory Boyington, United States Marine Corps, to be a prime example of the excellence that this university represents and strives to impart upon its students." In the heated discussion that followed its introduction, one student senator questioned the propriety of honoring someone who had killed so many others because "she didn't believe a member of the Marine Corps was an example of the sort of person UW wanted to produce." A second senator, who obviously knew nothing of Boyington's life and accomplishments, believed that monuments at the university only "commemorate rich white men" and that another one was unnecessary.[24] Despite the fierce support of the university's Republican Club, the resolution failed by a single vote. The Student Senate's action produced an avalanche of angry e-mails and postings on Internet blogs, most assailing the students for being out of touch and uneducated about our country's heroes. Calls swamped a Seattle morning radio talk show, with most criticizing the Student Senate for its rude treatment of a war hero.

"Tell Pappy that we love him"

Years of hard living, smoking, and alcohol abuse gradually wore down Boyington's body, which deteriorated from the effects of bronchitis, emphysema, and other ailments. Two operations to remove cancer failed to produce any significant changes in his lifestyle, and by the 1980s Boyington was a shell of the man who led the Black Sheep to their air victories.

"In 1980, he stood before us at our Washington meeting, no longer the barrel-chested, swashbuckling terror of the skies," Walton wrote. "His deeply lined face showed every mile of the tortuous road he'd traveled over the years: 'Enough booze to float a battleship' as he often said; the stress of combat flying; the ravages of 20 months of Japanese prison camps; the strains of multiple marriages and divorces; brushes with the law; bouncing from one job to another; medical problems, including the lung cancer operation; sessions with psychiatrists—a classic picture of a man driven toward self-destruction."[25]

One of the few pastimes he enjoyed was an occasional round of golf, often with his friend from Omori, Hap Halloran. In 1978 Halloran caddied for Boyington, who had been invited to participate in the Bing Crosby Pro-Am golf tournament held each year at famed Pebble Beach. Along with astronaut Alan Shepard, the first American into space, and professional golfers Doug Tewell and Bobby Watkins, and with actor Robert Conrad walking alongside, Boyington displayed a vestige of the flair that had marked his life. With a large gallery watching play on the sixteenth green, Boyington faced a forty-foot downhill putt with a sharp break. As if he felt no pressure, Boyington nonchalantly knocked in the putt for a birdie, much to the delight of the onlookers.

The ensuing years were not kind to the aviator. He golfed less frequently as a result of his health problems, even though Josephine helped him quit drinking in the final few years of his life. When he felt strong enough to head to the golf course, he had to cut short his play, joining every fourth hole while watching from the golf cart as Halloran and his buddies attacked the rest. "The final day we played golf together," recalled Halloran, "he was not up to it. I drove the cart, and he chatted. He was really hurting. We maybe played four holes, but he talked a lot."[26]

Chemotherapy treatment failed to slow the cancer, and at the end of 1987 Josephine had to place Boyington in a hospice in Fresno, California. Some of the Black Sheep traveled to California to see their commander one final time, departing with heavy hearts after seeing Boyington so near to death. "It was like a funeral home," said pilot Fred Losch of his January 10, 1988, visit to the hospice with another Black Sheep member. He had come in hopes of convincing his commander to move out of the depressing hospice, but he knew after one look at the feeble Boyington that he had only a few days remaining. Although he was hovering close to death, Boyington joked with those around him. When a nurse came in to check on the visitors, Boyington explained, "Just a couple of my boys coming to say goodbye."[27] With tears streaming down his cheeks, Losch said a few final words, then walked away from the hospice.

Determined to ensure that Boyington received the honor he deserved, Hap Halloran chatted with his friend about funeral arrangements. Boyington at first had no desire to be buried at Arlington National Cemetery, figuring that politicians would somehow ruin the occasion, but Halloran and Josephine convinced him that as a war hero, he had earned a place in the nation's most revered cemetery.

The day after Losch's visit, January 11, 1988, Boyington succumbed. A long line of mourners, many of whom had little association with the man but wanted to pay their respects, gathered throughout the day at the funeral home for a final glimpse of the aviator. "There were people coming into the funeral parlor," recalled Halloran, "and I stood by the casket and listened as parents with kids said 'we drove down because we used to see him at air shows.'" Halloran witnessed many other touching scenes at the funeral home and during the airplane journey that carried Boyington's remains to Washington, D.C. Pallbearers transported the coffin between two lines of Marines standing at attention at the Fresno Airport while jets from the current Black Sheep Squadron flew overhead in tribute. "The Marines sent a DC-9 for the body," said Halloran. "The plane was loaded with flowers. There was a chaplain, a colonel, and I think his job was to police me on what I wrote for the eulogy, that it was not brusque, like Boyington. I wrote the eulogy on the plane going to Washington, and every time I finished something the colonel asked if he could read it. I said, 'No, when I finish I'm only going to check with one person, Greg's wife.' But he didn't give up. I think he was under orders from the Commandant, but I never let him read it."

As the plane carrying Boyington's body across the country on January 14 neared Salt Lake City, Utah, the colonel told Halloran to put on the earphones. When he did, Halloran heard a ground controller tell the pilot, "You tell Pappy that we love him and we're really going to miss him." As the aircraft neared Kansas City, another controller called up his thanks for all Boyington did, as if the aviator could still hear his accolade. Even in death, Boyington, on the final trip he would make in an aircraft, made an impact on people around the country.

A horse-drawn caisson bore Boyington's body to his final resting place not far from the Tomb of the Unknowns, where a collection of mourners, including a group of his Black Sheep, gathered in the cold. "There were six of the Black Sheep at the funeral," said Halloran, "and they liked my eulogy because it gave them credit for being good pilots. Some people wondered why a Black Sheep didn't give the eulogy, but I just said I was a friend."[28] Fittingly, as Halloran concluded his eulogy, four Phantom fighters, the Navy's best fighter aircraft of the day, passed above.

"Some men step forward and lead"

What do we make of this man? Some say that Gregory Boyington was a larger-than-life hero; others consider him an abysmal failure. Boyington may have been a disappointment to family members and friends and the scourge of his superiors, but no one can deny his impact on those around him. To this day most of the members of the AVG have little good to say about him, and some of his own family members will say nothing at all. The men with whom he achieved his greatest renown, the Black Sheep pilots and his fellow captives in Japanese prison camps, unanimously acclaim him. "I think any of us Sheep would credit Pappy for making us what we were," asserts Robert McClurg, "and in fact influencing part of our adult lives well beyond our combat tours. With Pappy's passing, a part of each one of us was gone, as well."[29]

According to Frank Walton, the squadron totals support that second view. In fewer than ninety days of combat the squadron amassed a record equaled by few, shooting down or demolishing on the ground more than two hundred enemy aircraft while destroying an unknown number of barges and supply vessels. After compiling these impressive statistics under Boyington's guidance, the pilots moved on to productive postwar careers. John Bolt became a jet ace in the Korean War, making him the Marine's only propeller-jet double ace; seven Black Sheep owned or were presidents of firms; two became mayors; two continued to fly as airline pilots; three returned to school and earned their law degrees; and one held a position as a college professor.[30]

Walton attributes that success to one undeniable factor that Boyington nurtured.

The key word that keeps coming up in all our recollections about those days is "camaraderie": loyalty and warm, friendly feeling among comrades. Founded on our unique beginning, forged in the crucible of battle, our loyalties were firm; our desire to achieve intense. Friendships formed during those 84 days of combat, when the Black Sheep spearheaded the drive that broke the back of Japanese aerial opposition in the Solomons, have remained steady for 40 years. Black Sheep memorabilia adorn the walls of most of our homes or offices.

Some of the Black Sheep gave their lives; others their blood.

All gave something of themselves.[31]

People's lives are rarely influenced by brief encounters with other individuals. Habits and traits normally form after extended exposure to influential people—caring parents who nurture the person within, teachers who open minds to new possibilities and prod students to strive toward their full potential, mentors who illuminate the path to success. Boyington was, at least from 1943 to 1945, that sort of significant force for the Black Sheep and, to a lesser degree, for those in two prison camps. He helped men think of themselves as a team rather than as an odd collection of individuals, and his obvious influence on them lasted well beyond the handful of months they spent together in the South Pacific.

"As I look back," said Black Sheep aviator Bruce Matheson,

never before or since have I been in a situation that was a literal life-and-death effort, where you would knowingly place yourself repeatedly and routinely in these remote air battles hundreds of miles from your base and really think nothing of it. I don't believe it was a matter of stupidity; we had reliance on each other and the airplane. I never found anything subsequent to those two six-week tours that was nearly as challenging or completely demanding of me as a person. Other things were colorful and enjoyable, but in that crucible I made friendships and attachments and long relationships such as I've never again experienced. Never since that time have I been given the opportunity to achieve or attain or do anything as notable or noteworthy as I was able to do in those few short weeks with the Black Sheep Squadron.[32]

Hap Halloran, effusive in his praise for Boyington's contributions at Omori, noted the near-untouchable record Boyington set as an aviator, one on which other top pilots looked with admiration and even envy. Boyington was "one of their very best," a man Halloran looked up to as "an inspiration."[33]

Lest anyone think that only his World War II associates hold Boyington's memory in high regard, consider the words of actor Robert Conrad or the sentiments printed in *Fortitudine,* a respected military publication that focuses on Marine Corps history and tradition, on Boyington's death. When asked in 1978 to assess Boyington, Conrad told a reporter, "I would love to have flown for him, and I would have loved to have competed with him." *Fortitudine* went even further, stating in its obituary that Boyington was "by far the most colorful Marine aviator of any era, he was pugnacious, witty, rebellious, fun-loving, a disaster as a peacetime officer, a gifted pilot in both dog-fighting and gunnery, and a brilliant combat leader."[34] In August 2007 officials renamed the Coeur d'Alene, Idaho, airport Coeur d'Alene Airport–Pappy Boyington Field to honor the aviator.

Boyington himself admitted that he had taken a tortuous path through life, with incredible accomplishments sprinkled among his deplorable shortcomings. In 1977 he stated, "I might say this brings me here at the age of 65 kinda telling up my career as a military pilot, combat pilot, and life in aviation. I have enjoyed, I would say, all of it. Some of it was not too pleasant at the time but as time passes by it was not all that bad and it is a part of my life that I am very happy that I lived. There are certain parts that I would not want to re-live, but that is neither here nor there."[35]

Perhaps the best assessment comes from Ed Olander, a Black Sheep pilot who flew with Boyington during both combat tours and who, while admitting Boyington's obvious faults, also pointed to his strengths.

> I can say this with conviction, that when countries are facing a crisis such as war, inevitably some men step forward and lead when leadership is most needed. Greg Boyington was such a man. He inspired those fifty of us in his VMF-214 to achieve over and above our own most optimistic expectations. He also inspired others in squadrons with whom we fought side by side. He may have been a roughneck of sorts, he may have consumed too much whisky too often and he may not have been the classic

officer and a gentleman, but he loved and supported the men with whom he fought. And, on a daily basis, he provided a quality of leadership of which few others were capable. The pity is, I guess, that he was never able to reach the heights he could have. I'm grateful that I knew Greg Boyington at his best—in combat.[36]

An overall judgment of Boyington's life thus seems to depend on whether the person making the assessment associated with Boyington at his best or at his worst. Those who knew Boyington as a family member, during his early military period, during his time with the AVG, or in the postwar years have a justifiably negative opinion of him. Boyington failed to measure up during those times. He wallowed in self-pity, he ignored his children and cheated on his wives, he performed his duties lackadaisically, and he shifted the blame for his lack of integrity onto others.

Those who flew with Boyington in the South Pacific or suffered in a prison camp with him invariably offer a positive assessment that is equally as valid as the negative judgments. He was a skilled squadron commander, his uncontested courage and daring in combat earned accolades, and he attempted to help fellow prisoners live through one more difficult day. He performed so ably as a squadron commander that after his January 1944 disappearance his squadron members compiled a booklet about Boyington's tactics that the Marine Corps printed and distributed throughout the Pacific as an example of how to wage war. Black Sheep swear their loyalty to this day, and Hap Halloran depicts Boyington as one of the greatest men he has ever known.

Which evaluation is correct? Both and neither, for to properly assess an individual one must take into account the entirety of that person's years, not one or two segments. Many in the AVG condemned Boyington without knowledge of his later accomplishments. Those in the Black Sheep who praised him were unaware of his poor performance under Chennault. To judge a person on one portion of his life is to miss the totality of who that person was. The answer to how a man could prove so inept with one group and so gifted with another only a few months later rests in two of Boyington's ingrained characteristics— his alcoholism and his need for acceptance. In Burma, Boyington turned to alcohol and self-pity as props when he learned that he was not to be a squadron commander. His performance suffered, and he made highly disputable claims for downed enemy aircraft. Because Boyington lacked a reputation when he arrived in Burma, the AVG members judged him solely on what they observed —an unflattering but fair way of evaluating him. Boyington, who admitted in his autobiography the deep need for acceptance, never fit in with the AVG. Instead of determining how to remedy the situation, he buried himself in a bottle, which only made matters worse.

The Black Sheep, on the other hand, readily accepted Boyington as their commander. He arrived with an established reputation based on his exploits in China and Burma, where he had already engaged the enemy and achieved ace status. Unaware of Boyington's other failings during that period, the Black Sheep had no reason to doubt his abilities. To a man like Boyington, suffering from the maladies that tormented him, that acceptance made all the difference. The failure in China became a triumph in the South Pacific.

In researching this book I corresponded with Harry Foster, who knew Boyington's daughter. An October 2007 e-mail reflected his feelings for the aviator: "I hope you write well about the Col[onel]. He was always for the underdog and thought of himself as one."[37] Those words are as good as any to describe the complicated man that Gregory Boyington was.

Notes

Chapter 1. "A Chained Animal Just Striding to Get Loose"

1. Author's interview with Ray Halloran, October 4, 2007; Lt. Col. Robert W. McClurg, *On Boyington's Wing* (Westminster, Md.: Eagle Editions, 2006), 193.
2. Author's interview with James Hill, October 4, 2007.
3. Chuck Baisden, at http://forums.flyingtigersavg.com/ubb/Forum1/HTML/001870.html, November 18, 2003.
4. "'Pappy' Boyington Comes Home," *Life*, October 1, 1945, 29.
5. Gregory Boyington, *Pappy Boyington, World War II Ace*, Mark 56 Records, 1977.
6. Gregory Boyington, *Baa Baa Black Sheep* (New York: G. P. Putnam's Sons, 1958), 213–14.
7. Boyington, *Pappy Boyington, World War II Ace*.
8. Ibid.
9. Ibid.
10. Ibid.
11. Ibid.
12. Bruce Gamble, *Black Sheep One* (Novato, Calif.: Presidio Press, 2000), 13.
13. Boyington, *Pappy Boyington, World War II Ace*.
14. Ibid.
15. Thomas Coffey, *Hap* (New York: Viking Press, 1982), 40.
16. Ibid., 61.
17. Burke Davis, *The Billy Mitchell Affair* (New York: Random House, 1967), 58, 151.

18. John F. Wukovits, "Daredevil of the Air Gained Early Fame by Combining Airmanship and Showmanship," *Aviation Heritage,* January 1992, 60.

19. Ibid., 62.

20. Boyington, *Pappy Boyington, World War II Ace.*

21. Gamble, *Black Sheep One,* 20.

22. Boyington, *Pappy Boyington, World War II Ace.*

23. Ibid.

24. Ibid.

25. Gamble, *Black Sheep One,* 38.

26. Boyington, *Pappy Boyington, World War II Ace.*

27. Ibid.

28. Ibid.

29. Brig. Gen. John F. Kinney with James M. McCaffrey, *Wake Island Pilot* (Washington: Brassey's, 1995), 23.

30. Boyington, *Pappy Boyington, World War II Ace.*

31. Kinney, *Wake Island Pilot,* 26.

32. Ibid., 27.

33. Boyington, *Pappy Boyington, World War II Ace.*

34. Boyington, *Baa Baa Black Sheep,* 59.

35. Kinney, *Wake Island Pilot,* 29.

36. Gamble, *Black Sheep One,* 97–98.

37. Ibid., 87.

38. Ibid., 112.

39. Kinney, *Wake Island Pilot,* 34.

40. Boyington, *Pappy Boyington, World War II Ace.*

Chapter 2. "He Was Restless and Lonesome"

1. Russell Whelan, *The Flying Tigers* (New York: Viking Press, 1943), 29.

2. Daniel Ford, *Flying Tigers: Claire Chennault and His American Volunteers, 1941–1942* (New York: Smithsonian Books, 2007), 28.

3. Boyington, *Baa Baa Black Sheep,* 17.

4. Charles Baisden, *Flying Tiger to Air Commando* (Atglen, Pa.: Schiffer Military History, 1999), 12, 19.

5. Boyington, *Baa Baa Black Sheep,* 15–16; Boyington, *Pappy Boyington, World War II Ace.*

6. George Burgard, "Diary," September 24, 1941, at http://members.tripod. com/Flying-tiger-ace/id18.htm.

7. Boyington, *Pappy Boyington, World War II Ace.*

8. Boyington, *Baa Baa Black Sheep,* 20.

9. Burgard, "Diary," September 30, 1941.

10. Ed Overend, "Diary," October 1, 1941, at http://www.warbirdforum.com.

11. Burgard, "Diary," October 6, 1941.

12. Maj. Gen. Charles R. Bond Jr. and Terry H. Anderson, *A Flying Tiger's Diary* (College Station: Texas A&M University Press, 1984), 24.

13. Burgard, "Diary," October 13, 1941.

14. Bond and Anderson, *A Flying Tiger's Diary,* 25.

15. Boyington, *Baa Baa Black Sheep,* 25.

16. Overend, "Diary," October 1, 1941.

17. Burgard, "Diary," October 21, 1941.

18. Boyington, *Baa Baa Black Sheep,* 26–27.

19. Bond and Anderson, *A Flying Tiger's Diary,* 33.

20. Ibid., 33–34; Burgard, "Diary," November 5, 7, 1941.

21. Whelan, *The Flying Tigers,* 40.

22. Olga S. Greenlaw, *The Lady and the Tigers* (New York: E. P. Dutton, 1943), 32.

23. Claire Lee Chennault, *Way of a Fighter* (New York: G. P. Putnam's Sons, 1949), 109.

24. Boyington, *Baa Baa Black Sheep,* 39.

25. Bond and Anderson, *A Flying Tiger's Diary,* 37.

26. Ibid.

27. Olga Greenlaw, "Pappy," *Cosmopolitan,* April 1944, 29.

28. The preceding quotations are from Greenlaw, "Pappy," 28–29; Greenlaw, *The Lady and the Tigers,* 61–62.

29. Eve Curie, *Journey among Warriors* (Garden City, N.Y.: Doubleday, Doran, 1943), 395, 397.

30. Boyington, *Baa Baa Black Sheep,* 40.

31. Chennault, *Way of a Fighter,* 110.

32. Maj. Gen. Charles R. Bond Jr. "Oral History," Oral History Collection, Cushing Memorial Library and Archives, Texas A&M University, July 21–22, 1981, 29.

33. Ford, *Flying Tigers: Claire Chennault and His American Volunteers, 1941–1942,* 28.

34. Greenlaw, *The Lady and the Tigers*, 63–64.
35. "Magic from Waterproof," *Time*, June 8, 1942, 30.
36. Bond and Anderson, *A Flying Tiger's Diary*, 46.
37. Chennault, *Way of a Fighter*, 113.
38. James H. Howard, *Roar of the Tiger* (New York: Orion Books, 1991), 81.
39. Boyington, *Pappy Boyington, World War II Ace*.
40. Bond and Anderson, *A Flying Tiger's Diary*, 39.
41. Greenlaw, "Pappy," 29.
42. Boyington, *Baa Baa Black Sheep*, 28.
43. Bond and Anderson, *A Flying Tiger's Diary*, 45.
44. Boyington, *Pappy Boyington, World War II Ace*.
45. Chennault, *Way of a Fighter*, 111–12.
46. Burgard, "Diary," November 27, 1941.
47. David Lee "Tex" Hill and Maj. Reagan Schaupp, *"Tex" Hill: Flying Tiger* (San Antonio, Tex.: Universal Bookbindery, 2003), 97.
48. Greenlaw, "Pappy," 29.
49. Howard, *Roar of the Tiger*, 114.
50. Bond, "Oral History," 41.
51. Wanda Cornelius and Thayne Short, *Ding Hao: America's Air War in China, 1937–1945* (Gretna: Pelican Publishing, 1980), 103.

Chapter 3. "This Was Real. This Was War"

1. Bond and Anderson, *A Flying Tiger's Diary*, 51–52.
2. Greenlaw, *The Lady and the Tigers*, 69–70.
3. Boyington, *Baa Baa Black Sheep*, 44.
4. Frank S. Losonsky and Terry M. Losonsky, *Flying Tiger: A Crew Chief's Story* (Atglen, Pa.: Schiffer Military/Aviation History, 1996), 69.
5. Boyington, *Baa Baa Black Sheep*, 47.
6. Bond and Anderson, *A Flying Tiger's Diary*, 59; Burgard, "Diary," December 18, 1941.
7. Burgard, "Diary," December 18–19, 1941.
8. Gamble, *Black Sheep One*, 159.
9. C. Joseph Rosbert, *Flying Tiger Joe's Adventure Story Cookbook* (Franklin, N.C.: Giant Poplar Press, 1985), 75.
10. Boyington, *Baa Baa Black Sheep*, 51.

11. Gouichi Suzuki interview with Frank Christopher, quoted in Ford, *Flying Tigers: Claire Chennault and His American Volunteers, 1941–1942.*

12. Rosbert, *Flying Tiger Joe's Adventure Story Cookbook,* 77.

13. Burgard, "Diary," December 20, 1941.

14. Paul Frillmann and Graham Peck, *China: The Life Remembered* (Boston: Houghton Mifflin, 1968), 92; Bond, "Oral History," p. 36.

15. Harrison Forman, "Reinforcement of Flying Tigers Now Assured, Leader Declares," *New York Times,* April 4, 1942, 3.

16. "Echo from the West," *Time,* December 15, 1941, 26; "Tigers Prove It," *Time,* January 12, 1942, 25.

17. Greenlaw, *The Lady and the Tigers,* 48–49.

18. Boyington, *Baa Baa Black Sheep,* 53.

19. Burgard, "Diary," December 21, 23, 1941.

20. Boyington, *Baa Baa Black Sheep,* 53.

21. Bond and Anderson, *A Flying Tiger's Diary,* 70.

22. Ibid., 63.

23. Ibid., 63.

24. Burgard, "Diary," December 30, 1941.

25. Ibid., December 29, 31, 1941.

26. Bond and Anderson, *A Flying Tiger's Diary,* 74.

27. Boyington, *Baa Baa Black Sheep,* 56.

28. Burgard, "Diary," January 18, 20, 21, 1942.

29. Olga Greenlaw, "Pappy," 29.

30. Ford, *Flying Tigers: Claire Chennault and His American Volunteers, 1941–1942,* 180.

31. Boyington, *Pappy Boyington, World War II Ace.*

32. Colin Heaton, "Interview with Pappy Boyington," *Aviation History,* May 2001, 3, at http://www.historynet.com.

33. Boyington, *Pappy Boyington, World War II Ace.*

34. Heaton, "Interview with Pappy Boyington," 5.

35. Boyington, *Baa Baa Black Sheep,* 60.

36. Ibid., 60.

37. Ibid., 63.

38. Bond and Anderson, *A Flying Tiger's Diary,* 90; *Chicago Daily Tribune,* January 27, 1942, 10; *New York Times,* January 28, 1942, 7.

39. "Magic from Waterproof," 30.

40. Howard, *Roar of the Tiger,* 125.

41. "Tigers over Burma," *Time,* February 9, 1942, 25–26.

42. Larry M. Pistole, *The Pictorial History of the Flying Tigers* (Orange, Va.: Publisher's Press, Inc., 1981), 178.

43. Howard, *Roar of the Tiger,* 123.

44. Bond and Anderson, *A Flying Tiger's Diary,* 99–100.

45. Bond, "Oral History," p. 41.

46. Burgard, "Diary," February 10, 16, 1942.

47. Howard, *Roar of the Tiger,* 126.

48. Ibid., 130.

49. Burgard, "Diary," March 6, 1942.

50. Boyington, *Baa Baa Black Sheep,* 86.

51. Bond and Anderson, *A Flying Tiger's Diary,* 129.

52. Burgard, "Diary," March 22, 1942.

53. Bond and Anderson, *A Flying Tiger's Diary,* 132–33.

54. Bob Bergin, "Pearl Harbor Payback," *Flight Journal,* April 2005, 68.

55. Boyington, *Baa Baa Black Sheep,* 99.

56. Bond and Anderson, *A Flying Tiger's Diary,* 137.

57. "Flying Tigers Blast 40 Planes," *Chicago Daily Tribune,* March 25, 1942, 1; Forman, "Reinforcement of Flying Tigers Now Assured, Leader Declares," 3; "20 for 1," *Time,* April 6, 1942, 21.

58. "Flying Tigers," editorial, *New York Times,* March 30, 1942, 16.

59. "Magic from Waterproof," 30.

60. Harrison Forman, "Victories of A.V.G. Laid to Courage," *New York Times,* March 15, 1942, 5.

Chapter 4. "Only Have to Fight the Japs Now"

1. Bond and Anderson, *A Flying Tiger's Diary,* 141.

2. Greenlaw, *The Lady and the Tigers,* 213.

3. Heaton, "Interview with Pappy Boyington," 3.

4. Boyington, *Baa Baa Black Sheep,* 93.

5. Ibid., 101.

6. Leo J. Schramm, *Leo the Tiger* (Camp Hill, Pa.: GreenShield Services, 1992), 153.

7. Greenlaw, *The Lady and the Tigers*, 248.

8. Hill and Schaupp, *"Tex" Hill: Flying Tiger*, 147.

9. Greenlaw, "Pappy," 29.

10. Boyington, *Baa Baa Black Sheep*, 101.

11. Burgard, "Diary," April 22, 1942.

12. Howard, *Roar of the Tiger*, 147.

13. Greenlaw, *The Lady and the Tigers*, 283–84.

14. Howard, *Roar of the Tiger*, 147.

15. Boyington, *Pappy Boyington, World War II Ace*.

16. Boyington, *Baa Baa Black Sheep*, 112–13.

17. Ibid., 115.

18. Ibid., 120.

19. Gamble, *Black Sheep One*, 211.

20. Boyington, *Pappy Boyington, World War II Ace*.

21. Greenlaw, "Pappy," 139.

22. Robert Sherrod, *History of Marine Corps Aviation in World War II* (Baltimore, Md.: Nautical & Aviation Publishing Company of America, 1987), 65.

23. Boyington, *Baa Baa Black Sheep*, 125–26.

24. J. Hunter Reinburg, *A Pilot's Log Book: The True Combat Aerial Escapades of Colonel J. Hunter Reinburg* (Boynton Beach, Fla.: Star Publishing, 1966).

25. Marine Fighting Squadron 122, "War Diary," April 21, 1943.

26. Boyington, *Baa Baa Black Sheep*, 127.

27. Reinburg, *A Pilot's Log Book*, 75–76.

28. Heaton, "Interview with Pappy Boyington," 7.

29. Reinburg, *A Pilot's Log Book*, 76–77.

30. Boyington, *Baa Baa Black Sheep*, 132–33.

31. Heaton, "Interview with Pappy Boyington," 7–8.

32. Boyington, *Baa Baa Black Sheep*, 139.

33. Masatake Okumiya, Jiro Horikoshi, and Martin Caidin, *Zero* (New York: ibooks, 2002), 220.

34. Tom Bartlett, "Bolt out of the Blue," *Leatherneck*, September 1986, 1, at http://pqasb.pqarchiver.com/mca-marines/access.

35. Boyington, *Baa Baa Black Sheep*, 131.

36. Ibid., 139.

Chapter 5. "I Am Going to Save You Guys"

1. Frank E. Walton, *Once They Were Eagles* (Lexington: University Press of Kentucky, 1986), 8.
2. Ibid., 35.
3. Ibid., 10.
4. Boyington, *Pappy Boyington, World War II Ace.*
5. Hill interview, October 4, 2007.
6. Walton, *Once They Were Eagles*, 20–21.
7. Ibid.
8. Boyington, *Pappy Boyington, World War II Ace.*
9. Walton, *Once They Were Eagles*, 21.
10. Boyington, *Pappy Boyington, World War II Ace.*
11. McClurg, *On Boyington's Wing*, 26.
12. Hill interview, October 4, 2007.
13. Gamble, *Black Sheep One*, 234.
14. McClurg, *On Boyington's Wing*, 111.
15. Ibid., 39.
16. John A. De Chant, *Devilbirds: The Story of United States Marine Corps Aviation in World War II* (New York: Harper & Brothers, 1947), 113.
17. Walton, *Once They Were Eagles*, 20.
18. Hill interview, October 4, 2007.
19. Ibid.
20. Heaton, "Interview with Pappy Boyington," 8.
21. McClurg, *On Boyington's Wing*, 202.
22. Boyington, *Baa Baa Black Sheep*, 146.
23. VMF-214 Action Report, September 16, 1943, "Zeros Spilled out of the Clouds."
24. McClurg, *On Boyington's Wing*, 39–40.
25. Hill interview, October 4, 2007.
26. Walton, *Once They Were Eagles*, 55.
27. Oliver L. North with Joe Musser, *War Stories II: Heroism in the Pacific* (Washington, D.C.: Regnery Publishing, 2004), 217.
28. Hill interview, October 4, 2007.
29. VMF-214 Action Report, September 16, 1943, "Zeros Spilled out of the Clouds."

30. Ibid.
31. Boyington, *Pappy Boyington, World War II Ace.*
32. VMF-214 Combat Report, September 16, 1943.
33. McClurg, *On Boyington's Wing,* 41.
34. Hill interview, October 4, 2007.
35. Boyington, *Baa Baa Black Sheep,* 155, 158.
36. VMF-214 Combat Report, September 23, 1943.
37. McClurg, *On Boyington's Wing,* 59.
38. Walton, *Once They Were Eagles,* 36.
39. VMF-214 Combat Report, September 27, 1943.
40. VMF-214 Action Report, September 27, 1943, "Ten Corsairs Battle Fifty Zeros."
41. McClurg, *On Boyington's Wing,* 67.
42. De Chant, *Devilbirds: The Story of United States Marine Corps Aviation in World War II,* 113.
43. VMF-214 Action Reports: September 30, 1943, "PT Boat Report on Action of 30 September"; September 30, 1943, "Statement of Stanley R. Bailey, Major, re: Strafing PT Boats on North Shore, Kolombangara"; September 30, 1943, "Statement of First Lieutenant B. L. Tucker Concerning PT Boat Incident, 30 September 1943."
44. VMF-214 Monthly Report of Friendly & Enemy Losses, September 1943; VMF-214 War Diary, September 1, 1943, to September 30, 1943.

Chapter 6. "We Had Pride; We Had Class; and We Were Winners"

1. Boyington, *Baa Baa Black Sheep,* 167.
2. VMF-214 Action Report, October 4, 1943, "3 Zeros in 60 Seconds."
3. VMF-214 Combat Report, October 15, 1943.
4. Walton, *Once They Were Eagles,* 55.
5. VMF-214 Action Report, October 4, 1943, "3 Zeros in 60 Seconds."
6. VMF-214 Combat Report, October 4, 1943; VMF-214 Aircraft Action Report, October 4, 1943; VMF-214 Action Report, October 4, 1943, "3 Zeros in 60 Seconds."
7. Boyington, *Pappy Boyington, World War II Ace.*
8. VMF-214 Combat Report, October 15, 1943; VMF-214 Aircraft Action Report, October 15, 1943.

9. Gamble, *Black Sheep One,* 293.

10. Walton, *Once They Were Eagles,* 53.

11. VMF-214 Combat Report, October 17, 1943; VMF-214 Aircraft Action Report, October 17, 1943.

12. Walton, *Once They Were Eagles,* 55–56.

13. Boyington, *Baa Baa Black Sheep,* 163.

14. Walton, *Once They Were Eagles,* 50–51.

15. McClurg, *On Boyington's Wing,* 80.

16. VMF-214 Combat Report, October 15, 1943.

17. McClurg, *On Boyington's Wing,* 86, 202.

18. Hill interview, October 4, 2007.

19. Bob Reed, "A Golden Gathering of Black Sheep," *Leatherneck,* September 1993, 1, at http://pqasb.pqarchiver.com/mca-marines/access.

20. VMF-214 Aircraft Action Report, October 19, 1943; McClurg, *On Boyington's Wing,* 103.

21. VMF-214 Monthly Report of Friendly & Enemy Losses, October 1943.

22. McClurg, *On Boyington's Wing,* 91.

23. Okumiya, Horikoshi, and Caidin, *Zero,* 212–13.

24. VMF-214 War Diary, October 21–31, 1943.

25. McClurg, *On Boyington's Wing,* 101.

26. *The Combat Strategy and Tactics of Major Gregory Boyington, USMCR,* Headquarters, Marine Aircraft, South Pacific, Fleet Marine Force Intelligence Section, January 19, 1944, "VMF-214 January 1944" folder, National Archives and Records Administration, College Park, Md.

27. Ibid.

28. Gamble, *Black Sheep One,* 285–86.

29. McClurg, *On Boyington's Wing,* 203.

30. Walton, *Once They Were Eagles,* 119.

31. Bartlett, "Bolt out of the Blue," 3–4; Walton, *Once They Were Eagles,* 110.

32. *The Combat Strategy and Tactics of Major Gregory Boyington, USMCR.*

33. Boyington, *Pappy Boyington, World War II Ace.*

34. *The Combat Strategy and Tactics of Major Gregory Boyington, USMCR.*

35. Walton, *Once They Were Eagles,* 114; *The Combat Strategy and Tactics of Major Gregory Boyington, USMCR.*

36. McClurg, *On Boyington's Wing,* 25.

37. *The Combat Strategy and Tactics of Major Gregory Boyington, USMCR.*

38. Ibid.

39. Ibid.

40. McClurg, *On Boyington's Wing,* 56.

41. *The Combat Strategy and Tactics of Major Gregory Boyington, USMCR.*

42. VMF-214 Action Report, September 16, 1943, "Zeros Spilled out of the Clouds."

43. Capt. John M. Foster, *Hell in the Heavens* (New York: G. P. Putnam's Sons, 1961), 195.

44. VMF-214 Action Report, September 16, 1943, "Zeros Spilled out of the Clouds"; *The Combat Strategy and Tactics of Major Gregory Boyington, USMCR.*

45. VMF-214 Action Report, September 16, 1943, "Zeros Spilled out of the Clouds"; *The Combat Strategy and Tactics of Major Gregory Boyington, USMCR;* Foster, *Hell in the Heavens,* 195.

46. VMF-214 Action Report, September 16, 1943, "Zeros Spilled out of the Clouds."

47. Walton, *Once They Were Eagles,* 17.

48. Boyington, *Pappy Boyington, World War II Ace;* Boyington, *Baa Baa Black Sheep,* 198.

49. Boyington, *Pappy Boyington, World War II Ace.*

50. Walton, *Once They Were Eagles,* 113, 129.

51. Ibid., 129.

52. Foster, *Hell in the Heavens,* 312.

53. McClurg, *On Boyington's Wing,* 203.

54. Gamble, *Black Sheep One,* 273.

55. Walton, *Once They Were Eagles,* 160.

56. Ibid., 158.

57. Ibid., 111, 115.

58. Ibid., 123.

59. McClurg, *On Boyington's Wing,* iii, 106.

60. North and Musser, *War Stories II: Heroism in the Pacific,* 217.

61. Walton, *Once They Were Eagles,* 57.

62. Sherrod, *History of Marine Corps Aviation in World War II,* xii.

63. Hill interview, October 4, 2007.

Chapter 7. "They Can't Kill Me"

1. Boyington, *Baa Baa Black Sheep,* 206.
2. Walton, *Once They Were Eagles,* 61–62.
3. Boyington, *Baa Baa Black Sheep,* 238.
4. Hill interview, October 4, 2007.
5. McClurg, *On Boyington's Wing,* 119.
6. Walton, *Once They Were Eagles,* 76.
7. Ibid., 121.
8. Foster, *Hell in the Heavens,* 193.
9. McClurg, *On Boyington's Wing,* 125.
10. Foster, *Hell in the Heavens,* 196.
11. Author's interview with Fred Avey, October 1989.
12. Ibid.
13. Hill interview, October 4, 2007.
14. Avey interview, October 1989.
15. Henry Sakaida, *Pacific Air Combat WWII: Voices from the Past* (St. Paul, Minn.: Phalanx Publishing, 1993), 74; Henry Sakaida, *The Siege of Rabaul* (St. Paul, Minn.: Phalanx Publishing, 1996), 13.
16. Mark Styling, *Corsair Aces of World War 2* (London: Osprey Publishing, 1995), 54.
17. Sherrod, *History of Marine Corps Aviation in World War II,* 195.
18. Boyington, *Baa Baa Black Sheep,* 212; Foster, *Hell in the Heavens,* 195.
19. VMF-214 Combat Report, December 17, 1943.
20. Walton, *Once They Were Eagles,* 90.
21. Boyington, *Baa Baa Black Sheep,* 217.
22. McClurg, *On Boyington's Wing,* 149.
23. Marine Corps Press Release, Gregory Boyington Personal File, Marine Corps Research Center, Quantico, Va.
24. Walton, *Once They Were Eagles,* 93–94.
25. Boyington, *Baa Baa Black Sheep,* 223.
26. Avey interview, October 1989.
27. Greenlaw, "Pappy," 139.
28. Maj. Gen. Marion E. Carl with Barrett Tillman, *Pushing the Envelope* (Annapolis, Md.: Naval Institute Press, 1994), 46.
29. Boyington, *Baa Baa Black Sheep,* 230.

30. Ibid., 231; Boyington, *Pappy Boyington, World War II Ace.*

31. Boyington, *Baa Baa Black Sheep,* 231.

32. Robert T. Reed, *Lost Black Sheep* (Central Point, Ore.: Hellgate Press/PSI Research, 2001), 74.

33. McClurg, *On Boyington's Wing,* 162.

34. Foster, *Hell in the Heavens,* 203–4.

35. Reed, *Lost Black Sheep,* 74.

36. "Lost Sheep," *Time,* January 17, 1944, 62; "Ace Lost; Downed 26 Japs," *Chicago Daily Tribune,* January 7, 1944, 1; Gamble, *Black Sheep One,* 311.

37. Walton, *Once They Were Eagles,* 96.

38. McClurg, *On Boyington's Wing,* 164.

39. Col. Clyde H. Metcalf, ed., *The Marine Corps Reader* (New York: G. P. Putnam's Sons, 1944), 397.

40. Maj. Henry S. Miller to the Commanding General, 1st Marine Aircraft Wing, "Flight echelon known until recently as VMF-214, disposition of," January 12, 1944, National Archives and Records Administration, College Park, Md.

41. Handwritten note found with a copy of *The Combat Strategy and Tactics of Major Gregory Boyington, USMCR,* in "VMF-214 January 1944" folder, National Archives and Records Administration, College Park, Md..

42. Heaton, "Interview with Pappy Boyington," 10.

43. Sakaida, *The Siege of Rabaul,* p. 21.

44. Boyington, *Baa Baa Black Sheep,* 258.

45. Ibid., 271.

46. Ibid., 272.

Chapter 8. "I'll Meet You Guys in a San Diego Bar"

1. Louis Zamperini with Helen Itria, *Devil at My Heels* (New York: E. P. Dutton, 1956), 92.

2. *New York Post,* August 31, 1945; "Deposition of Ens. John Bertrang," Record Group 153, Records of the Office of the Judge Advocate General, War Crimes Branch, Reports of Interviews with American Servicemen Who Were Prisoners of War, 1943–47, National Archives and Records Administration, College Park, Md. (hereafter cited as Prisoner of War Depositions).

3. "Deposition of Lt. John M. Arbuckle," Prisoner of War Depositions.

4. "Deposition of Lt. (jg) Edwin Walasek," Prisoner of War Depositions.

5. Heaton, "Interview with Pappy Boyington," 11.

6. "Ace Boyington May Yet Keep that Bar Date; Missing Flyer again Rumored Alive," *Chicago Daily Tribune*, May 16, 1944, 2.

7. Heaton, "Interview with Pappy Boyington," 10.

8. Boyington, *Baa Baa Black Sheep*, 318.

9. Ibid., 322.

10. "Deposition of TSgt. Harry C. Liskowsky," Prisoner of War Depositions.

11. Halloran interview, October 4, 2007.

12. Ibid.

13. Author's interview with Joseph Goicoechea, April 12, 2002; Joseph Goicoechea, "Memoirs," handwritten, June 14, 2001, 68.

14. Ray "Hap" Halloran with Chester Marshall, *Hap's War* (Menlo Park, Calif.: Hallmark Press, 1998), 144.

15. Halloran interview, October 4, 2007.

16. "Deposition of Sgt. James E. Hinkle," Prisoner of War Depositions.

17. "Deposition of TSgt. Harry C. Liskowsky," Prisoner of War Depositions; "Deposition of Lt. John M. Arbuckle," Prisoner of War Depositions, italics in original.

18. Halloran interview, October 4, 2007.

19. McClurg, *On Boyington's Wing*, 193; Halloran interview, October 4, 2007.

20. McClurg, *On Boyington's Wing*, 193; Joe Morang, "Boyington Here; Pale, Tired, but Still Grinning," *Chicago Daily Tribune*, October 1, 1945, 5.

21. Boyington, *Baa Baa Black Sheep*, 324; Halloran interview, October 4, 2007; Halloran and Marshall, *Hap's War*, 145.

22. Robert R. Martindale, *The 13th Mission* (Austin, Tex.: Eakin Press, 1998), 212–13.

23. Boyington, *Baa Baa Black Sheep*, 325–26, 330.

24. Ibid., 330.

25. Linda Goetz Holmes, *Unjust Enrichment: How Japan's Companies Built Postwar Fortunes Using American POWs* (Mechanicsburg, Pa.: Stackpole Books, 2001), 116.

26. Martindale, *The 13th Mission*, 227.

27. Boyington, *Baa Baa Black Sheep*, 341.

28. Martindale, *The 13th Mission*, 237.

29. John E. Jones, "Stassen's Full Part in Rescues of Captives in Japan Revealed," *Pittsburgh Post-Gazette,* January 22, 1946.

30. Boyington, *Baa Baa Black Sheep,* 343.

31. Fleet Adm. William F. Halsey and Lt. Cdr. J. Bryan III, *Admiral Halsey's Story* (New York: McGraw-Hill, 1947), 278.

32. "Ace Boyington Safe in Tokyo, 3d Fleet Told," *Chicago Daily Tribune,* August 29, 1945, 1.

33. Boyington, *Baa Baa Black Sheep,* 349.

34. Heaton, "Interview with Pappy Boyington," 11.

35. Gamble, *Black Sheep One,* 344.

36. Boyington, *Baa Baa Black Sheep,* 347, italics in original.

37. Sakaida, *The Siege of Rabaul,* 26.

38. Heaton, "Interview with Pappy Boyington," 10–11.

39. "18 Black Sheep Welcome 'Pappy' Back to Fold," *Chicago Daily Tribune,* September 13, 1945, 3.

40. Boyington, *Baa Baa Black Sheep,* 351.

Chapter 9. "I Knew Greg Boyington at His Best—in Combat"

1. Walton, *Once They Were Eagles,* 188.

2. Boyington, *Baa Baa Black Sheep,* 356.

3. Gamble, *Black Sheep One,* 355.

4. Boyington, *Baa Baa Black Sheep,* 364–67.

5. VMF-214 Aircraft Action Report, January 3, 1944, Supplemental Report filed October 4, 1945.

6. Sherrod, *History of Marine Corps Aviation in World War II,* xii; Howard, *Roar of the Tiger,* 147–48.

7. Carl and Tillman, *Pushing the Envelope,* 48–49.

8. Gregory Boyington Personal File, Marine Corps Research Center, Quantico, Va.

9. Gamble, *Black Sheep One,* 348.

10. McClurg, *On Boyington's Wing,* 197.

11. Boyington, *Baa Baa Black Sheep,* 12.

12. "Woman in Reno Says She'll Wed Marine Ace," *Chicago Daily Tribune,* January 6, 1946, 1; "Woman Jilted by Pappy Will Cling to Mate," *Chicago Daily*

Tribune, January 8, 1946, 1; "Pappy's Lucy 'Amazed' as He Weds Another," *Chicago Daily Tribune,* January 10, 1946, 3.

13. Gamble, *Black Sheep One,* 361; Walton, *Once They Were Eagles,* 188.

14. "Born to Fight," *Time,* September 2, 1946.

15. Seymour Korman, "Pappy Wins His Toughest Fight," *Chicago Daily Tribune,* April 28, 1957, C39.

16. Boyington, *Baa Baa Black Sheep,* 384.

17. Avey interview, October 1989.

18. McClurg, *On Boyington's Wing,* 37, 183–84.

19. Frank Walton, "'Baa Baa Black Sheep' Is Pulling the Wool over Our Eyes," *TV Guide,* April 23, 1977, pp. 15–20.

20. Walton, *Once They Were Eagles,* xi.

21. Hill interview, October 4, 2007.

22. Masajiro Kawato, *Bye Bye Black Sheep* (Phoenix, Ariz.: Printing Dynamics, 1978), 76.

23. May 25, 1981, letter from the Zero Fighter Pilots Association to Mr. Strickland, Gregory Boyington Personal File, Marine Corps Research Center, Quantico, Va.

24. University of Washington Student Senate Minutes, February 7, 2006, at senate.asuw.org.

25. Walton, *Once They Were Eagles,* 189.

26. Halloran interview, October 4, 2007.

27. Reed, "A Golden Gathering of Black Sheep," 1–2.

28. Halloran interview, October 4, 2007.

29. McClurg, *On Boyington's Wing,* 197.

30. Walton, "'Baa Baa Black Sheep' Is Pulling the Wool over Our Eyes," 20.

31. Walton, *Once They Were Eagles,* 191.

32. Ibid., 164.

33. McClurg, *On Boyington's Wing,* 193.

34. Mary Daniels, "Robert Conrad Is Flying High as 'Pappy' Boyington," *Chicago Daily Tribune,* January 8, 1978, K3; Col. Charles J. Quilter II, "'One-of-a-Kind' Marine Aviator 'Pappy' Boyington Dies," *Fortitudine,* 1988, 17.

35. Boyington, *Pappy Boyington, World War II Ace.*

36. Styling, *Corsair Aces of World War 2,* 56.

37. E-mail from Harry Foster to the author, October 31, 2007.

Bibliography

Official Sources

"American Interests—Japan, Transmission of report no. 1, main Tokyo prisoner of war camp (Omori)," February 19, 1945. National Archives and Records Administration, College Park, Md.

The Combat Strategy and Tactics of Major Gregory Boyington, USMCR. Headquarters, Marine Aircraft, South Pacific, Fleet Marine Force Intelligence Section, January 19, 1944. "VMF-214 January 1944" folder, National Archives and Records Administration, College Park, Md.

Maj. Henry S. Miller to the Commanding General, First Marine Aircraft Wing. "Flight echelon known until recently as VMF-214, disposition of," January 12, 1944. National Archives and Records Administration, College Park, Md.

Record Group 153, Records of the Office of the Judge Advocate General, War Crimes Branch. Reports of Interviews with American Servicemen Who Were Prisoners of War, 1943–1947. National Archives and Records Administration, College Park, Md.

Ofuna

Lt. John M. Arbuckle, USN

Lt. Charles August

Motor Machinist's Mate 2nd Class James N. Baker Jr., USN

1st Lt. Gordon Bennett, Air Corps

Ens. John Bertrang, USN

Lt. Cdr. Carlton H. Clark

Joseph E. Cross, rank not stated, USN

Lt. William A. Daindson, USN

TSgt. Walter G. Gomer, AAF

Lt. Cdr. J. J. Vandegrift

Lt. (jg) Edwin Walasek

Chief Gunner's Mate Fred Zufelt, USN

Omori

TM Norman Albertson, USN

Lt. John M. Arbuckle, USN

Cpl. Dale Coulson, USMC

SSgt. Robert A. Franz, AAF

Sgt. James E. Hinkle

Chief Machinist's Mate Howard W. Koviak, USN

EM2/c James D. Landrum

Lt. (jg) Herbert Law

TM2/c John Leskovsky, USNR

TSgt. Harry C. Liskowsy, USA

Capt. Arthur L. Maher, USN

1st Lt. James Martin

Pfc. Herbert Schroer

1st Lt. Gordon H. Scott

Pfc. George H. Smith Jr., USMC

SSgt. Stephen Spege Jr., AAF

VMF-122 War Diary, April 1, 1943, to April 30, 1943." National Archives and Records Administration, College Park, Md.

VMF-122 War Diary, June 1, 1943, to June 30, 1943. National Archives and Records Administration, College Park, Md.

VMF-122 War Diary, July 1, 1943, to July 31, 1943. National Archives and Records Administration, College Park, Md.

VMF-214 Combat Reports

September 14, 1943

September 15, 1943

September 16, 1943

September 17, 1943

September 18, 1943

September 19, 1943

September 20, 1943

September 21, 1943

September 22, 1943

September 23, 1943

September 24, 1943

September 25, 1943

September 26, 1943

September 27, 1943

October 4, 1943

October 10, 1943

October 11, 1943

October 15, 1943

October 16, 1943

October 17, 1943

October 18, 1943

December 1–16, 1943

December 17, 1943

December 23, 1943

January 2, 1944

January 3, 1944

January 4, 1944

VMF-214 Action Reports

September 16, 1943, "Zeros Spilled out of the Clouds"

September 18, 1943, "One Corsair Scatters 15 Jap Dive Bombers"

September 23, 1943, "I Got that Old Feelin!"

September 26, 1943, "Zeros Snapped At Their Heels"

September 27, 1943, "Ten Corsairs Battle Fifty Zeros"

September 30, 1943, "PT Boat Report on Action of 30 September"

September 30, 1943, "Statement of Stanley R. Bailey, Major, re: Strafing PT Boats on North Shore, Kolombangara"

September 30, 1943, "Statement of First Lieutenant B. L. Tucker Concerning PT Boat Incident, 30 September 1943"

October 4, 1943, "3 Zeros in 60 Seconds"

VMF-214 Aircraft Action Reports

October 4, 1943

October 10, 1943

October 11, 1943

October 14, 1943

October 15, 1943

October 17, 1943

October 18, 1943

October 19, 1943

December 17, 1943

December 23. 1943

January 2, 1944

January 3, 1944

January 3, 1944, Supplemental Report, filed October 4, 1945

January 4, 1944

VMF-214 Monthly Report of Friendly & Enemy Losses

September 1943

October 1943

November 1943

December 1943

January 1944

VMF-214 Tour of Duty

September 1, 1943, to September 30, 1943

October 1, 1943, to October 31, 1943

November 1, 1943, to November 30, 1943

December 1, 1943, to December 31, 1943

January 1, 1944, to January 31, 1944

VMF-214 War Diary

September 1, 1943, to September 30, 1943

October 1, 1943, to October 31, 1943

November 1, 1943, to November 30, 1943

December 1, 1943, to December 31, 1943

January 1, 1944, to January 31, 1944

Publications

"Ace Asks Divorce." *Chicago Daily Tribune,* August 21, 1959, p. 7.

"Ace Boyington May Yet Keep that Bar Date; Missing Flyer again Rumored Alive." *Chicago Daily Tribune,* May 16, 1944, p. 2.

"Ace Boyington Safe in Tokyo, 3d Fleet Told." *Chicago Daily Tribune,* August 29, 1945, p. 1.

"Ace Lost; Downed 26 Japs." *Chicago Daily Tribune,* January 7, 1944, pp. 1, 3.

"Aces." *Time,* March 20, 1944, p. 65.

"Actress Wed to Boyington, War Air Hero." *Chicago Daily Tribune,* October 28, 1959, p. A1.

"Allied Fliers Rout Column in Burma." *New York Times,* January 28, 1942, p. 7.

"American Pilots Rout Forty Jap Planes in Burma." *Chicago Daily Tribune,* January 27, 1942, p. 10.

Anderson, N. J. "Baa Baa Black Sheep." *Marine Corps Gazette,* September 1958, pp. 1–2. At http://pqasb.pqarchiver.com/mca-marines/access.

Anonymous. "'Black Sheep' Squadron Flies Again." *Marine Corps Gazette,* February 1978, p. 1. At http://pqasb.pqarchiver.com/mca-marines/access.

Anonymous. "Boyington Receives Medal of Honor." *Marine Corps Gazette,* May 1944, pp. 1–3. At http://pqasb.pqarchiver.com/mca-marines/access.

Anonymous. "'Pappy' Boyington Flies Again." *Marine Corps Gazette,* November 1976, p. 1. At http://pqasb.pqarchiver.com/mca-marines/access.

"A.V.G. Fliers Bag at Least Three." *New York Times,* February 23, 1942, p. 4.

"A.V.G. Gets a Tribute." *New York Times,* April 18, 1942, p. 4.

Baisden, Charles. *Flying Tiger to Air Commando.* Atglen, Pa.: Schiffer Military History, 1999.

Bartlett, Tom. "Baa Baa Black Sheep." *Leatherneck,* May 1986, p. 1. At http://pqasb.pqarchiver.com/mca-marines/access.

———. "Bolt out of the Blue." *Leatherneck,* September 1986, pp. 1–5. At http://pqasb.pqarchiver.com/mca-marines/access.

Bergerud, Eric M. *Fire in the Sky: The Air War in the South Pacific.* Boulder, Colo.: Westview Press, 2000.

Bergin, Bob. "Pearl Harbor Payback." *Flight Journal,* April 2005, pp. 64–70.

"Blood for the Tigers." *Time,* December 29, 1941, p. 19.

Bond, Maj. Gen. Charles R. Jr. "Oral History." Oral History Collection, Cushing Memorial Library and Archives, Texas A&M University, July 21–22, 1981.

Bond, Maj. Gen. Charles R. Jr., and Terry H. Anderson. *A Flying Tiger's Diary.* College Station: Texas A&M University Press, 1984.

"Born to Fight." *Time,* September 2, 1946.

Boyington, Col. Gregory. *Baa Baa Black Sheep.* New York: G. P. Putnam's Sons, 1958.

————. *Pappy Boyington, World War II Ace.* Mark 56 Records, 1977.

"Boyington, Kawato: A Tale of Two Warriors." *Tacoma News Tribune,* December 19, 2001, at TheNewsTribune.com, p. 1.

"Boyington, War Ace, Is Divorced by Wife." *Chicago Daily Tribune,* October 14, 1959, p. B14.

"Bright Days for a 'Bum.'" *Life,* January 26, 1959, pp. 67–72.

Burgard, George. "Diary." At http://members.tripod.com/Flying-tiger-ace/ id18.htm.

Callaghan, Peter. "It's Time to Honor Tacoma's Flying Ace." *Tacoma News Tribune,* May 28, 2006, at http://www.thenewstribune.com.

"Calling All Fronts." *Time,* April 13, 1942, p. 43.

Caporale, Louis G. "Marine Air in the Solomons." *Marine Corps Gazette,* May 1993, pp. 1–4. At http://pqasb.pqarchiver.com/mca-marines/access.

Carl, Maj. Gen. Marion E., with Barrett Tillman. *Pushing the Envelope.* Annapolis, Md.: Naval Institute Press, 1994.

Chennault, Claire Lee. *Way of A Fighter.* New York: G. P. Putnam's Sons, 1949.

Christenson, Sig, and Carmina Danini. "'Giant Figure in Heroic Aviation,' 'Tex' Hill, Dies." *San Antonio Express-News,* October 12, 2007, pp. 1–4. At http://www.mysanantonio.com/news/MYSA101207_01A_NZOBITHILL DAVIDTEX_347c060_html5873.html

Christopher, Frank. *Fei Hu: The Script.* Fei Hu Films and Jordan Publishing, 1998. At http://home.att.net/~ww2aviation/Fei-Hu.html.

Cockfield, Jamie H. "Interview with General Robert L. Scott." *World War II,* January 1996, pp. 1–8. At http://www.historynet.com.

Coffey, Thomas. *Hap.* New York: Viking Press, 1982.

"Col. Boyington Is Flying Home to See Squadron." *Chicago Daily Tribune,* September 7, 1945, p. 6.

Connor, John. "Bouquets from Boyington." *Leatherneck,* July 1945, pp. 1–2. At http://pqasb.pqarchiver.com/mca-marines/access.

"Controversial War Hero Bares His Soul." *Chicago Daily Tribune,* July 27, 1958, p. B1.

Coons, Jerry. "The Fabulous Pappy Boyington." *Air Classics,* February 1979, pp. 42–43, 90–91.

Cornelius, Wanda, and Thayne Short. *Ding Hao: America's Air War in China, 1937–1945.* Gretna: Pelican Publishing, 1980.

"'Cuddle-Bum' Weeps over Pappy's Notes." *Chicago Daily Tribune,* August 21, 1946, p. 1.

Curie, Eve. *Journey among Warriors.* Garden City, N.Y.: Doubleday, Doran, 1943.

Daniels, Mary. "Robert Conrad Is Flying High as 'Pappy' Boyington." *Chicago Daily Tribune,* January 8, 1978, p. K3.

Davis, Burke. *The Billy Mitchell Affair.* New York: Random House, 1967.

De Chant, John. "Devil Birds." *Marine Corps Gazette,* April 1947, pp. 1–7. At http://pqasb.pqarchiver.com/mca-marines/access.

———. *Devilbirds: The Story of United States Marine Corps Aviation in World War II.* New York: Harper & Brothers, 1947.

DeLuce, Daniel. "Chicagoans Help Destroy 15 Jap Planes in Burma." *Chicago Daily Tribune,* April 24, 1942, p. 7.

"Echo from the West." *Time,* December 15, 1941, p. 26.

"18 Black Sheep Welcome 'Pappy' Back to Fold." *Chicago Daily Tribune,* September 13, 1945, p. 3.

Evans, Rev. John. "Fighting Parson Tells of Flying Tigers' Deeds." *Chicago Daily Tribune,* July 22, 1942, p. 4.

"500 Jap Planes Downed by Corsair-Flying Marines; Spectacular Scores Uphold Traditions of the Corps." *Chicago Daily Tribune,* January 5, 1944, p. 15.

"Flying Tigers." Editorial. *New York Times,* March 30, 1942, p. 16.

"Flying Tigers Blast 40 Planes." *Chicago Daily Tribune,* March 25, 1942, p. 1.

Folkart, Bruce A. "Flying Ace Pappy Boyington, Who Shot Down 28 Zeros, Dies at 75." *Los Angeles Times,* January 12, 1988, pp. 3–4.

Ford, Daniel. *Flying Tigers: Claire Chennault and His American Volunteers, 1941–1942.* New York: Smithsonian Books, 2007.

Forman, Harrison. "Reinforcement of Flying Tigers Now Assured, Leader Declares." *New York Times,* April 4, 1942, p. 3.

———. "Victories of A.V.G. Laid to Courage." *New York Times,* March 15, 1942, p. 5.

Foster, Capt. John M. *Hell in the Heavens.* New York: G. P. Putnam's Sons, 1961.

"Free Woman of 'Pappy's' Theft Charge." *Chicago Daily Tribune,* August 22, 1946, p. 1.

Frey, Christine. "UW Students Face Barbs of Free Speech." *Seattle Post-Intelligencer,* February 16, 2006. At http://www.seattlepi.nwsource.com.

Frillmann, Paul, and Graham Peck. *China: The Life Remembered.* Boston: Houghton Mifflin, 1968.

Gamble, Bruce. *The Black Sheep.* Novato, Calif.: Presidio Press, 1998.

———. *Black Sheep One.* Novato, Calif.: Presidio Press, 2000.

Goicoechea, Joseph. "Memoirs." June 14, 2001. Handwritten reminiscences of a prisoner of war.

Gowran, Clay. "Former 'Tiger' Gets 5 Zeros in 1st Pacific Bout." *Chicago Daily Tribune,* September 21, 1943, p. 4. As posted at http://pqasb.pqarchiver.com/chicagotribune/access.

Greenlaw, Olga S. *The Lady and the Tigers.* New York: E. P. Dutton, 1943.

———. "Pappy." *Cosmopolitan,* April 1944, pp. 28–29, 139.

Guyton, Boone T. *Whistling Death: The Test Pilot's Story of the F4U Corsair.* New York: Orion Books, 1990.

Halloran, Ray "Hap," with Chester Marshall. *Hap's War.* Menlo Park, Calif.: Hallmark Press, 1998.

Halsey, Fleet Adm. William F., and Lt. Cdr. J. Bryan III. *Admiral Halsey's Story.* New York: McGraw-Hill, 1947.

Hammel, Eric. "50 Years Ago: Marine Air at Rabaul." *Leatherneck,* part 1, January 1994, pp. 1–4; part 2, February 1994, pp. 1–4. At http://pqasb.pqarchiver.com/mca-marines/access.

Heaton, Colin. "Interview with Pappy Boyington." *Aviation History,* May 2001, pp. 1–13. At http://www.historynet.com.

Hill, David Lee "Tex," and Major Reagan Schaupp. *"Tex" Hill: Flying Tiger.* San Antonio, Tex.: Universal Bookbindery, 2003.

Hofrichter, Paul. "Television Brought Back Memories of WWII Glory for Old Corsair Pilots." *Marine Corps Gazette,* May 1979, pp. 1–5. At http://pqasb.pqarchiver.com/mca-marines/access.

Holmes, Linda Goetz. *Unjust Enrichment: How Japan's Companies Built Postwar Fortunes Using American POWs.* Mechanicsburg, Pa.: Stackpole Books, 2001.

Hotz, Robert B. *With General Chennault: The Story of the Flying Tigers.* New York: Coward-McCann, 1943.

Howard, James H. *Roar of the Tiger.* New York: Orion Books, 1991.

"Hurry, Hurry." *Time,* June 29, 1942, p. 25.

"The Incident Becomes a Crisis." *Time,* June 1, 1942, pp. 18–21.

"It's Just Luck, Say 'Tigers' Who Bag 400 Planes." *Chicago Daily Tribune,* April 28, 1942, p. 4.

Jones, John E. "Stassen's Full Part in Rescues of Captives in Japan Revealed." *Pittsburgh Post-Gazette,* January 22, 1946.

Karig, Capt. Walter, Lt. Cdr. Russell L. Harris, and Lt. Cdr. Frank A. Manson. *Battle Report: The End of an Empire.* New York: Rinehart, 1948.

Kawato, Masajiro. *Bye Bye Black Sheep.* Phoenix, Ariz.: Printing Dynamics, 1978.

Kerr, E. Bartlett. *Surrender and Survival: The Experience of American POWs in the Pacific 1941–1945.* New York: William Morrow, 1985.

Kinney, Brig. Gen. John F., with James M. McCaffrey. *Wake Island Pilot.* Washington, D.C.: Brassey's, 1995.

Korman, Symour. "Pappy Wins His Toughest Fight." *Chicago Daily Tribune,* April 28, 1957, p. C38–C40.

"Labels Americans 'Flying Tigers.'" *New York Times,* January 27, 1942, p. 10.

Leckie, Robert. *Strong Men Armed.* New York: Da Capo Press, 1997.

Losonsky, Frank S., and Terry M. Losonsky. *Flying Tiger: A Crew Chief's Story.* Atglen, Pa.: Schiffer Military/Aviation History, 1996.

"Lost Sheep." *Time,* January 17, 1944, p. 62.

"Magic from Waterproof." *Time,* June 8, 1942, p. 30.

"Maj. Boyington Freed." *Chicago Daily Tribune,* August 31, 1945, p. 4.

"The Major Shaves." *Time,* February 21, 1944, p. 68.

Martindale, Robert R. *The 13th Mission.* Austin, Tex.: Eakin Press, 1998.

McClurg, Lt. Col. Robert W. *On Boyington's Wing.* Westminster, Md.: Eagle Editions, 2006.

Melson, Maj. Charles D. *Up the Slot: Marines in the Central Solomons.* Washington, D.C.: Marine Corps Historical Center, 1993.

Mersky, Peter B. *Time of the Aces: Marine Pilots in the Solomons, 1942–1944.* Washington, D.C.: Marine Corps Historical Center, 1993.

———. *U.S. Marine Corps Aviation: 1912 to the Present.* Annapolis, Md.: Nautical & Aviation Publishing Company of America, 1983.

Metcalf, Col. Clyde H., ed. *The Marine Corps Reader.* New York: G. P. Putnam's Sons, 1944.

Morang, Joe. "Boyington Here; Pale, Tired, but Still Grinning." *Chicago Daily Tribune,* October 1, 1945, p. 5.

"Mrs. Boyington Changes Mind and Gets Married." *Chicago Daily Tribune,* March 21, 1946, p. 27.

Murphy, John R. "A Tragic Hero." *Marine Corps Gazette,* November 2001, pp. 1–3. At http://pqasb.pqarchiver.com/mca-marines/access.

North, Oliver L., with Joe Musser. *War Stories II: Heroism in the Pacific.* Washington, D.C.: Regnery, 2004.

"Offer Zeroes for Caps." *New York Times,* October 8, 1943, p. 23.

O'Kane, Rear Adm. Richard H. *Clear the Bridge! The War Patrols of the U.S.S. Tang.* Chicago: Rand McNally, 1977.

Okumiya, Masatake, Jiro Horikoshi, and Martin Caidin. *Zero.* New York: ibooks, 2002.

"'Pappy' Accuses 'Jilted' Friend of $9,000 Theft." *Chicago Daily Tribune,* May 21, 1946, p. 4.

"'Pappy' Boyington Comes Home." *Life,* October 1, 1945, pp. 29–31.

"'Pappy' Boyington, Famed Flier." *Washington Times,* January 12, 1988, p. B4.

"'Pappy' Boyington Is Dead at 75; Hero of the Black Sheep Squadron." *New York Times,* January 12, 1988, p. A25.

"Pappy Boyington, World War II Hero." *New York Newsday,* January 12, 1988, p. 35.

"'Pappy' Boyington, WWII Pilot 'Black Sheep' Squadron Leader Shot Down 28 Planes." *Chicago Tribune,* January 12, 1988, p. 1. At http://pqasb.pqarchiver.com/chicagotribune/access.

"Pappy of the Black Sheep." *Time,* January 10, 1944, pp. 68, 70.

"Pappy's Jilted Brunette Asks Reno Divorce." *Chicago Daily Tribune,* March 30, 1947, p. 33.

"Pappy's Lucy 'Amazed' as He Weds Another." *Chicago Daily Tribune,* January 10, 1946, p. 3.

"'Pappy' Tells Court Woman Misused $9,000." *Chicago Daily Tribune,* June 27, 1946, p. 18.

Pearson, Richard. "WWII Pilot 'Pappy' Boyington Dies." *Washington Post,* January 12, 1988, p. D5.

Phillips, James Atlee. "The Man from Everywhere." *Leatherneck,* December 1945, pp. 1–4. At http://pqasb.pqarchiver.com/mca-marines/access.

Pistole, Larry M. *The Pictorial History of the Flying Tigers.* Orange, Va.: Publisher's Press, 1981.

Quilter, Col. Charles J. II. "'One-of-a-Kind' Marine Aviator 'Pappy' Boyington Dies." *Fortitudine,* 1988, pp. 17–19.

"Reach for Glory." *Time,* April 17, 1944, p. 68.

Reed, Bob. "A Golden Gathering of Black Sheep." *Leatherneck,* September 1993, pp. 1–2. At http://pqasb.pqarchiver.com/mca-marines/access.

———. "Winged Warriors." *Leatherneck*, May 1976, pp. 1–5. At http://pqasb .pqarchiver.com/mca-marines/access.

Reed, Robert T. *Lost Black Sheep*. Central Point, Ore.: Hellgate Press/PSI Research, 2001.

Reinburg, J. Hunter. *A Pilot's Log Book: The True Combat Aerial Escapades of Colonel J. Hunter Reinburg*. Boynton Beach, Fla.: Star Publishing, 1966.

"Resolution to Calling for a Tribute for Col. Gregory 'Pappy' Boyington, USMC." At http://www.senate.asuw.org.

Richardson, Herb. "Giants of the Corps." *Leatherneck*, May 1976, pp. 1–3. At http://pqasb.pqarchiver.com/mca-marines/access.

Rosbert, C. Joseph. *Flying Tiger Joe's Adventure Story Cookbook*. Franklin, N.C.: Giant Poplar Press, 1985.

Rossi, Dick. *A Flying Tiger's Story*. Jordan Publishing, 1995. Available at http:// home.att.net/~C.C.Jordan/Rossi-AVG2.html.

Sakaida, Henry. *Pacific Air Combat WWII: Voices from the Past*. St. Paul, Minn.: Phalanx Publishing, 1993.

———. *The Siege of Rabaul*. St. Paul, Minn.: Phalanx Publishing, 1996.

Schaller, Michael. *The U.S. Crusade in China, 1938–1945*. New York: Columbia University Press, 1979.

Schramm, Leo J. *Leo the Tiger*. Camp Hill, Pa.: GreenShield Services, 1992.

Shaw, Henry I. Jr., and Maj. Douglas T. Kane. *History of U.S. Marine Corps Operations in World War II*. Vol. 2: *Isolation of Rabaul*. Washington, D.C.: Historical Branch, G-3 Division, Headquarters, U.S. Marine Corps, 1963.

Sherrod, Robert. *History of Marine Corps Aviation in World War II*. Baltimore, Md.: Nautical & Aviation Publishing Company of America, 1987.

Shilling, Erik. *Erik Shilling: Flying Tiger*. Jordan Publishing, 1993 and 1998. Available at http://home.att.net/~C.C.Jordan/Shilling.html.

"Six A.V.G. Pilots Tackle 100 of Foe." *New York Times*, March 27, 1942, p. 4.

Smith, Robert M., with Philip D. Smith. *With Chennault in China: A Flying Tiger's Diary*. Blue Ridge Summit, Pa.: Tab Books, 1984.

Smith, Robert T. *Tale of a Tiger*. Jordan Publishing, 1986. Available at http:// home.att.net/~ww2aircraft/RTSmith1.html.

"Students Reject Honor to 'Baa Baa Black Sheep' Hero." *WorldNetDaily*, April 21, 2007, at http://www.worldnetdaily.com.

Styling, Mark. *Corsair Aces of World War 2*. London: Osprey Publishing, 1995.

"Tigers over Burma." *Time*, February 9, 1942, pp. 25–26.

"Tigers Prove It." *Time*, January 12, 1942, p. 25.

Tillman, Barrett. *Corsair: The F4U in World War II and Korea*. Annapolis, Md.: Naval Institute Press, 1979.

———. "The Incredible Corsair." *World War II*, March 2008, pp. 36–41.

"Tinsel & Ribbon." *Time*, January 24, 1944, p. 66.

Toland, John. *The Flying Tigers*. New York: Random House, 1963.

"To Wed Boyington." *Chicago Daily Tribune*, January 7, 1946, p. 4.

"20 for 1." *Time*, April 6, 1942, pp. 20–21.

"Two Soldiers and a Marine." *Time*, April 24, 1944, pp. 66, 68.

"U.S. Flying Tigers Bag 7 Jap Planes in Air Battles." *Chicago Daily Tribune*, April 14, 1942, p. 4.

"U.S. Rule for 20 Years Jap Need, Says Boyington." *Chicago Daily Tribune*, January 24, 1946, p. 7.

Wachhorst, Wyn. "Never Give Up: The Odyssey of Hap Halloran." *Gentry*, August 2007, pp. 97–103.

Walton, Frank. "'Baa Baa Black Sheep' Is Pulling the Wool over Our Eyes." *TV Guide*, April 23, 1977, pp. 15–20.

———. *Once They Were Eagles*. Lexington: University Press of Kentucky, 1986.

Whelan, Russell. *The Flying Tigers*. New York: Viking Press, 1943.

Wolters, Larry. "How U.S. Fights Enemies Shown by Army Hour." *Chicago Daily Tribune*, July 19, 1942, p. N4.

"Woman in Reno Says She'll Wed Marine Ace." *Chicago Daily Tribune*, January 6, 1946, p. 1.

"Woman Jilted by Pappy Will Cling to Mate." *Chicago Daily Tribune*, January 8, 1946, p. 1.

"World War II Flying Ace Gregory Boyington, 75." *Chicago Tribune*, January 12, 1988.

Wukovits, John F. "Corsairs above the Coral." *Aviation Heritage*, May 1991, pp. 30–37.

———. "Daredevil of the Air Gained Early Fame by Combining Airmanship and Showmanship." *Aviation Heritage*, January 1992, pp. 10–12, 60–62.

Zamperini, Louis, with Helen Itria. *Devil at My Heels*. New York: E. P. Dutton, 1956.

Interviews

Avey, Fred. Black Sheep Squadron. Personal interview, October 1989.

Brown, Carl. Flying Tiger. Telephone interviews, January 28, 2008; January 29, 2008.

Goicoechea, Joseph. Omori prison camp inmate. Telephone interviews, February 26, 2002; March 5, 2002; personal interviews, April 10, 2002; April 12, 2002.

Halloran, Ray "Hap." Omori prison camp inmate. Telephone interview, September 26, 2007; personal interview, October 4, 2007.

Hill, James. Black Sheep Squadron. Personal interview, October 4, 2007.

Losonsky, Frank. Flying Tiger. Telephone interview, September 21, 2007.

Zamperini, Lou. Omori prison camp inmate. Personal interview, March 6, 2008.

Videos

Fei Hu: The Story of the Flying Tigers. Fei Hu Films, 2003.

War Stories with Oliver North: The Black Sheep Squadron. Fox News, 2003.

Web Sites

http://forums.flyingtigersavg.com. This is the web site for the American Volunteer Group (AVG), the unit of American aviators dubbed the Flying Tigers. The site contains a wonderful collection of reminiscences, photos, information, and a lively forum in which members post comments on matters regarding the AVG. A close-knit group, the AVG family was of immense help to me as I researched this book.

http://www.warbirdforum.com. This site, maintained by author Daniel Ford, contains an abundance of material about the Flying Tigers, including information from the Japanese vantage.

Index

Aichi D3A "Val" dive-bomber, 98
air shows, 198–99
aircraft and aviation: aircraft approaching out of the sun, tactic to prevent surprise from, 76, 118; claims of aircraft shot down while with Flying Tigers, 71, 72, 76, 80, 88–90; early interest in, 6–12, 13; enthusiasm and talent for flying, 2, 44–45, 74, 113, 118–19, 130; first flight, 9–10; flight training and solo flight, 15–16; hazards of flying, 8–9, 11–12; instruments, flying by, 19–20; Pensacola flight training, 16–21. *See also specific aircraft*
aircraft carriers: Corsair fighters for, 98–99; Japan, raid on, 174; learning to land on, 20; qualifying for carrier landings, 22–23
Alcoholics Anonymous, 197
Aldworth, Richard, 32
Alexander, Robert, 117, 123
Alsop, Joseph, 31
American Volunteer Group (AVG)/ Flying Tigers: achievements of,

2; airfields for, 41, 42–43; attitude of members toward Boyington, 2, 73–74, 86, 87–88, 89–90, 145, 206–7; barracks for in Burma, 41–42; Burma, withdrawal from, 77; Chiang Mai raid, 77–82, 89; dangers faced by, 57; disbanding of, 84; dismissal from, 31; drinking by members, 37, 38; dropouts from program, 38, 49; equipment for, 32; escort and scout missions by, 75, 76–77, 83–84; esprit de corps of, 53; events leading to formation of, 25–30; financial inducements, 31, 32; flying and fighting, readiness for, 40; formation of, 29–30; Japanese bombers, first encounter with, 62–63; leadership and command methods, 45–46; leisure activities for, 54–55; military demeanor of, 35; morale of, 83–84; physical condition of pilots, 47; pilot recruitment, 30–32; pilot training activities, 46–52, 54, 57–58; pilots, experience of, 47; pilots for, 29–30;

239

About the Author

John F. Wukovits is a military expert specializing in the Pacific theater of World War II. He is the author of many books, including *Devotion to Duty: A Biography of Admiral Clifton A. F. Sprague; Eisenhower: A Biography; Pacific Alamo: The Battle for Wake Island; One Square Mile of Hell: The Battle for Tarawa;* and *American Commando: Evans Carlson, His WWII Marine Raiders, and America's First Special Forces Mission.* He has also written numerous articles for such publications as *WWII History, Naval History,* and *World War II.* A native of Trenton, MI, and a graduate of the University of Notre Dame, Wukovits is the father of three daughters—Amy, Julie, and Karen—and the grandfather of Matthew, Megan, Emma, and Kaitlyn.

The **Naval Institute Press** is the book-publishing arm of the U.S. Naval Institute, a private, nonprofit, membership society for sea service professionals and others who share an interest in naval and maritime affairs. Established in 1873 at the U.S. Naval Academy in Annapolis, Maryland, where its offices remain today, the Naval Institute has members worldwide.

Members of the Naval Institute support the education programs of the society and receive the influential monthly magazine *Proceedings* or the colorful bimonthly magazine *Naval History* and discounts on fine nautical prints and on ship and aircraft photos. They also have access to the transcripts of the Institute's Oral History Program and get discounted admission to any of the Institute-sponsored seminars offered around the country.

The Naval Institute's book-publishing program, begun in 1898 with basic guides to naval practices, has broadened its scope to include books of more general interest. Now the Naval Institute Press publishes about seventy titles each year, ranging from how-to books on boating and navigation to battle histories, biographies, ship and aircraft guides, and novels. Institute members receive significant discounts on the more than eight hundred Press books in print.

Full-time students are eligible for special half-price membership rates. Life memberships are also available.

For a free catalog describing Naval Institute Press books currently available, and for further information about joining the U.S. Naval Institute, please write to:

Member Services
U.S. NAVAL INSTITUTE
291 Wood Road
Annapolis, MD 21402-5034
Telephone: (800) 233-8764
Fax: (410) 571-1703
Web address: www.usni.org